Finding the Source in Sociology and Anthropology

Finding the Source in Sociology and Anthropology

A Thesaurus-Index to the Reference Collection

Compiled by Samuel R. Brown

Finding the Source, Number 1

GREENWOOD PRESS
New York • Westport, Connecticut • London

Library of Congress Cataloging-in-Publication Data

Brown, Samuel R.
Finding the source in sociology and anthropology.

(Finding the source, ISSN 0891-1843 ; no. 1)
Includes indexes.
1. Reference books—Sociology—Bibliography.
2. Sociology—Bibliography. 3. Reference books—
Sociology—Indexes. 4. Sociology—Indexes.
5. Reference books—Anthropology—Bibliography.
6. Anthropology—Bibliography. 7. Reference books—
Anthropology—Indexes. 8. Anthropology—Indexes.
I. Title. II. Series.
Z7164.S68B75 1987 [HM51] 016.301 86-31879
ISBN 0-313-25263-7 (lib. bdg. : alk. paper)

Library of Congress Catalog Card Number: 86-31879
ISBN: 0-313-25263-7
ISSN: 0891-1843

First published in 1987

Greenwood Press, Inc.
88 Post Road West, Westport, Connecticut 06881

Printed in the United States of America

The paper used in this book complies with the Permanent Paper Standard issued by the National Information Standards Organization (Z39.48-1984).

10 9 8 7 6 5 4 3 2 1

To Mom and Dad for being there

CONTENTS

PREFACE ix

ACKNOWLEDGMENTS xi

INTRODUCTION xiii

CITATIONS

General Sources 3

Atlases 3
Foundations, organizations and research centers 4
Indexes 5
Yearbooks, almanacs and directories 5

Social Sciences 6

General topics 6
Research methods 8

Anthropology 9

General topics 9
Archaeology 11
Ethnography 12
Social and cultural anthropology 13

Sociology 13

General topics 13
Statistics 16
Subfields 17
Criminology 18

Population and Life Cycle 19

Death and dying 19
Divorce 20
Marriage and family 21
Population 23

Racial, Ethnic and Social Groups 25

American Indians 25
Black-Americans 26
Communities and urban groups 28
Elderly 30
Ethnic groups -- general topics 32
Ethnic groups -- specific topics 33
Hispanics 35
Race relations 36
Women -- general topics 37
Women -- by region 39
Youth 40

Sexuality 41

Sexual abuse 41
Sexual behavior, attitudes and deviations 41

Social Issues 43

Alcoholism 43
Crime 44
Drug abuse 45
Poverty 45

Social Forces 46

Popular culture 46
Public opinion 47
Social change and conflict 48
Social indicators 48
Social policy 49

Social Welfare 49

Criminal justice 49
Mental health 51
Social work 52

TITLE/SUBTITLE INDEX 55

AUTHOR INDEX 69

THESAURUS-INDEX 77

PREFACE

Sociology and anthropology cover a variety of broad topics. Often however, researchers, graduate students and librarians need to focus in from such general and abstract ideas to issues of particular concern. Guides to reference sources in these disciplines, employing annotated citations arranged within a broad framework of knowledge, often are not a sufficient resource. These classified arrangements and seemingly limited subject indexes often fail to provide the quickest and/or most efficient means of finding information.

The purpose of FINDING THE SOURCE IN SOCIOLOGY AND ANTHROPOLOGY is to offer a guide with which one can efficiently locate specific information. Up-to-date free text descriptors and extensive subject indexing, made possible by a thesaurus-index, enable the user to easily find what s/he is looking for. An added feature to FINDING THE SOURCE, when used in conjunction with the card catalog and/or automated system, is direct access to sources. Once call numbers are penciled in margins in the citation section the user may proceed straight from FINDING THE SOURCE to that section of the collection.

Sheehy's GUIDE TO REFERENCE BOOKS and its supplements provided the initial core list for the writing of this text. The core list was made more extensive by adding selected sources from: FINDING THE SOURCE: A THESAURUS INDEX TO THE REFERENCE COLLECTION, Carl White's SOURCES OF INFORMATION IN THE SOCIAL SCIENCES, Tze-chung Li's SOCIAL SCIENCE REFERENCE SOURCES, A.L.A.'s REFERENCE SOURCES FOR SMALL AND MEDIUM-SIZED LIBRARIES, AMERICAN REFERENCE BOOKS ANNUAL, GOVERNMENT REFERENCE BOOKS and reference books review sections from CHOICE and RQ. Additional citations were gathered from the reference sections of the Library of Congress and the libraries of George Washington University and Georgetown University. All 1,200 titles in the ensuing core list were entered into the OCLC data base for holdings information. The decision for inclusion in the final list of 578 titles was based on the author's professional judgment of a books's quality and its importance to the reference collection, reviews that have appeared in the above-mentioned sources, and its availability as indicated from the OCLC holdings information. Scope notes were written based upon the author's professional experience and in consultation with the following sources: Mitchell's A DICTIONARY OF SOCIOLOGY, Theodorson and Theodorson's A MODERN DICTIONARY OF SOCIOLOGY, Zadrozny's DICTIONARY OF SOCIAL SCIENCE, Gould and Kolb's A DICTIONARY OF THE SOCIAL SCIENCES, THESAURUS OF ERIC DESCRIPTORS, and THE AMERICAN HERITAGE DICTIONARY OF THE ENGLISH LANGUAGE.

This book is directed to librarians, researchers, graduate students and faculty, in addition to those involved in public policy matters, members of applied research centers and those in the general public interested in current issues.

ACKNOWLEDGMENTS

The impetus for this book came from Ben and Barb Shearer, the editors for the FINDING THE SOURCE series. I thank them for their advice and assistance. In the course of research I made extensive use of the excellent reference collections of George Washington University, Georgetown University and the Library of Congress. James D. Anderson, Associate Dean and Professor at the School of Communication, Information and Library Studies, Rutgers University, provided helpful suggestions regarding the citation section. I am especially grateful to friends and colleagues at Spring Hill College Library, and faculty and fellow graduate students at the University of Pennsylvania for their support.

INTRODUCTION

How to use this book

FINDING THE SOURCE IN SOCIOLOGY AND ANTHROPOLOGY is the third book in the FINDING THE SOURCE series. Like its predecessors, this volume consists of two sections: bibliographic citations to selected reference books and a thesaurus-index to the contents of the books cited. In section one, citations are listed by broad subjects and by title with indexes for authors and titles/subtitles at the end of the section. Each bibliographic citation is given a distinct entry number further cited in the thesaurus-index. Section two combines the concept of thesaurus-building and detailed subject-indexing in a thesaurus index. Every book cited in section two is indexed in multiple natural language terms or descriptors. The terms are matched with the entry numbers of the appropriate citations in section one. The following abbreviations are used throughout the thesaurus-index to describe the hierarchical relationships of descriptors: UF-Used For; BT-Broader Term; NT-Narrower Term; and RT-Related Term. The word "see" is employed to refer from a term not used for indexing to the preferred term used. SN signifies a Scope Note.

The provision of multiple tiers used extensively throughout the thesaurus allowed for a thorough index to the core collection. A case by case determination was made regarding the most appropriate hierarchy of terms within each thesaurus entry. For effective use of the index, it is necessary to scan the entire thesaurus entry before going on to another thesaurus access point. Using cross references and other index terms found beneath thesaurus entries as additional entry points and scanning nearby thesaurus entries will further enhance the effectiveness of the search process. Not all index terms under thesaurus entries are themselves thesaurus entries since this would have made the index much too cumbersome. An effort was made to include as many access points as possible while maintaining a consistent use of the index terms.

There are two types of subject access to the contents of the core collection: by broad subject areas under which citations are arranged, and by specific topic or type of information in the thesaurus. While beginning a search with general descriptors such as "Bibliographies," "Encyclopedias," or "Dictionaries" will lead into the thesaurus, it is not particularly efficient. Not only may one step be added to the search process, but the index entries are listed alphabetically rather than hierarchically. With the index terms unrelated under general descriptors, some useful vocabulary could be overlooked or lost.

The geographic focus of this book is the United States. However, a small portion of the sources include Canada, the United Kingdom, Europe, and other international sources. This is often indicated in the title of the book. In addition, there are separate entries established for topics covering specific countries or geographic regions. Unless otherwise noted broad subject areas are to be considered of American origin. Specific groups other than American are listed separately. For example "Ethnic groups (Soviet Union)" would be listed as such, whereas "Ethnic groups (U.S.)" would appear simply as "Ethnic groups."

The following sample search explains how to use the thesaurus index effectively.

"WHERE CAN I FIND INFORMATION ON THE MENTAL HEALTH OF WOMEN?"

Step 1. Choose the most particular word or words of the question.

The two major elements of this question are "mental health" and "women". The most specific approach is "mental health."

MENTAL HEALTH

UF Emotional health
BT Social welfare
.
.
.
Women
Abstracts 421
Bibliographies 412

Note that two sources are given that provide information on the subject.

Step 2. Find entry numbers 421 and 412 in section one.

412. Women and deviance: issues in social conflict and change: an annotated bibliography, by Nanette J. Davis and Jone M. Keith. New York: Garland, 1984.

421. Women studies abstracts. Rush, NY: Rush, 1972 --. quarterly.

At this point, it might be to the user's advantage to go ahead and check the broader term "Social welfare."

SOCIAL WELFARE

UF Public welfare
NT Child welfare
NT Criminal justice
NT Mental health

.
.
.

Women
  Almanacs 422
  Indexes 420

Note that there are two books on the subject.

420. Women, 1965-1975, edited by Cynthia Crippen. Glen Rock, NJ: Microfilming Corporation of America, 1978.

422. Women's action almanac: a complete resource guide, edited by Jane Williamson et al. New York: William Morrow, 1979.

The term "Women" is also a thesaurus entry and the same information could have been located by going there first. However, the multiple tiers make it more difficult to use this procedure than the direct subject approach.

In this instance the thesaurus could have been passed over by going directly to the citation section. Such a strategy is time-consuming and is recommended only to complement a more extensive thesaurus search or to obtain a brief overview of the citations in the section.

Finding the Source in Sociology and Anthropology

CITATIONS

General Sources

Atlases

1. Atlas of ancient archaeology, edited by Jacquetta Hawkes. New York: McGraw-Hill, 1974.

2. Atlas of archaeology, edited by Keith Branigan. New York: St. Martin's, 1982.

3. Atlas of demographics: U.S. by county, from the 1980 census. Boulder, CO: Infomap, 1982.

4. Atlas of human evolution, edited by C. Loring Brace, et al. 2nd ed. New York: Holt, Rinehart & Winston, 1979.

5. Atlas of world cultures, by George Peter Murdock. Pittsburgh, PA: University of Pittsburgh, 1981.

6. Atlas of world population history, by Colin McEvedy and Richard Jones. Harmondsworth, NY: Penguin, 1978.

7. Cultural atlas of Africa, edited by Jocelyn Murray. New York: Facts on File, 1981.

8. Ethnographic atlas, by George Peter Murdock. Pittsburgh, PA: University of Pittsburgh, 1967.

9. Urban atlas; tract data for standard metropolitan statistical areas. U.S. Bureau of the Census. Washington, DC: Government Printing Office, 1974--.

Foundations, organizations and research centers

10. A dictionary of secret and other societies, compiled by Arthur Preuss. Detroit: Gale, 1966.

11. Directory of associations in Canada. Repertoire des associations du Canada, edited by Brian Land. 6th ed. Toronto: Micromedia, 1985.

12. Directory of European associations. Detroit: Gale, 1971--.

13. Directory of national information sources on handicapping conditions and related services. Washington, DC: U.S. Department of Education, 1982.

14. Encyclopedia of associations. Detroit: Gale, 1956--.

15. Foundation directory, compiled by the Foundation Center. 9th ed. New York: The Center (dist. by Columbia University), 1983.

16. Foundation grants index, 1970/71--; a cumulative listing of foundation grants, compiled by the Foundation Center. New York: The Center (dist. by Columbia University), 1972--. annual.

17. Foundation grants to individuals, compiled by the Foundation Center. 4th ed. New York: The Center, 1984.

18. Fraternal organizations, by Alvin J. Schmidt. Westport, CT: Greenwood, 1980.

19. Handbook of secret organizations, by William Joseph Whalen. Milwaukee: Bruce, 1966.

20. The international foundation directory, edited by H. V. Hodson. 2nd ed. Detroit: Gale, 1979.

21. Research centers directory. Detroit: Gale, 1960--. biennial.

22. User's guide to funding resources. Human Resources Network. Radnor, PA: Chilton, 1975.

23. World directory of social science institutions: research, advanced training, documentation, professional bodies. Paris: UNESCO, 1977.

24. World guide to scientific associations and learned societies, edited by Michael Zils. 2nd ed. New York: Bowker, 1978.

Indexes

25. Book review index to social science periodicals. Ann Arbor, MI: Pierian, 1978-1981. (4v.)

26. Bulletin of the Public Affairs Information Service. Annual cumulation. New York: Public Affairs Information Service, 1915--.

27. Social sciences citation index. Philadelphia: Institute for Scientific Information, 1973--.

28. Social sciences index. New York: H. W. Wilson, June 1974--.

Yearbooks, almanacs and directories

29. Colombo's Canadian references, by John Robert Colombo. Toronto: Oxford University, 1976.

30. Community resources directory: a guide to U.S. volunteer organizations and other resource groups, services, training events and courses, and local program models, edited by Harriet Clyde Kipps. 2nd ed. Detroit: Gale, 1984.

31. Directory of information resources for the handicapped: a guide to information resources and services for the handicapped. Santa Barbara, CA: Ready Reference, 1980.

32. Europa yearbook. London: Europa Publications, 1959--. annual. (2v.)

33. Federal assistance for programs serving the handicapped. Washington, DC: U.S. Department of Education, 1980.

34. Handicapped funding directory: a guide to sources of funding in the United States for handicapped programs and services, by Burton J. Eckstein. Oceanside, NY: Research Grant Guides, 1978.

35. The help book, by Janet L. Barkas. New York: Scribner, 1979.

36. Hotline: crisis intervention directory, by J. L. Greenstone and S. Leviton. New York: Facts on File, 1981.

37. Irregular serials and annuals; an international directory. New York: Bowker, 1967--. biennial.

38. Municipal year book. Chicago: International city management association, 1934--.

39. The source book for the disabled: an illustrated guide to easier and more independent living ..., by Glorya Hale. New York: Paddington, 1979.

40. Statesman's year-book; statistical and historical annual of the states of the world. New York: St. Martin's, 1864--.

41. Ulrich's international periodicals directory. New York: Bowker, 1932--. biennial.

42. Washington information directory. Washington, DC: Congressional Quarterly, 1975--. annual.

43. World almanac and book of facts. New York: Newspaper Enterprise Association, 1868--. annual.

44. Yearbook of international organizations. Annuaire des organisations internationales. Brussels: Union of International Associations, 1949--.

Social Sciences

General topics

45. American men and women of science: social and behavioral sciences, edited by Jaques Cattell Press. 13th ed. New York: Bowker, 1978.

46. Bibliography of the Soviet social sciences 1965-1975, by William S. Heiliger. Troy, NY: Whitston, 1978. (2v.)

47. Dictionary of social science, by John Thomas Zadrozny. Washington, DC: Public Affairs, 1959.

48. A dictionary of the social sciences, edited by Julius Gould and William L. Kolb. New York: Free Press, 1964.

49. A dictionary of the social sciences, by Hugo F. Reading. London: Routledge & Kegan Paul, 1977.

50. Directory of published proceedings. Series SSH: Social sciences/Humanities. White Plains, NY: InterDok, 1968--. quarterly.

51. Encyclopaedia of the social sciences. Editor-in-chief, E. R. A. Seligman, associate editor, Alvin Johnson. New York: Macmillan, 1930-35. (15v.)

52. Guide to reference material, by Albert John Walford. 4th ed. London: Library Association, 1982.

53. A guide to writing and publishing in the social and behavioral sciences, by Carolyn J. Mullins. Reprint. Malabar, FL: Krieger, 1983.

54. International encyclopedia of the social sciences, edited by David L. Sills. New York: Macmillan, 1968-1979. (18v.)

55. Latin America: social science information sources, 1967-1979, by Robert L. Delorme. Santa Barbara, CA: ABC-Clio, 1981.

56. Latin America 1979-1983: a social science bibliography, by Robert L. Delorme. Santa Barbara, CA: ABC-Clio, 1984.

57. A London bibliography of the social sciences. 18th supplement. New York: Mansell, 1984.

58. A new dictionary of the social sciences, by Geoffrey Duncan Mitchell. Hawthorne, NY: Aldine, 1979.

59. A reader's guide to the social sciences, by Berthold Frank Hoselitz. New York: Free Press, 1970.

60. Reading lists in radical social science, edited by Mark Maier and Dan Gilroy. New York: Monthly Review, 1982.

61. Social science reference sources: a practical guide, by Tze-chung Li. Westport, CT: Greenwood, 1980.

62. Sources of information in the social sciences, edited by William H. Webb. 3rd ed. Chicago: American Library Association, 1985.

63. Use of social sciences literature, edited by N. Roberts. London: Butterworth, 1977.

64. World list of social science periodicals, by International Committee for Social Science Information and Documentation. 6th ed. Paris: UNESCO, 1982.

Research methods

65. Bibliography on methods of social and business research, by William A. Belson and Beryl-Anne Thompson. London: London School of Economics and Political Science, 1973.

66. A dictionary of social science methods, by P. McC. Miller and M. J. Wilson. New York: Wiley, 1983.

67. Ethics in social research; protecting the interests of human subjects, by Robert T. Bower and Priscilla DeGasparis. New York: Praeger, 1978.

68. Handbook for social research in urban areas, edited by Philip Morris Hauser. Paris: UNESCO, 1965.

69. Handbook of research design and social measurement, by Delbert Charles Miller. 4th ed. New York: Longman, 1983.

70. Handbook of small group research, by A. Paul Hare. 2nd ed. New York: Free Press, 1976.

71. Library research guide to sociology: illustrated search strategy and sources, by Patricia McMillan and James R. Kennedy, Jr. Ann Arbor, MI: Pieran, 1981.

72. Methods for the social sciences: a handbook for students and non-specialists, by John J. Hartman and Jack H. Hedblom. Westport, CT: Greenwood, 1979.

73. Questionnaires for research; an annotated bibliography on design, construction and use, by Dale R. Potter. Portland, OR: Pacific Northwest Forest and Range Experiment Station, 1972.

74. Research resources: annotated guide to the social sciences, by John Brown Mason. Santa Barbara, CA: ABC-Clio, 1968-1971 (2v.)

75. Social science research handbook, by Raymond G. McInnis and James William Scott. New York: Barnes and Noble, 1975.

Anthropology

General topics

76. Abstracts in anthropology. Westport, CT: Greenwood, 1970--. quarterly.

77. Anthropological bibliography of Negro Africa, by Heinrich Albert Wieschhoff. Reprint. New York: Kraus, 1970.

78. An anthropological bibliography of South Asia, compiled by Elizabeth von Furer-Haimendorf. Paris: Mouton, 1958-1970. (3v.)

79. An anthropological bibliography of South Asia, compiled by Helen A. Kanitkar. The Hague: Mouton, 1976--.

80. Anthropological literature: an index to periodical articles and essays. Pleasantville, NY: Redgrave, 1979--. quarterly.

81. Anthropology in the New Guinea highlands: an annotated bibliography, by Terence A. Hays. New York: Garland, 1976.

82. Anthropology in use: a bibliographic chronology of the development of applied anthropology, by John Van Willigen. Pleasantville, NY: Redgrave, 1980.

83. Anthropology of southern Africa in periodicals to 1950, compiled by N. J. van Warmelo. Johannesburg: Witwatersrand University, 1977.

84. Bibliography for cross-cultural workers, compiled by Alan Richard Tippett. South Pasadena, CA: William Carey Library, 1971.

85. A cross-cultural summary, compiled by Robert B. Textor. New Haven, CT: HRAF, 1967.

86. Dictionary of anthropology, by Charles Winick. Ames, IA: Littlefield, Adams & Co., 1958.

87. Education and anthropology: an annotated bibliography, by Annette Rosenstiel. New York: Garland, 1977.

88. Encyclopedia of anthropology, edited by David E. Hunter and Phillip Whitten. New York: Harper and Row, 1976.

89. The history of anthropology: a research bibliography, by Robert V. Kemper and John F. S. Phinney. New York: Garland, 1977.

90. International directory of anthropologists. 5th ed. Chicago: University of Chicago, 1975.

91. Language in culture and society; a reader in linguistics and anthropology, by Dell Hymes. New York: Harper and Row, 1964.

92. Masters' theses in anthropology: a bibliography of theses from United States colleges and universities, by David R. McDonald. New Haven, CT: HRAF, 1977.

93. Micronesia 1944-1974; a bibliography of anthropological and related source materials, by Mac Marshall and James D. Nason. New Haven, CT: HRAF, 1975.

94. Notes and queries on anthropology. Royal Anthropological Institute. 6th ed. London: Routledge & Paul, 1951.

95. Research in ritual studies: a programmatic essay and bibliography, by Ronald L. Grimes. Metuchen, NJ: Scarecrow, 1985.

96. Selected bibliography of the anthropology and ethnology of Europe, by William Zebina Ripley. Boston: Public Library, 1899.

97. Serial publications in anthropology, compiled by Library-Anthropology Resource Group, edited by F. X. Grollig and Sol Tax. 2nd ed. Pleasantville, NY: Redgrave, 1982.

98. Source book for African anthropology, by Wilfrid Dyson Hambly. Reprint. New York: Kraus, 1968.

99. The student anthropologist's handbook; a guide to research, training and career, by Charles Frantz. Cambridge, MA: Schenkman, 1972.

100. Warfare in primitive societies: a bibliography, by William Tulio Divale. Rev. ed. Santa Barbara, CA: ABC-Clio, 1973.

Archaeology

101. The amateur archaeologist's handbook, by Maurice Robbins with Mary B. Irving. 3rd ed. Cambridge, MA: Harper and Row, 1981.

102. Archaeology: a bibliographical guide to the basic literature, by Robert F. Heizer et al. New York: Garland, 1980.

103. The Cambridge encyclopedia of archaeology, edited by Andrew Sherratt. New York: Crown, 1980.

104. A dictionary of terms and techniques in archaeology, by Sara Champion. New York: Facts on File, 1980.

105. The MacMillan dictionary of archaeology, edited by Ruth D. Whitehouse. London: MacMillan, 1983.

106. A thesaurus of British archaeology, by Lesley Adkins and Roy A. Adkins. Totowa, NJ: Barnes and Noble, 1982.

Ethnography

107. Aboriginal tribes of Australia: their terrain, environmental controls, distribution, limits, and proper names, by Norman Barnett Tindale. Berkeley, CA: University of California, 1974.

108. An annotated bibliography of Northern Plains ethnohistory, compiled by Katherine M. Weist and Susan R. Sharrock. Missoula, MT: University of Montana, 1985.

109. Eastern European national minorities, 1919-1980: a handbook, by Stephan M. Horak, et al. Littleton, CO: Libraries Unlimited, 1985.

110. Ethnicity and nationality: a bibliographic guide, by G. Carter Bentley. Seattle: University of Washington, 1982.

111. Ethnographic bibliography of North America, by George Peter Murdock and Timothy J. O'Leary. 4th ed. New Haven, CT: Human Relations Area Files Press, 1975. (5v.)

112. Ethnographic bibliography of South America, by Timothy J. O'Leary. New Haven, CT: Human Relations Area Files Press, 1963.

113. Europe: a selected ethnographic bibliography, by Robert J. Theodoratus. New Haven, CT: Human Relations Area Files Press, 1969.

114. Handbook of major Soviet nationalities, edited by Zev Katz. New York: Free Press, 1975.

115. Muslim peoples: a world ethnographic survey, edited by Richard V. Weekes. 2nd ed. Westport, CT: Greenwood, 1984. (2v.)

116. The peoples of the USSR: an ethnographic handbook, by Ronald Wixman. Armonk, NY: M.E. Sharpe, 1984.

117. Philippine ethnography: a critically annotated and selected bibliography, by Shiro Saito. Honolulu, HI: University of Hawaii, 1972.

Social and cultural anthropology

118. Folk classification: a topically arranged bibliography of contemporary and background references through 1971, by Harold C. Conklin. New Haven, CT: Yale University, 1980.

119. A handbook of method in cultural anthropology, edited by Raoul Naroll and Ronald Cohen. Garden City, NY: Natural History Press, 1970.

120. Handbook of social and cultural anthropology, by John J. Honigmann. Chicago: Rand McNally, 1973.

121. The illustrated encyclopedia of mankind. New York: Marshall Cavendish, 1978. (20v.)

122. International bibliography of social and cultural anthropology. London: Tavistock, 1955--. annual.

123. International dictionary of regional European ethnology and folklore. Copenhagen: Rosenkilde and Bagger, 1960-65. (2v.)

124. Sixty cultures: a guide to the HRAF probability sample files, edited by Robert O. Lagace. Appendix by David Levinson. New Haven, CT: Human Relations Area Files Press, 1977-.

Sociology

General topics

125. Author's guide to journals in sociology and related fields, by Marvin B. Sussman. New York: Haworth, 1978.

126. C.R.I.S.: combined retrospective index set to journals in sociology, 1895-1974, Annadel N. Wile, exec. editor. Washington, DC: Carrollton, 1978. (6v.)

127. Changes in American society, 1960-1978: an annotated bibliography of official government publications, by David W. Parish. Metuchen, NJ: Scarecrow, 1980.

128. Dictionary of modern sociology, by Thomas Ford Hoult. Totowa, NJ: Littlefield, Adams, 1969.

129. Dictionary of quotations in sociology, by Panos Bardis. Westport, CT: Greenwood, 1985.

130. Directory of members. New York: American Sociological Association, 1950--.

131. Durkheimian school: a systematic and comprehensive bibliography, by Yash Nandan. Westport, CT: Greenwood, 1977.

132. Encyclopedia of sociology. Guilford, CT: DPG Reference Publications, 1981.

133. An encyclopedic dictionary of Marxism, socialism and communism: economic, philosophical, political and sociological theories, concepts, institutions and practices -- classical and modern, East-West relations included, by Jozef Wilczynski. Hawthorne, NY: Walter de Gruyter, 1981.

134. Encyclopedic handbook of cults in America, by J. Gordon Melton. New York: Garland, 1985.

135. Guide to graduate departments of sociology. Washington, DC: American Sociological Association, 1965--.

136. Handbook of contemporary developments in world sociology, edited by Raj P. Mohan and Don Martindale. Westport, CT: Greenwood, 1975.

137. Handbook of socialization theory and research, edited by David A. Goslin. Chicago: Rand McNally, 1969.

138. A handbook of sociology, by William F. Ogburn and Meyer F. Nimkoff. 5th ed. London: Routledge & Kegan Paul, 1965.

139. Index to sociology readers, 1960-1965, by Harold J. Abramson and Nicholas Sofios. Metuchen, NJ: Scarecrow, 1973. (2v.)

140. International bibliography of sociology. London: Tavistock, 1952--.

141. The international encyclopedia of sociology, edited by Michael Mann. New York: Continuum, 1984.

142. Marx-Engels dictionary, by James Russell. Westport, CT: Greenwood, 1980.

143. Marxist philosophy: a bibliographical guide, by John Lachs. Chapel Hill, NC: University of North Carolina, 1967.

144. Modern British society: a bibliography, by John H. Westergaard et al. New York: St. Martin's Press, 1977.

145. A modern dictionary of sociology, by George A. Theodorson and Achilles G. Theodorson. New York: Barnes and Noble, 1979.

146. The Penguin dictionary of sociology, by Nicholas Abercrombie et al. London: Allen Lane, 1984.

147. Social stratification: a research bibliography, by Norval D. Glenn et al. Berkeley, CA: Glendessary, 1970.

148. Sociological abstracts. San Diego, CA: Sociological abstracts, 1952--.

149. Sociology: an international bibliography of serial publications, 1880-1980. London: Mansell, 1983.

150. Sociology dissertations in American universities, 1893-1966, by G. Albert Lunday. Commerce, TX: East Texas State University, 1969.

151. Sociology of America: a guide to information sources, by Charles Mark. Detroit: Gale, 1976.

152. Sociology theses register, edited by Frances Wakeford. London: Social Science Research Council and British Sociological Association, 1976--. annual.

153. Soviet sociology, 1964-75: a bibliography, by Mervyn Matthews and Thomas A. Jones. New York: Praeger, 1978.

154. The student sociologist's handbook, by Pauline Bart and Linda Frankel. 3rd ed. Glenview, IL: Scott, Foresman, 1981.

Statistics

155. Annual abstract of statistics. London: Central Statistical Office, 1854--. annual.

156. Congressional districts in the 1980s. Washington, DC: Congressional Quarterly, 1983.

157. Congressional districts of the 98th Congress. U.S. Bureau of the Census. Washington, DC: Government Printing Office, 1983.

158. County and city data book. U.S. Bureau of the Census. Washington, DC: Government Printing Office, 1952--.

159. DataMap: index of published tables of statistical data 1985-86, by Jarol B. Manheim and Allison Ondrasik. Phoenix, AZ: Oryx, 1986.

160. Demographic yearbook. New York: United Nations, 1949--. annual.

161. Directory of federal statistics for local areas: a guide to sources, 1976-1978. U.S. Bureau of the Census. Washington, DC: Government Printing Office, 1978, 1979. (2v.)

162. The East European and Soviet data handbook: political, social, and developmental indicators, 1945-1975, by Paul S. Shoup. New York: Columbia University, 1981.

163. Historical statistics of the United States, colonial times to 1970. U.S. Department of Commerce. Washington, DC: Government Printing Office, 1975. (2v.)

164. 1980 census of population. U.S. Bureau of the Census. Washington, DC: Government Printing Office, 1980--.

165. Perspective Canada II: a compendium of social statistics. Statistics Canada. Ottawa: Information Canada, 1977.

166. Population abstract of the United States, by John L. Andriot. McLean, VA: Andriot Associates, 1983. (2v.)

167. Sources of social statistics, by Bernard Edwards. London: Heinemann, 1974.

168. State and metropolitan area databook. U.S. Bureau of the Census. Washington, DC: Government Printing Office, 1980--.

169. Statistical abstract of the United States. U.S. Bureau of the Census. Washington, DC: Government Printing Office, 1879--.

170. Statistical yearbook. New York: United Nations, 1949--. annual.

171. Statistics sources, edited by Paul Wasserman and Jacqueline O'Brien. Detroit: Gale, 1962--.

172. Township atlas of the United States, by John L. Andriot. McLean, VA: Andriot Associates, 1979.

173. Vital statistics of the United States. U.S. National Vital Statistics Division. Washington, DC: Government Printing Office, 1939--. annual.

Subfields

174. The clinical sociology handbook, by Jan M. Fritz. Edited by Dan A. Chekki. New York: Garland, 1985.

175. Handbook of medical sociology, edited by Howard E. Freeman et al. 3rd ed. Englewood Cliffs, NJ: Prentice-Hall, 1979.

176. Handbook of theory and research for the sociology of education, edited by John G. Richardson. Westport, CT: Greenwood, 1986.

177. Issues in the sociology of religion: a bibliography, by Anthony J. Blasi and Michael W. Cuneo. New York: Garland, 1986.

178. Mathematical sociology: a selective annotated bibliography, by Janet Holland and Max D. Steuer. New York: Schocken, 1970.

179. Medical sociology: an annotated bibliography, 1972-1982, by John G. Bruhn et al. New York: Garland, 1985.

180. The social sciences in educational studies: a selective guide to the literature, edited by Anthony Hartnett. London: Heinemann, 1982.

181. Social scientific studies of religion, by Morris I. Berkowitz and J. Edmund Johnson. Pittsburgh, PA: University of Pittsburgh, 1967.

182. The sociology of aging: an annotated bibliography and sourcebook, by Diana K. Harris. New York: Garland, 1985.

183. Sociology of education: a guide to information sources, by Francesco Cordasco. Detroit: Gale, 1979.

184. Sociology of poverty in the United States: an annotated bibliography, compiled by H. Paul Chalfant. Westport, CT: Greenwood, 1985.

185. Sociology of sciences: an annotated bibliography on invisible colleges, 1972-1981, by Daryl E. Chubin. New York: Garland, 1983.

186. Sociology of the law: a research bibliography, by William J. Chambliss and Robert B. Seidman. Berkeley, CA: Glendessary, 1970.

Criminology

187. A bibliography on general deterrence, by Deryck Beyleveld. Hampshire, England: Saxon House, 1980.

188. Criminological bibliographies: uniform citations to bibliographies, indexes, and review articles of the literature of crime study in the United States, by Bruce L. Davis. Westport, CT: Greenwood, 1978.

189. Criminology: a cross-cultural perspective, edited by Dae H. Chang. Durham, NC: Carolina Academic Press, 1976. (2v.)

190. Criminology and penology abstracts. Amsterdam: Excerpta Criminologica Foundation, 1961--. bimonthly.

191. Criminology and the administration of criminal justice: a bibliography, by Leon Radzinowicz and Roger Hood. Westport, CT: Greenwood, 1976.

192. Criminology in the world, by Denis Szabo. Montreal: Universite de Montreal, 1977.

193. Criminology index: research and theory in criminology in the United States, 1945-1972, by Marvin E. Wolfgang et al. New York: Elsevier, 1975. (2v.)

194. A dictionary of criminology, edited by Dermot Walsh and Adrian Poole. London: Routledge & Kegan Paul, 1983.

195. Elsevier's dictionary of criminal science, in eight languages: English/American, French, Italian, Spanish, Portuguese, Dutch, Swedish, and German, compiled by Johann Anton Adler. Amersterdam: Elsevier, 1960.

196. Encyclopedia of criminology, by Vernon Carnegie Branham and Samuel B. Kutash. New York: Philosophical Library, 1949.

197. International handbook of contemporary developments in criminology, edited by Elmer H. Johnson. Westport, CT: Greenwood, 1983. (2v.)

198. Use of criminology literature, by Martin Wright. Hamden, CT: Archon Books, 1974.

Population and Life Cycle

Death and dying

199. Adjustment to widowhood and some related problems: a selective and annotated bibliography, by Cecile Strugnell. New York: Health Sciences Publ. Corp., 1974.

200. Bibliography on suicide and suicide prevention, 1897-1957, 1958-1970, by Norman L. Farberow. Rockville, MD: National Institute of Mental Health, 1972.

201. Death: a bibliographical guide, by Albert Jay Miller and Michael James Acri. Metuchen, NJ: Scarecrow, 1977.

202. Death and dying A to Z: a loose-leaf encyclopedic handbook on death and dying and related subjects, by Isaac A. Bleckman. Queens Village, NY: Croner, 1980.

203. Death education: an annotated resource guide, compiled by Hannelore Wass et al. Washington, DC: Hemisphere Publ. Corp., 1980.

204. Dying and death: an annotated bibliography, by Irene L. Sell. New York: Tiresias, 1977.

205. Dying, death, and grief: a critically annotated bibliography and source book of thanatology and terminal care, by Michael A. Simpson. 4th ed. New York: Plenum, 1979.

206. The euthanasia controversy, 1812-1974: a bibliography with select annotations, by Charles W. Triche and Diane Samson Triche. Troy, NY: Whitston, 1975.

207. Research on suicide: a bibliography, compiled by John L. McIntosh. Westport, CT: Greenwood, 1985.

208. Sourcebook on death and dying, James A. Fruehling, consulting editor. Chicago: Marquis, 1982.

209. Suicide: a guide to information sources, by David Lester et al. Detroit: Gale, 1980.

210. Suicide: a selective bibliography of over 2,200 items, by Ann E. Prentice. Metuchen, NJ: Scarecrow, 1974.

Divorce

211. Children and divorce: an annotated bibliography and guide, by Evelyn B. Hausslein. New York: Garland, 1983.

212. Divorce: a selected annotated bibliography, by Mary McKenney. Metuchen, NJ: Scarecrow, 1975.

213. Divorce in the 70s: a subject bibliography, by Kenneth D. Sell. Phoenix, AZ: Oryx, 1981.

214. Divorce in the United States, Canada, and Great Britain: a guide to information sources, by Kenneth D. Sell and Betty H. Sell. Detroit: Gale, 1978.

215. One-parent children: the growing minority. An annotated bibliography, by Mary Noel Gouke and Arline McClarty Rollins. New York: Garland, 1985.

216. The one-parent family: perspectives and annotated bibliography, by Benjamin Schlesinger. 4th ed. Toronto: University of Toronto, 1978.

Marriage and family

217. Adoption bibliography and multi-ethnic sourcebook, by Elizabeth Wharton van Why. Hartford, CT: Open Door Society of Connecticut, 1977.

218. Child care issues for parents and society: a guide to information sources, by Andrew Garoogian and Rhoda Garoogian. Detroit: Gale, 1977.

219. Families under the flag: a review of military literature, compiled by Edna J. Hunter, et al. New York: Praeger, 1982.

220. Family factbook, Helena Znaniecki, consulting editor. Chicago: Marquis Academic Media, 1978.

221. Family measurement techniques: abstracts of published instruments, 1935-1974, by Murray A. Straus and Bruce W. Brown. Minneapolis: University of Minnesota, 1978.

222. Family research: a source book, analysis, and guide to federal funding, edited by Rowan A. Wakefield et al. Westport, CT: Greenwood, 1979. (2v.)

223. History of the family and kinship: a select international bibliography, edited by Gerald L. Soliday et al. Millwood, NY: Kraus International, 1980.

224. International bibliography of research in marriage and the family, 1900-1964, by Joan Aldous and Reuben Hill. Minneapolis: Minnesota Family Study Center and the Institute of Life Insurance, 1967.

225. International bibliography of research in marriage and the family, volume II, 1965-1972, by Joan Aldous and Nancy Dahl. Minneapolis: University of Minnesota, 1974.

226. International family-planning programs, 1966-1975: a bibliography, edited by Katherine Ch'iu Lyle and Sheldon J. Segal. University, AL: University of Alabama, 1977.

227. Inventory of marriage and family literature, 1973/74--. St. Paul, MN: University of Minnesota, 1975--. annual.

228. The Jewish family: a survey and annotated bibliography, by Benjamin Schlesinger. Toronto: University of Toronto, 1971.

229. The multi-problem family: a review and annotated bibliography, by Benjamin Schlesinger. 3rd ed. Toronto: University of Toronto, 1970.

230. Parent-child separation: psychosocial effects on development: an abstracted bibliography, by Faren R. Akins et al. New York: IFI/Plenum, 1981.

231. Problems of early childhood: an annotated bibliography and guide, by Elisabeth S. Hirsch. New York: Garland, 1983.

232. Sage family studies abstracts. Beverly Hills, CA: Sage, 1979--. quarterly.

233. Sources of information on population/family planning: a handbook for Asia, by Sumiye Konoshima et al. Honolulu, HI: East-West Communication Institute, 1975.

234. Special adoptions: an annotated bibliography on transracial, transcultural, and nonconventional adoption and minority children. Washington, DC: Government Printing Office, 1981.

235. The troubled family: sources of information, by Theodore P. Peck. Jefferson, NC: McFarland, 1982.

236. Two-career families: an annotated bibliography of relevant readings. New York: Catalyst, 1981.

237. Violence in the family: an annotated bibliography, by Elizabeth Kemmer. New York: Garland, 1984.

238. Work and family: an annotated bibliography, 1978-1980, compiled by Clifford Baden. Boston: Wheelock College Center for Parenting Studies, 1981.

Population

239. The baby boom: a selective annotated bibliography, by Greg Byerly and Richard E. Rubin. Lexington, MA: Lexington Books, D.C. Heath, 1985.

240. The dictionary of demography, by Roland Pressat. Edited by Christopher Wilson. New York: Blackwell, 1985.

241. Dictionary of demography: biographies, by William Petersen. Westport, CT: Greenwood, 1985. (2v.)

242. Dictionary of demography: multilingual glossary, by William Petersen. Westport, CT: Greenwood, 1985.

243. Dictionary of demography: terms, concepts, and institutions, by William Petersen. Westport, CT: Greenwood, 1986. (2v.)

244. Glossary of population and housing: English-French-Italian-Dutch-German-Swedish, by Gordon Logie. Amersterdam: Elsevier, 1978.

245. The handbook of national population censuses: Latin America and the Caribbean, North America, and Oceania, by Doreen S. Goyer and Eliane Domschke. Westport, CT: Greenwood, 1983.

246. Human migration: a guide to migration literature in English, 1955-1962, by J.J. Mangalam. Lexington, KY: University of Kentucky, 1968.

247. Immigration literature: abstracts of demographic, economic, and policy studies, by Jeannette H. North and Susan J. Grodsky. Washington, DC: U.S. Department of Justice, Immigration and Naturalization Service, 1979.

248. International directory of population information and library resources, by Catherine Fogle et al. Chapel Hill, NC: Carolina Population Center, 1972.

249. International encyclopedia of population, edited by John A. Ross. New York: Free Press, 1982. (2v.)

250. International population census bibliography. Austin, TX: University of Texas, 1965-68. no. 1-7.

251. Latin American population and urbanization analysis: maps and statistics, 1950-1982, by Richard W. Wilkie. Los Angeles: University of California, 1984.

252. The materials of demography: a selected and annotated bibliography, by Hope T. Eldridge. Reprint. Westport, CT: Greenwood, 1975.

253. The methods and materials of demography, by Henry S. Shryock et al. Condensed edition by Edward G. Stockwell. New York: Academic, 1976.

254. Multilingual demographic dictionary. English section, adapted by Etienne van de Walle from the French section edited by Louis Henry. 2nd ed. Liege, Belgium: Ordina Editions, 1982.

255. Population: an international directory of organizations and information resources, by Thaddeus C. Trzyna. Claremont, CA: Public Affairs Clearinghouse, 1976.

256. Population and the population explosion: a bibliography for 1970--. Troy, NY: Whitston, 1973--. annual.

257. Population, environment and resources, and Third World development, edited by P.K. Ghosh. Westport, CT: Greenwood, 1984.

258. Population in development planning: background and bibliography, by Richard E. Bilsborrow. Chapel Hill, NC: University of North Carolina, 1976.

259. Population index. Princeton, NJ: Princeton University and the Population Association of America, 1935--. quarterly.

260. Population information in nineteenth century census volumes, by Suzanne Schulze. Phoenix, AZ: Oryx, 1984.

261. Population information in twentieth century census volumes: 1900-1940, by Suzanne Schulze. Phoenix, AZ: Oryx, 1985.

262. Social change and internal migration: a review of research findings from Africa, Asia, and Latin America, compiled by Alan Simmons et al. Ottawa: International Development Research Centre, 1977.

263. The sociology of human fertility: an annotated bibliography, by Ronald Freedman. New York: Irvington, 1975.

264. Union list of population/family planning periodicals, edited and compiled by Susan Kingsley Pasquariella. Clarion, PA: Association for Population/Family Planning Libraries and Information Centers, 1978.

265. World population policy: an annotated bibliography, by Edwin D. Driver. Lexington, MA: Lexington Books, 1971.

Racial, Ethnic and Social Groups

American Indians

266. The Alaska Eskimos: a selected, annotated bibliography, by Arthur E. Hippler and John Richard Wood. Fairbanks, AK: University of Alaska, 1977.

267. American Indian almanac, by John Upton Terrell. New York: World Publishing, 1971.

268. A Canadian Indian bibliography 1960-1970, by Thomas S. Abler and Sally M. Weaver. Toronto: University of Toronto, 1974.

269. A concise dictionary of Indian tribes of North America, by Barbara A. Leitch. Algonac, MI: Reference Publications, 1979.

270. Guide to research on North American Indians, by Arlene B. Hirschfelder et al. Chicago: American Library Association, 1983.

271. Handbook of Middle American Indians, Robert Wauchope, general editor. Austin, TX: University of Texas, 1964-1976. (16v.)

272. Index to literature on the American Indian, 1970--. San Francisco: Indian Historian Press, 1972--. annual.

273. Indians of North America: methods and sources for library research, by Marilyn L. Haas. Hamden, CT: Shoestring, 1983.

274. Indians of North and South America: a bibliography based on the collection at the Willard E. Yager Library-Museum ..., by Carolyn E. Wolf and Karen R. Folk. Metuchen, NJ: Scarecrow, 1977.

275. Native American women: a contextual bibliography, by Rayna Green. Bloomington, IN: Indiana University, 1983.

276. Native Americans of North America: a bibliography based on collections in the Libraries of California State University, Northridge, compiled by David Perkins and Norman Tanis. Metuchen, NJ: Scarecrow, 1975.

277. Reference encyclopedia of the American Indian, by Barry Klein. 3rd ed. Rye, NY: Todd Publications, 1978. (2v.)

278. Tulapai to Tokay: a bibliography of alcohol use and abuse among native Americans of North America, compiled by Patricia D. Mail and David R. McDonald. New Haven, CT: HRAF Press, 1981.

279. The urbanization of American Indians: a critical bibliography, by Russell Thornton et al. Bloomington, IN: Indiana University, 1982.

Black-Americans

280. The black American reference book, edited by Mabel M. Smythe. Englewood Cliffs, NJ: Prentice-Hall, 1976.

281. Black child development in America, 1927-1977: an annotated bibliography, by Hector F. Myers et al. Westport, CT: Greenwood, 1979.

282. Black children and their families: a bibliography, by Charlotte Dunmore. San Francisco: R & E Research Associates, 1976.

283. The black family and the black woman: a bibliography, compiled by Phyllis Rauch Klotman and Wilmer H. Baatz. New York: Arno, 1978.

284. The black family in the United States: a selected bibliography of annotated books, articles, and dissertations on black families in America, by Lenwood G. Davis. Westport, CT: Greenwood, 1978.

285. Black immigration and ethnicity in the United States: an annotated bibliography, by Center for Afroamerican Studies, University of Michigan. Westport, CT: Greenwood, 1985.

286. Black lesbians: an annotated bibliography, compiled by J.R. Roberts. Tallahassee, FL: Naiad, 1981.

287. Black separatism: a bibliography, by Betty Lanier Jenkins and Susan Phillis. Westport, CT: Greenwood, 1976.

288. Black-white racial attitudes: an annotated bibliography, by Constance E. Obudho. Westport, CT: Greenwood, 1976.

289. The black woman in American society: a selected annotated bibliography, by Lenwood G. Davis. Boston: G.K. Hall, 1975.

290. Demography of the black population in the United States: an annotated bibliography with a review essay, by Jamshid A. Momeni. Westport, CT: Greenwood, 1983.

291. The Ebony handbook, edited by Doris E. Saunders. Chicago: Johnson, 1974.

292. Encyclopedia of black America, edited by W. Augustus Low. New York: McGraw-Hill, 1981.

293. Negro almanac, edited by Harry A. Ploski and James Williams. 4th ed. New York: Wiley, 1983.

294. The Negro in America: a bibliography, by Elizabeth W. Miller. Compiled by Mary L. Fisher. 2nd ed. Cambridge, MA: Harvard University, 1970.

295. The Negro in the United States: a selected bibliography, by Dorothy Burnett Porter. Washington, DC: Library of Congress, 1970.

296. The progress of Afro-American women: a selected bibliography and resource guide, compiled by Janet L. Sims. Westport, CT: Greenwood, 1980.

297. The social and economic status of the black population in the United States: an historical view, 1790-1978. U.S. Bureau of the Census. Washington, DC: U.S. Government Printing Office, 1979.

298. A working bibliography on the Negro in the United States, by Dorothy Burnett Porter. Ann Arbor, MI: Xerox/University Microfilms, 1969.

Communities and urban groups

299. Bibliography on the urban crisis: the behavioral, psychological, and sociological aspects of the urban crisis, by Jon K. Meyer. Chevy Chase, MD: National Institute of Mental Health, 1969.

300. Cities, by Dwight W. Hoover. New York: Bowker, 1976.

301. Directory of urban affairs information and research centers, by Eric V.A. Winston. Metuchen, NJ: Scarecrow, 1970.

302. Encyclopedia of urban planning, edited by Arnold Whittick. Huntington, NY: Krieger, 1980.

303. The Indian city: a bibliographic guide to the literature on urban India, by John Van Willigen. New Haven, CT: Human Relations Area Files, 1979. (2v.)

304. The Kibbutz: a bibliography of scientific and professional publications in English, by Shimon Shur et al. Darby, PA: Norwood Editions, 1981.

305. The language of cities: a glossary of terms, by Charles Abrams. New York: Viking, 1971.

306. Latin American urbanization: a guide to the literature, organizations, and personnel, by Martin Howard Sable. Metuchen, NJ: Scarecrow, 1971.

307. Minority groups and housing: a bibliography, 1950-1970, by Byrl N. Boyce and Sidney Turoff. Morristown, NJ: General Learning, 1972.

308. Periodical literature on United States cities: a bibliography and subject guide, compiled by Barbara Smith Shearer and Benjamin F. Shearer. Westport, CT: Greenwood, 1983.

309. Sage urban studies abstracts. Beverly Hills, CA: Sage, 1973--. quarterly.

310. Suburbia: a guide to information sources, by Joseph Zikmund and Deborah Ellis Dennis. Detroit: Gale, 1979.

311. University urban research centers. 2nd ed. Washington, DC: Urban Institute, 1971.

312. Urban affairs abstracts. Washington, DC: National League of Cities, 1971--.

313. Urban America examined: a bibliography, by Dale E. Casper. New York: Garland, 1985.

314. Urban community: a guide to information sources, by Anthony J. Filipovitch and Earl J. Reeves. Detroit: Gale, 1978.

315. Urban environments and human behavior: an annotated bibliography, by Gwen Bell et al. Stroudsburg, PA: Dowden, Hutchinson & Ross, 1973.

316. Urban needs: a bibliography and directory for community resource centers, by Paula Kline. Metuchen, NJ: Scarecrow, 1978.

317. Urbanization in developing countries: an international bibliography, by Stanley D. Brunn. East Lansing, MI: Michigan State University, 1971.

318. Urbanization in tropical Africa: an annotated bibliography, by Anthony Michael O'Connor. Boston: G.K. Hall, 1981.

319. Village studies data analysis and bibliography. Epping, Essex, England: University of Sussex, 1976-78. (2v.)

Elderly

320. Abuse of the elderly: a guide to resources and services, edited by Joseph J. Costa. Lexington, MA: Lexington Books, D.C. Heath, 1984.

321. Aging: a guide to reference sources, journals and government publications, by B. McIlvaine and Mohini Mundkur. Storrs, CT: University of Connecticut Library, 1978.

322. Aging: a guide to resources, edited by John B. Balkema. Syracuse, NY: Gaylord, 1983.

323. Aging and the aged: an annotated bibliography and library research guide, by Linna Funk Place et al. Boulder, CO: Westview, 1981.

324. Alternatives to institutionalization: a selective review of the literature, by Anthony N. Maluccio. Saratoga, CA: Century Twenty One, 1980.

325. The black aged in the United States: an annotated bibliography, by Lenwood G. Davis. Westport, CT: Greenwood, 1980.

326. The challenge of aging: a bibliography, compiled by Margaret E. Monroe and Rhea Joyce Rubin. Littleton, CO: Libraries Unlimited, 1983.

327. Disaffiliated man: essays and bibliography on skid row, vagrancy, and outsiders, by Howard M. Bahr. Toronto: University of Toronto, 1970.

328. Elder neglect and abuse: an annotated bibliography, compiled by Tanya F. Johnson et al. Westport, CT: Greenwood, 1985.

329. Ethnicity and aging: a bibliography, compiled by Edward Murguia et al. San Antonio, TX: Trinity University, 1984.

330. Fact book on aging: a profile of America's older population. Washington, DC: National Council on the Aging, 1978.

331. Funding in aging: public, private and voluntary, by Lilly Cohen et al. 2nd ed. Garden City, NY: Adelphi University, 1979.

332. Gerontology: a cross-national core list of significant works, by Willie M. Edwards and Frances Flynn. Ann Arbor, MI: University of Michigan, 1982.

333. Gerontology: an annotated bibliography, by M. Leigh Rooke and C. Ray Wingrove. Washington, DC: University Press of America, 1978.

334. A guide to minority aging references, by Jose B. Cuellar and E. Percil Stanford. Washington, DC: Federal Council on Aging, 1983.

335. Handbook of aging and the social sciences, edited by Robert H. Binstock and Ethel Shanas. 2nd ed. New York: Van Nostrand Reinhold, 1985.

336. Handbook on the aged in the United States, edited by Erdman B. Palmore. Westport, CT: Greenwood, 1984.

337. International directory of organizations concerned with the aging. New York: United Nations, 1977.

338. International handbook on aging: contemporary developments and research, edited by Erdman Palmore. Westport, CT: Greenwood, 1980.

339. The national senior citizens directory, by Deborah J. Stither and Mary Lee Bundy. College Park, MD: Urban Information Interpreters, 1982.

340. Religion & aging: an annotated bibliography, by Vincent John Fecher. San Antonio, TX: Trinity University, 1982.

341. The rural elderly: an annotated bibliography of social science research, by John A. Krout. Westport, CT: Greenwood, 1983.

342. Sourcebook on aging. 2nd ed. Chicago: Marquis Academic Media, 1979.

Ethnic groups -- general topics

343. American ethnic groups and the revival of cultural pluralism, by Jack F. Kinton. 4th ed. Aurora, IL: Social Science & Sociological Resources, 1974.

344. Canadian ethnic groups bibliography: a selected bibliography of ethno-cultural groups in Canada and the province of Ontario, by Andrew Gregorovich. Toronto: Department of the Provincial Secretary and Citizenship of Ontario, 1972.

345. Comprehensive bibliography for the study of American minorities, by Wayne Charles Miller et al. New York: New York University, 1976. (2v.)

346. Demography of racial and ethnic minorities in the United States: an annotated bibliography with a review essay, by Jamshid A. Momeni. Westport, CT: Greenwood, 1984.

347. Encyclopedic directory of ethnic organizations in the United States, by Lubomyr R. Wynar. Littleton, CO: Libraries Unlimited, 1975.

348. The ethnic almanac, by Stephanie Bernardo. Garden City, NY: Doubleday, 1981.

349. Ethnic film and filmstrip guide for libraries and media centers: a selective filmography, by Lubomyr R. Wynar and Lois Butler. Littleton, CO: Libraries Unlimited, 1980.

350. Ethnic information sources of the United States, edited by Paul Wasserman. 2nd ed. Detroit: Gale, 1983. (2v.)

351. Ethnic studies bibliography. Pittsburgh: University of Pittsburgh, v.1-2, 1975-76.

352. European immigration and ethnicity in the United States and Canada: a historical bibliography, edited by David L. Brye. Santa Barbara, CA: ABC-Clio, 1983.

353. Harvard encyclopedia of American ethnic groups, edited by Stephan Thernstrom. Cambridge, MA: Harvard University, 1980.

354. Immigrants and their children in the United States: a bibliography of doctoral dissertations, 1885-1982, by A. William Hoglund. New York: Garland, 1985.

355. Immigration and ethnicity: a guide to information sources, by John D. Buenker and Nicholas C. Burckel. Detroit: Gale, 1978.

356. Minorities in America, the annual bibliography, 1976, edited by Wayne Charles Miller. University Park, PA: Pennsylvania State University, 1985.

357. The Oxbridge directory of ethnic periodicals. New York: Oxbridge Communications, 1979.

358. Refugees in the United States: a reference handbook, edited by David W. Haines. Westport, CT: Greenwood, 1985.

Ethnic groups -- specific topics

359. American Jewish yearbook. Philadelphia, PA: The Jewish Publication Society of America and the American Jewish Committee, 1899--. annual.

360. Asian American reference data directory, by Rj Associates. Washington, DC: U.S. Department of Health, Education, and Welfare, 1976.

361. The cultural heritage of the Swedish immigrant: selected references, by O. Fritiof Ander. New York: Arno, 1979.

362. Dutch Americans: a guide to information sources, by Linda Pegman Doezema. Detroit: Gale, 1979.

363. Filipinos overseas: a bibliography, by Shiro Saito. New York: Center for Migration Studies, 1977.

364. German-American history and life: a guide to information sources, by Michael Keresztesi and Gary Cocozzoli. Detroit: Gale, 1980.

365. German-Americana: a bibliography, by Don Heinrich Tolzmann. Metuchen, NJ: Scarecrow, 1975.

366. Guide to the study of the Soviet nationalities: non-Russian peoples of the USSR, edited by Stephan M. Horak. Littleton, CO: Libraries Unlimited, 1982.

367. Hungarians in the United States and Canada: a bibliography, compiled and edited by Joseph Szeplaki. Minneapolis: University of Minnesota, 1977.

368. The Irish-American experience: a guide to the literature, by Seamus P. Metress. Washington, DC: University Press of America, 1981.

369. Italian Americans: a guide to information sources, by Francesco Cordasco. Detroit: Gale, 1978.

370. Italians in the United States, by Francesco Cordasco and Michael Vaughn Cordasco. Fairview, NJ: Junius, 1981.

371. The Japanese in Hawaii: an annotated bibliography of Japanese Americans, by Dennis M. Ogawa and Jerry Y. Fujioka. Rev. ed. Honolulu, HI: University of Hawaii, 1975.

372. The Jewish experience in America: a historical bibliography. Santa Barbara, CA: ABC-Clio, 1983.

373. Literature of the Filipino-American in the United States: a selective and annotated bibliography, by Irene P. Norell. San Francisco: R and E Research Associates, 1976.

374. Polish American history and culture: a classified bibliography, by Joseph W. Zurawski. Chicago: Polish Museum of America, 1975.

375. Refugee resettlement in the United States: an annotated bibliography on the adjustment of Cuban, Soviet and Southeast Asian refugees. Washington, DC: Government Printing Office, 1981.

376. The Romanians in America and Canada: a guide to information sources, by Vladimir Wertsman. Detroit: Gale, 1980.

377. Social research on Arabs in Israel, 1948-1977: trends and an annotated bibliography, by Sammy Smooha and Ora Cibulski. Tel Aviv: Turtledove, 1978.

378. The third Americans: a select bibliography on Asians in America with annotations, by Tekong Tong, with the assistance of Robert Wu. Oak Park, IL: CHCUS, 1980.

379. Ukrainians in Canada and the United States: a guide to information sources, by Aleksander Sokolyszyn and Vladimir Wertsman. Detroit: Gale, 1981.

Hispanics

380. Basque Americans: a guide to information sources, by William A. Douglass and Richard W. Etulain. Detroit: Gale, 1981.

381. Bibliografia chicana: a guide to information sources, by Arnulfo D. Trejo. Detroit: Gale, 1975.

382. The Chicana: a comprehensive bibliographic study, edited by Robert Cabello-Argandona et al. Los Angeles: Aztlan, 1975.

383. A comprehensive Chicano bibliography, 1960-1972, by Jane Mitchell Talbot and Gilbert R. Cruz. Austin, TX: Jenkins, 1973.

384. Cubans in the United States: a bibliography for research in the social and behavioral sciences, 1960-1983, compiled by Lyn MacCorkle. Westport, CT: Greenwood, 1984.

385. Hispanic American voluntary organizations, by Sylvia Alicia Gonzales. Westport, CT: Greenwood, 1985.

386. The Mexican American: a critical guide to research aids, by Barbara J. Robinson and Joy C. Robinson. Greenwich, CT: JAI, 1980.

387. The Mexican American: a selected and annotated bibliography, edited by Luis G. Nogales. 2nd ed. Stanford, CA: Stanford University, 1971.

388. Mexican Americans: a research bibliography, by Frank Pino. East Lansing, MI: Michigan State University, 1974. (2v.)

389. Mexican Americans: an annotated bibliography of bibliographies, by Julio A. Martinez and Ada Burns. Saratoga, CA: R & E Publishers, 1984.

390. The Puerto Rican community and its children on the mainland: a source book for teachers, social workers, and other professionals, edited by Francesco Cordasco and Eugene Bucchioni. Metuchen, NJ: Scarecrow, 1982.

391. The Puerto Ricans: an annotated bibliography, edited by Paquita Vivo. New York: Bowker, 1973.

392. Sourcebook of Hispanic culture in the United States, edited by David William Foster. Chicago: American Library Association, 1982.

Race relations

393. Bibliography on racism. Rockville, MD: National Institute of Mental Health, 1972-78. (2v.)

394. Dictionary of race and ethnic relations, by E. Ellis Cashmore. London: Routledge & Kegan Paul, 1984.

395. The invisible empire: a bibliography of the Ku Klux Klan, by William H. Fisher. Metuchen, NJ: Scarecrow, 1980.

396. The Ku Klux Klan: a bibliography, compiled by Lenwood G. Davis and Janet L. Sims-Wood. Westport, CT: Greenwood, 1984.

397. Race and ethnic relations: an annotated bibliography, by Graham C. Kinloch. New York: Garland, 1984.

398. Race and ethnic relations in Latin America and the Caribbean: an historical dictionary and bibliography, by Robert M. Levine. Metuchen, NJ: Scarecrow, 1980.

399. Sage race relations abstracts. Beverly Hills, CA: Sage, 1976--. quarterly.

Women -- general topics

400. Abortion: an annotated indexed bibliography, by Maureen Muldoon. New York: E. Mellen, 1980.

401. Abortion bibliography for 1970--. Troy, NY: Whitston, 1972--. annual.

402. Determinants and consequences of maternal employment: an annotated bibliography, 1968-1980, by Marsha Hurst and Ruth E. Zambrana. Washington, DC: Business and Professional Women's Foundation, 1981.

403. Development as if women mattered: an annotated bibliography with a Third World focus, by May Rihani and Jody Joy. Washington, DC: New TransCentury Foundation, 1978.

404. Guide to social science resources in women's studies, by Elizabeth H. Oakes and Kathleen E. Sheldon. Santa Barbara, CA: ABC-Clio, 1978.

405. Handbook of international data on women, by Elise Boulding et al. Los Angeles: Sage, 1976.

406. Minorities and women: a guide to reference literature in the social sciences, by Gail A. Schlachter and Donna Belli. Los Angeles: Reference Services, 1977.

407. The nature of woman: an encyclopedia & guide to the literature, by Mary Anne Warren. Inverness, CA: Edgepress, 1979.

408. New feminist scholarship: a guide to bibliographies, edited by Jane Williamson. Old Westbury, NY: Feminist Press, 1979.

409. A statistical portrait of women in the U.S., 1978. U.S. Bureau of the Census. Washington, DC: U.S. Government Printing Office, 1980.

410. Women: a bibliography of bibliographies, by Patricia K. Ballou. Boston: G.K. Hall, 1980.

411. Women and ambition: a bibliography, by Patricia S. Faunce. Metuchen, NJ: Scarecrow, 1980.

412. Women and deviance: issues in social conflict and change: an annotated bibliography, by Nanette J. Davis and Jone M. Keith. New York: Garland, 1984.

413. Women and society: a critical review of the literature with a selected annotated bibliography, by Marie Barovic Rosenberg and Len V. Bergstrom. Beverly Hills, CA: Sage, 1975.

414. Women and society, citations 3601 to 6000: an annotated bibliography, by JoAnn Delores Een and Marie B. Rosenberg-Dishman. Beverly Hills, CA: Sage, 1978.

415. Women and urban society: a guide to information sources, by Hasia R. Diner. Detroit: Gale, 1979.

416. Women and world development: an annotated bibliography, by Mayra Buvinic. Washington, DC: Overseas Development Council, 1976.

417. Women at work: an annotated bibliography, by Mei Liang Bickner. Los Angeles: University of California, 1974-77. (2v.)

418. Women helping women: a state-by-state directory of services. New York: Women's Action Alliance, 1981.

419. Women in perspective: a guide for cross-cultural studies, by Sue-Ellen Jacobs. Urbana, IL: University of Illinois, 1974.

420. Women, 1965-1975, edited by Cynthia Crippen. Glen Rock, NJ: Microfilming Corporation of America, 1978.

421. Women studies abstracts. Rush, NY: Rush, 1972--. quarterly.

422. Women's action almanac: a complete resource guide, edited by Jane Williamson et al. New York: William Morrow, 1979.

423. The women's movement in the seventies: an international English-language bibliography, by Albert Krichmar et al. Metuchen, NJ: Scarecrow, 1977.

424. Women's organizations & leaders directory, edited by Lester A. Barrer. Washington, DC: World Today, 1973--.

425. Women's studies: a checklist of bibliographies, compiled by Maureen Ritchie. London: Mansell, 1980.

426. Women's studies: a recommended core bibliography, by Esther Stineman with the assistance of Catherine Loeb. Littleton, CO: Libraries Unlimited, 1979.

Women -- by region

427. African women: a select bibliography, by Laura Kratochvil and Shauna Shaw. Cambridge, England: African Studies Centre, 1974.

428. Appalachian women: an annotated bibliography, by Sidney Saylor Farr. Lexington, KY: University Press of Kentucky, 1981.

429. Korean and Japanese women: an analytic bibliographical guide, compiled and edited by Hesung Chun Koh. Westport, CT: Greenwood, 1982.

430. The modern Arab woman: a bibliography, by Michelle Raccagni. Metuchen, NJ: Scarecrow, 1978.

431. The status of the Arab woman: a select bibliography, compiled by Samira Rafidi Meghdessian. Westport, CT: Greenwood, 1980.

432. Women in America: a guide to information sources, by Virginia R. Terris. Detroit: Gale, 1980.

433. Women in China: a selected and annotated bibliography, by Karen T. Wei. Westport, CT: Greenwood, 1984.

434. Women in Southeast Asia: a bibliography, by Kok Sim Fan. Boston: G.K. Hall, 1982.

435. Women in Spanish America: an annotated bibliography from pre-conquest to contemporary times, by Meri Knaster. Boston: G.K. Hall, 1977.

436. Women in the Caribbean: a bibliography, by Bertie A. Cohen Stuart. Leiden, Netherlands: Royal Institute of Linguistics and Anthropology, 1979.

437. Women in the Middle East and North Africa: an annotated bibliography, by Ayad al-Qazzaz. Austin, TX: Center for Middle Eastern Studies, 1977.

438. Women of India: an annotated bibliography, by Harshida Pandit. New York: Garland, 1985.

439. Women of South Asia: a guide to resources, by Carol Sakala. Millwood, NY: Kraus International, 1980.

Youth

440. American childhood: a research guide and historical handbook, by Joseph M. Hawes and N. Ray Hiner. Westport, CT: Greenwood, 1985.

441. Child abuse: an annotated bibliography, by Dorothy P. Wells. Metuchen, NJ: Scarecrow, 1980.

442. Child abuse and neglect: an annotated bibliography, by Beatrice J. Kalisch. Westport, CT: Greenwood, 1978.

443. Child abuse and neglect programs: practice and theory. Rockville, MD: National Institute of Mental Health, 1977.

444. Child welfare training and practice: an annotated bibliography, compiled by John T. Pardeck et al. Westport, CT: Greenwood, 1982.

445. The emergence of youth societies: a cross-cultural approach, by David Gottlieb et al. New York: Free Press, 1966.

446. Juvenile delinquency: a critical annotated bibliography, by Phillippe Sidney de Q. Cabot. Reprint. Westport, CT: Greenwood, 1971.

447. The national children's directory: an organizational directory and reference guide for changing conditions for children and youth, edited by Mary Lee Bundy and Rebecca Glenn Whaley. College Park, MD: Urban Information Interpreters, 1977.

448. Selected and annotated bibliography of youth, youth work, and provision for youth, by Deborah Derrick. Leicester, England: National Youth Bureau, 1976.

Sexuality

Sexual abuse

449. Abuse of women: legislation, reporting, and prevention, by Joseph J. Costa. Lexington, MA: Lexington Books, D.C. Heath, 1983.

450. Incest: an annotated bibliography, by Mary de Young. Jefferson, NC: McFarland, 1985.

451. Incest: the last taboo: an annotated bibliography, by Rick Rubin and Greg Byerly. New York: Garland, 1983.

452. National directory: rape prevention and treatment resources. Compiled by National Center for the Prevention and Control of Rape. Washington, DC: National Institute of Mental Health, 1981.

453. Rape: a bibliography, 1965-1975, by Dorothy L. Barnes. Troy, NY: Whitston, 1977.

454. Rape and rape-related issues, by Elizabeth Jane Kemmer. New York: Garland, 1977.

455. Rape and sexual assault: a research handbook, edited by Ann Wolbert Burgess. New York: Garland, 1985.

456. Sexual abuse of children: a resource guide and annotated bibliography, by Benjamin Schlesinger. Buffalo, NY: University of Toronto, 1982.

457. Violence against women: an annotated bibliography, by Carolyn F. Wilson. Boston: G.K. Hall, 1981.

Sexual behavior, attitudes and deviations

458. An annotated bibliography of homosexuality, by Vern L. Bullough et al. New York: Garland, 1976. (2v.)

459. A bibliography of prostitution, edited by Vern L. Bullough et al. New York: Garland, 1977.

460. Homosexuality: a selective bibliography of over 3,000 items, by William Parker. Metuchen, NJ: Scarecrow, 1971.

461. Homosexuality: an annotated bibliography, edited by Martin S. Weinberg and Alan P. Bell. New York: Harper & Row, 1972.

462. Homosexuality bibliography: supplement, 1970-1975, by William Parker. Metuchen, NJ: Scarecrow, 1977.

463. Homosexuality bibliography: second supplement, 1976-1982, by William Parker. Metuchen, NJ: Scarecrow, 1985.

464. Homosexuality in Canada: a bibliography, compiled by William Crawford. 2nd ed. Ontario: Canadian Gay Archives, 1984.

465. Human sexuality: a bibliography and critical evaluation of recent texts, by Mervyn L. Mason. Westport, CT: Greenwood, 1983.

466. The male sex role: a selected and annotated bibliography, by Kathleen E. Grady et al. Rockville, MD: National Institutes of Health, 1979.

467. Men's studies: a selected and annotated interdisciplinary bibliography, compiled by Eugene R. August. Littleton, CO: Libraries Unlimited, 1985.

468. Pornography: the conflict over sexually explicit materials in the United States: an annotated bibliography, by Greg Byerly and Rick Rubin. New York: Garland, 1980.

469. Sex research: bibliographies from the Institute for Sex Research, compiled by Joan Scherer Brewer and Rod W. Wright. Phoenix, AZ: Oryx, 1979.

470. Sex role stereotyping in the mass media: an annotated bibliography, by Leslie Friedman. New York: Garland, 1977.

471. Sex roles: a research bibliography, by Helen S. Astin et al. Rockville, MD: National Institute of Mental Health, 1975.

472. The sexual barrier: legal, medical, economic and social aspects of sex discrimination, by Marija Matich Hughes. Washington, DC: Hughes, 1977.

473. Sexuality and aging: an annotated bibliography, by George F. Wharton. Metuchen, NJ: Scarecrow, 1981.

474. Women and sexuality in America: a bibliography, by Nancy Sahli. Boston: G.K. Hall, 1984.

Social Issues

Alcoholism

475. Alcohol and sexuality: an annotated bibliography on alcohol use, alcoholism, and human sexual behavior, by Timothy J. O'Farrell et al. Phoenix, AZ: Oryx, 1983.

476. Alcohol and the elderly: a comprehensive bibliography, by Grace M. Barnes et al. Westport, CT: Greenwood, 1980.

477. Alcohol and youth: a comprehensive bibliography, by Grace M. Barnes. Westport, CT: Greenwood, 1982.

478. Alcohol use and alcoholism: a guide to the literature, by Penny Booth Page. New York: Garland, 1985.

479. Comprehensive bibliography of existing literature on alcohol, 1969-1974, by Robert S. Gold et al. Dubuque, IA: Kendall/Hunt, 1975.

480. Dictionary of alcohol use and abuse: slang, terms, and terminology, by Ernest L. Abel. Westport, CT: Greenwood, 1985.

481. A dictionary of words about alcohol, edited by Mark Keller et al. 2nd ed. New Brunswick, NJ: Rutgers Center of Alcohol Studies, 1982.

482. The encyclopedia of alcoholism, by Robert O'Brien and Morris Chafetz. New York: Facts on File, 1982.

483. International bibliography of studies on alcohol, edited by Mark Keller. New Brunswick, NJ: Rutgers Center of Alcohol Studies, 1966-67.

484. Social and behavioral aspects of female alcoholism: an annotated bibliography, compiled by H. Paul Chalfant et al. Westport, CT: Greenwood, 1980.

Crime

485. Arson: a selected bibliography, compiled by J.T. Skip Duncan et al. Washington, DC: U.S. Government Printing Office, 1979.

486. Computer crime, abuse, liability and security: a comprehensive bibliography, 1970-1984, compiled by Reba A. Best and D. Cheryn Picquet. Jefferson, NC: McFarland, 1985.

487. Crime dictionary, by Ralph DeSola. New York: Facts on File, 1982.

488. The encyclopedia of American crime, by Carl Sifakis. New York: Facts on File, 1982.

489. International terrorism: an annotated bibliography and research guide, by Augustus R. Norton and Martin H. Greenberg. Boulder, CO: Westview, 1980.

490. Language of the underworld, edited by David W. Maurer. Lexington, KY: University Press of Kentucky, 1981.

491. The literature of police corruption, by Antony E. Simpson and Nina Duchaine. New York: John Jay, 1977-79. (2v.)

492. Mafia: a select annotated bibliography, by Lloyd Trott. Cambridge, England: Cambridge University, 1977.

493. Organized crime: a selected bibliography, by Isabella Hopkins et al. Austin, TX: University of Texas, 1973.

Drug abuse

494. A bibliography of drug abuse, including alcohol and tobacco, by Theodora Andrews. Littleton, CO: Libraries Unlimited, 1977.

495. A bibliography of drug abuse: supplement 1977-1980, by Theodora Andrews. Littleton, CO: Libraries Unlimited, 1981.

496. A bibliography on drug dependence, compiled by Helen F. Sells. Fort Worth, TX: Texas Christian University, 1967.

497. A comprehensive guide to the cannabis literature, by Ernest L. Abel. Westport, CT: Greenwood, 1979.

498. A dictionary of drug abuse terms and terminology, by Ernest L. Abel. Westport, CT: Greenwood, 1984.

499. Drug abuse bibliography. Troy, NY: Whitston, 1971--. annual.

500. Drug use and abuse: a guide to research findings, by Gregory A. Austin and Michael L. Prendergast. Santa Barbara, CA: ABC-Clio, 1984. (2v.)

501. Drug use and abuse among U.S. minorities, by Patti Iiyama et al. New York: Praeger, 1976.

502. The encyclopedia of drug abuse, by Robert O'Brien and Sidney Cohen, M.D. New York: Facts on File, 1984.

503. Marihuana: an annotated bibliography, by Coy W. Waller et al. New York: Macmillan, 1976, 1982. (2v.)

504. A marihuana dictionary: words, terms, events, and persons relating to cannabis, by Ernest L. Abel. Westport, CT: Greenwood, 1982.

Poverty

505. Attitudes of the poor and attitudes toward the poor: an annotated bibliography, by Colin Cameron. Madison, WI: University of Wisconsin, 1975.

506. Background material on poverty. Washington, DC: U.S. Government Printing Office, 1983.

507. Characteristics of the population below the poverty level: 1983. Washington, DC: U.S. Government Printing Office, 1985.

508. Culturally disadvantaged: a bibliography and Keyword-Out-of-Context (KWOC) index, by Robert E. Booth et al. Detroit: Wayne State University, 1967.

509. The definition and measurement of poverty, by Sharon M. Oster et al. Boulder, CO: Westview, 1978. (2v.)

510. Human resources abstracts. Beverly Hills, CA: Sage, 1966--. quarterly.

511. Measuring the condition of the world's poor: the physical quality of life index, by Morris David Morris. New York: Pergamon, 1979.

512. Poverty: an annotated bibliography and references, by Freda L. Paltiel. Ottawa: Canadian Welfare Council, 1966.

513. Poverty/pauvrete, supplements 1-3, by Agnes Woodward. Ottawa: Canadian Welfare Council, 1967-68.

514. Poverty in Canada and the United States: overview and annotated bibliography, by Benjamin Schlesinger. Toronto: University of Toronto, 1966.

515. Poverty in the United States during the sixties: a bibliography, compiled by Dorothy Tompkins. Berkeley, CA: Institute of Governmental Studies, 1970.

516. Southern poor whites: a selected annotated bibliography of published sources, by J. Wayne Flynt and Dorothy S. Flynt. New York: Garland, 1981.

Social Forces

Popular culture

517. Blacks on television: a selectively annotated bibliography, by George H. Hill and Sylvia Saverson Hill. Metuchen, NJ: Scarecrow, 1985.

518. Effects and functions of television: children and adolescents: a bibliography of selected research literature 1970-1978, compiled by Manfred Meyer and Ursula Nissen. Revised edition. New York: K. G. Saur, 1979.

519. Handbook of American popular culture, edited by Thomas M. Inge. Westport, CT: Greenwood, 1978-81. (3v.)

520. Role portrayal and stereotyping on television: an annotated bibliography of studies relating to women, minorities, aging, sexual behavior, health and handicaps, compiled and edited by Nancy Signorielli. Westport, CT: Greenwood, 1985.

521. Where does the time go?: the United Media Enterprises report on leisure in America, by Research & Forecasts, Inc. New York: Newspaper Enterprise Association, 1983.

522. Women in popular culture: a reference guide, by Katherine Fishburn. Westport, CT: Greenwood, 1982.

Public opinion

523. American public opinion index. Louisville, KY: Opinion Research Service, 1981--.

524. American social attitudes data sourcebook, 1947-1978, by Philip E. Converse et al. Cambridge, MA: Harvard University, 1980.

525. The Gallup poll: public opinion, 1935-1971, by George Horace Gallup. New York: Random House, 1972. (3v.)

526. The Gallup poll: public opinion, 1972-1977, by George Horace Gallup. Wilmington, DE: Scholarly Resources, 1978. (2v.)

527. The Gallup poll: public opinion, 1978--, by George Horace Gallup. Wilmington, DE: Scholarly Resources, 1979--. annual.

528. Index to international public opinion, by Survey Research Consultants International, Inc. Westport, CT: Greenwood, 1978/79--.

Social change and conflict

529. Collective behavior: a bibliography, by Denton E. Morrison and Kenneth E. Hornback. New York: Garland, 1976.

530. Conflict and conflict resolution: a historical bibliography, by Jack Nusan Porter. New York: Garland, 1982.

531. Confrontation, conflict, and dissent: a bibliography of a decade of controversy, 1960-1970, by Albert Jay Miller. Metuchen, NJ: Scarecrow, 1972.

532. A dictionary of American social change, by Louis Filler. Malabar, FL: Krieger, 1982.

533. Life change events research, 1966-1978: an annotated bibliography of the periodical literature, edited by Thomas H. Holmes and Ella M. David. New York: Praeger, 1984.

534. The process of modernization: an annotated bibliography on the sociocultural aspects of development, by John Brode. Cambridge, MA: Harvard University, 1969.

535. Survey research on comparative social change: a bibliography, by Frederick W. Frey. Cambridge, MA: M.I.T. Press, 1969.

Social indicators

536. Handbook of Soviet social science data, edited by Ellen Propper Mickiewicz. New York: Free Press, 1973.

537. Social impact assessment and management, by F. Larry Leistritz and Brenda Ekstrom. New York: Garland, 1985.

538. Social indicators: an annotated bibliography of current literature, edited by Kevin J. Gilmartin et al. New York: Garland, 1979.

539. Social indicators for the European Community, 1960-1978, by Statistical Office of the European Communities. Luxembourg: Office des Publications Officielles des Communautes Europeennes, 1980.

540. Social indicators III: selected data on social conditions and trends in the United States. Washington, DC: U.S. Department of Commerce, 1980.

541. Urban indicators: a guide to information sources, by Thomas P. Murphy. Detroit, MI: Gale, 1980.

542. World handbook of political and social indicators, by Charles Lewis Taylor and David A. Jodice. 3rd ed. New Haven, CT: Yale University, 1983.

Social policy

543. The policy analysis source book for social programs, by Arnold Kotz and Julia Graham Lear. Washington, DC: National Planning Association, 1975. (2v.)

544. Social policy and administration in Britain: a bibliography, by Tessa Blackstone. London: Frances Pinter, 1975.

545. Social policy and its administration: a survey of the Australian literature, 1950-1975, by Joanna Monie and Adrienne Wise. Rushcutters Bay, N.S.W., Australia: Pergamon, 1977.

546. Urban policy: a guide to information sources, by Dennis James Palumbo and George Albert Taylor. Detroit, MI: Gale, 1978.

Social Welfare

Criminal justice

547. Alternatives to institutionalization: a definitive bibliography, by James R. Brantley and Marjorie Kravitz. Rockville, MD: U.S. Department of Justice, 1979.

548. Criminal justice abstracts. Hackensack, NJ: National Council on Crime and Delinquency, 1977--. quarterly.

549. The criminal justice dictionary, compiled by Erik Beckman. 2nd ed. Ann Arbor, MI: Pierian, 1983.

550. Criminal justice in America, 1959-1984: an annotated bibliography, by John D. Hewitt et al. New York: Garland, 1985.

551. Criminal justice periodical index. Ann Arbor, MI: University Microfilms, 1975--.

552. Criminal justice research sources, by Robert L. O'Block. 2nd ed. Cincinnati, OH: Anderson, 1986.

553. The criminal justice systems of the Latin American nations: a bibliography of the primary and secondary literature, by Richard Rank. South Hackensack, NJ: Rothman, 1974.

554. Criminal justice vocabulary, by Julian A. Martin and Nicholas A. Astone. Springfield, IL: C.C. Thomas, 1980.

555. Dictionary of American penology, by Vergil L. Williams. Westport, CT: Greenwood, 1979.

556. Dictionary of criminal justice, by George Eugene Rush. Boston: Holbrook, 1977.

557. Directory of criminal justice information sources, by Thomas Ketterman. 3rd ed. Washington, DC: U.S. Department of Justice, 1979.

558. Encyclopedia of crime and justice, edited by Sanford H. Kadish. New York: Free Press, 1983. (4v.)

559. Information sources in criminal justice: an annotated guide to directories, journals, newsletters, by Anne Newton et al. Hackensack, NJ: National Council on Crime and Delinquency, 1976.

560. The national prison directory: a prison reform, organizational, and resource directory, edited by Mary Lee Bundy. 2nd ed. College Park, MD: Urban Information Interpreters, 1979.

561. The prison and the prisoner, by Dorothy Campbell Tompkins. Berkeley, CA: University of California, 1972.

562. Sourcebook of criminal justice statistics -- 1983, edited by Edward J. Brown et al. Washington, DC: U.S. Government Printing Office, 1984.

Mental health

563. Anthropological and cross-cultural themes in mental health: an annotated bibliography, 1925-1974, by Armando R. Favazza and Mary Oman. Columbia, MO: University of Missouri, 1977.

564. Bibliography of North American Indian mental health, compiled by Dianne R. Kelso and Carolyn L. Attneave. Westport, CT: Greenwood, 1981.

565. Biological, psychological, and environmental factors in delinquency and mental disorder: an interdisciplinary bibliography, compiled by Deborah W. Denno and Ruth M. Schwarz. Westport, CT: Greenwood, 1985.

566. Hispanic mental health research: a reference guide, by Frank Newton et al. Berkeley, CA: University of California, 1982.

567. The national directory of mental health: a guide to adult outpatient mental health facilities and services throughout the United States, edited by Ellen Gay Detlefsen. New York: Wiley, 1980.

568. Social behavior of the mentally retarded: an annotated bibliography, by Manny Sternlicht and George Windholz. New York: Garland, 1984.

569. Social networks and mental health: an annotated bibliography, compiled by David E. Biegel et al. Beverley Hills, CA: Sage, 1985.

570. The sociology and anthropology of mental illness: a reference guide, by Edwin D. Driver. Revised ed. Amherst, MA: University of Massachusetts, 1972.

Social work

571. Directory of agencies: U.S. voluntary, international voluntary, intergovernmental. Washington, DC: National Association of Social Workers, 1980.

572. Directory of social welfare research capabilities: a working guide to organizations engaged in social work and social welfare research, by Richard J. Estes. Ardmore, PA: Dorrance, 1981.

573. Encyclopedia of social work: successor to the social work year book. New York: National Association of Social Workers, 1965--.

574. Family counseling: an annotated bibliography, edited by Kristi Brown. Cambridge, MA: Oelgeschlager, Gunn & Hain, 1981.

575. Group work in the helping professions: a bibliography, by David G. Zimpfer. Muncie, IN: Accelerated Development, 1984.

576. Handbook of the social services, edited by Neil Gilbert and Harry Specht. Englewood Cliffs, NJ: Prentice-Hall, 1981.

577. The Project Share Collection, 1976-1979. Rockville, MD: U.S. Department of Health, Education, and Welfare, 1979.

578. Reference sources in social work: an annotated bibliography, by James H. Conrad. Metuchen, NJ: Scarecrow, 1982.

579. Rural social welfare: educators and practitioners, by Dennis L. Poole. New York: Praeger, 1981.

580. Social service organizations. Peter Romanofsky, editor-in-chief. Westport, CT: Greenwood, 1978. (2v.)

581. Social service organizations and agencies directory, compiled and edited by Anthony T. Kruzas. Detroit: Gale, 1982.

582. Social welfare in America: an annotated bibliography, edited by Walter I. Trattner and W. Andrew Achenbaum. Westport, CT: Greenwood, 1983.

583. Social work education: a bibliography, by Hong-Chan Li. Metuchen, NJ: Scarecrow, 1978.

584. Social work research & abstracts. New York: National Association of Social Workers, 1977. quarterly.

585. Working with people: a selected social casework bibliography, by Marion S. Blank. 2nd rev. ed. New York: Family Service Association of America, 1982.

586. World guide to social work education, compiled by Vijaya Rao. Edited by Katherine A. Kendall. 2nd ed. New York: International Association of Schools of Social Work, 1984.

TITLE/SUBTITLE INDEX

Aboriginal tribes of Australia 107
Abortion 400
Abortion bibliography for 1970-- 401
Abstracts in anthropology 76
Abuse of the elderly 320
Abuse of women 449
Adjustment to widowhood and some related problems 199
Adoption bibliography and multi-ethnic sourcebook 217
African women 427
Aging 321
Aging: a guide to resources 322
Aging and the aged 323
The Alaska Eskimos 266
Alcohol and sexuality 475
Alcohol and the elderly 476
Alcohol and youth 477
Alcohol use and alcoholism 478
Alternatives to institutionalization 324
Alternatives to institutionalization: a definitive bibliography 547
The amateur archaeologist's handbook 101
American childhood 440
American ethnic groups and the revival of cultural pluralism 343
American Indian almanac 267
American Jewish yearbook 359
American men and women of science 45
American public opinion index 523
American social attitudes data sourcebook 524
An annotated bibliography of homosexuality 458
An annotated bibliography of Northern Plains ethnohistory 108
An annotated bibliography of studies relating to women, minorities, aging, sexual behavior, health and handicaps 520
An annotated bibliography on invisible colleges 185
An annotated bibliography on the adjustment of Cuban, Soviet and Southeast Asian refugees 375
An annotated bibliography on the sociocultural aspects of development 534
An annotated bibliography on transracial, transcultural, and nonconventional adoption and minority children 234
Annuaire des organisations internationales 44

Annual abstract of statistics 155
Anthropological and cross-cultural themes in mental health 563
Anthropological bibliography of Negro Africa 77
An anthropological bibliography of South Asia 78, 79
Anthropological literature 80
Anthropology in the New Guinea highlands 81
Anthropology in use 82
Anthropology of southern Africa in periodicals to 1950 83
Appalachian women 428
Archaeology 102
Arson 485
Asian American reference data directory 360
Atlas of ancient archaeology 1
Atlas of archaeology 2
Atlas of demographics 3
Atlas of human evolution 4
Atlas of world cultures 5
Atlas of world population history 6
Attitudes of the poor and attitudes toward the poor 505
Author's guide to journals in sociology and related fields 125
The baby boom 239
Background material on poverty 506
Basque Americans 380
The behavioral, psychological, and sociological aspects of the urban crisis 299
Bibliografia chicana 381
A bibliographic chronology of the development of applied anthropology 82
A bibliographic guide to the literature on urban India 303
Bibliography for cross-cultural workers 84
A bibliography of a decade of controversy, 1960-1970 531
A bibliography of alcohol use and abuse among native Americans of North America 278
A bibliography of drug abuse, including alcohol and tobacco 494
A bibliography of drug abuse: supplement 1977-1980 495
Bibliography of North American Indian mental health 564
A bibliography of prostitution 459
A bibliography of the Ku Klux Klan 395
Bibliography of the Soviet social sciences 46
A bibliography of theses from United States colleges and universities 92
A bibliography on drug dependence 496
A bibliography on general deterrence 187
Bibliography on methods of social and business research 65
Bibliography on racism 393
Bibliography on suicide and suicide prevention 200
Bibliography on the urban crisis 299
Biological, psychological, and environmental factors in delinquency and mental disorder 565
The black aged in the United States 325
The black American reference book 280
Black child development in America 281

Black children and their families 282
The black family and the black woman 283
The black family in the United States 284
Black immigration and ethnicity in the United States 285
Black lesbians 286
Black separatism 287
Black-white racial attitudes 288
The black woman in American society 289
Blacks on television 517
Book review index to social science periodicals 25
Bulletin of the Public Affairs Information Service 26
The Cambridge encyclopedia of archaeology 103
Canadian ethnic groups bibliography 344
A Canadian Indian bibliography 268
The challenge of aging 326
Changes in American society 127
Characteristics of the population below the poverty level: 1983 507
The Chicana 382
Child abuse 441
Child abuse and neglect 442
Child abuse and neglect programs 443
Child care issues for parents and society 218
Child welfare training and practice 444
Children and divorce 211
Cities 300
The clinical sociology handbook 174
Collective behavior 529
Colombo's Canadian references 29
Combined retrospective index set to journals in sociology 126
Community resources directory 30
A compendium of social statistics 165
Comprehensive bibliography for the study of American minorities 345
Comprehensive bibliography of existing literature on alcohol 479
A comprehensive Chicano bibliography 383
A comprehensive guide to the cannabis literature 497
Computer crime, abuse, liability and security 486
A concise dictionary of Indian tribes of North America 269
Conflict and conflict resolution 530
The conflict over sexually explicit materials in the United States 468
Confrontation, conflict, and dissent 531
Congressional districts in the 1980's 156
Congressional districts of the 98th Congress 157
County and city data book 158
Crime dictionary 487
Criminal justice abstracts 548
The criminal justice dictionary 549
Criminal justice in America 550
Criminal justice periodical index 551
Criminal justice research sources 552
The criminal justice systems of the Latin American nations 553
Criminal justice vocabulary 554

Criminological bibliographies 188
Criminology: a cross-cultural perspective 189
Criminology and penology abstracts 190
Criminology and the administration of criminal justice 191
Criminology in the world 192
Criminology index 193
Crisis intervention directory 36
C.R.I.S.: combined retrospective index set to journals in sociology 126
A critically annotated bibliography and source book of thanatology and terminal care 205
A cross-cultural summary 85
Cubans in the United States 384
Cultural atlas of Africa 7
The cultural heritage of the Swedish immigrant 361
Culturally disadvantaged 508
A cumulative listing of foundation grants 16
DataMap 159
Death 201
Death and dying A to Z 202
Death education 203
The definition and measurement of poverty 509
Demographic yearbook 160
Demography of racial and ethnic minorities in the United States 346
Demography of the black population in the United States 290
Determinants and consequences of maternal employment 402
Development as if women mattered 403
Dictionary of alcohol use and abuse 480
Dictionary of American penology 555
A dictionary of American social change 532
Dictionary of anthropology 86
Dictionary of criminal justice 556
A dictionary of criminology 194
The dictionary of demography 240
Dictionary of demography: biographies 241
Dictionary of demography: multilingual glossary 242
Dictionary of demography: terms, concepts, and institutions 243
A dictionary of drug abuse terms and terminology 498
Dictionary of modern sociology 128
Dictionary of quotations in sociology 129
Dictionary of race and ethnic relations 394
A dictionary of secret and other societies 10
Dictionary of social science 47
A dictionary of social science methods 66
A dictionary of terms and techniques in archaeology 104
A dictionary of the social sciences 48, 49
A dictionary of words about alcohol 481
Directory of agencies: U.S. voluntary, international voluntary, intergovernmental 571
Directory of associations in Canada 11
Directory of criminal justice information sources 557
Directory of European

associations 12
Directory of federal statistics for local areas 161
Directory of information resources for the handicapped 31
Directory of members (American Sociological Association) 130
Directory of national information sources on handicapping conditions and related services 13
Directory of published proceedings. Series SSH 50
Directory of social welfare research capabilities 572
Directory of urban affairs information and research centers 301
Disaffiliated man 327
Divorce 212
Divorce in the 70's 213
Divorce in the United States, Canada, and Great Britain 214
Drug abuse bibliography 499
Drug use and abuse 500
Drug use and abuse among U.S. minorities 501
Durkheimian school 131
Dutch Americans 362
Dying and death 204
Dying, death and grief 205
The East European and Soviet data handbook 162
Eastern European national minorities 109
The Ebony handbook 291
Education and anthropology 87
Effects and functions of television 518
Elder neglect and abuse 328
Elsevier's dictionary of criminal science 195
The emergence of youth societies 445
Encyclopaedia of the social sciences 51
The encyclopedia of alcoholism 482
The encyclopedia of American crime 488
Encyclopedia of anthropology 88
Encyclopedia of associations 14
Encyclopedia of black America 292
Encyclopedia of crime and justice 558
Encyclopedia of criminology 196
The encyclopedia of drug abuse 502
Encyclopedia of social work 573
Encyclopedia of sociology 132
Encyclopedia of urban planning 302
An encyclopedic dictionary of Marxism, socialism and communism 133
Encyclopedic directory of ethnic organizations in the United States 347
Encyclopedic handbook of cults in America 134
Essays and bibliography on skid row, vagrancy, and outsiders 327
Ethics in social research 67
The ethnic almanac 348
Ethnic film and filmstrip guide for libraries and media centers 349
Ethnic information sources of the United States 350
Ethnic studies bibliography 351
Ethnicity and aging 329
Ethnicity and nationality 110
Ethnographic atlas 8
Ethnographic bibliography of North America 111
Ethnographic bibliography of South America 112

Europa yearbook 32
Europe: a selected ethnographic bibliography 113
European immigration and ethnicity in the United States and Canada 352
The euthanasia controversy 206
Fact book on aging 330
Families under the flag 219
Family counseling 574
Family factbook 220
Family measurement techniques 221
Family research 222
Federal assistance for programs serving the handicapped 33
Filipinos overseas 363
Folk classification 118
Foundation directory 15
Foundation grants index 16
Foundation grants to individuals 17
Fraternal organizations 18
Funding in aging 331
The Gallup poll: public opinion, 1935-1971 525
The Gallup poll: public opinion, 1972-1977 526
The Gallup poll: public opinion, 1978-- 527
German-American history and life 364
German-Americana 365
Gerontology: a cross-national core list of significant works 332
Gerontology: an annotated bibliography 333
Glossary of population and housing 244
Group work in the helping professions 575
A guide to adult outpatient mental health facilities and services throughout the United States 567
Guide to graduate departments of sociology 135
A guide to information resources and services for the handicapped 31
A guide to minority aging references 334
Guide to reference material 52
Guide to research on North American Indians 270
Guide to social science resources in women's studies 404
A guide to sources of funding in the United States for handicapped programs and services 34
A guide to the HRAF probability sample files 124
Guide to the study of the Soviet nationalities 366
A guide to U.S. volunteer organizations 30
A guide to writing and publishing in the social and behavioral sciences 53
Handbook for social research in urban areas 68
Handbook of aging and the social sciences 335
Handbook of American popular culture 519
Handbook of contemporary developments in world sociology 136
Handbook of international data on women 405
Handbook of major Soviet nationalities 114
Handbook of medical sociology 175
A handbook of method in cultural anthropology 119
Handbook of Middle American Indians 271
The handbook of national population censuses 245
Handbook of research design and social measurement 69

Handbook of secret organizations 19
Handbook of small group research 70
Handbook of social and cultural anthropology 120
Handbook of socialization theory and research 137
A handbook of sociology 138
Handbook of Soviet social science data 536
Handbook of the social services 576
Handbook of theory and research for the sociology of education 176
Handbook on the aged in the United States 336
Handicapped funding directory 34
Harvard encyclopedia of American ethnic groups 353
The help book 35
Hispanic American voluntary organizations 385
Hispanic mental health research 566
Historical statistics of the United States, colonial times to 1970 163
The history of anthropology 89
History of the family and kinship 223
Homosexuality: a selective bibliography of over 3,000 items 460
Homosexuality: an annotated bibliography 461
Homosexuality bibliography: second supplement 1976-1982 463
Homosexuality bibliography: supplement, 1970-1975 462
Homosexuality in Canada 464
Hotline 36
Human migration 246
Human resources abstracts 510
Human sexuality 465
Hungarians in the United States and Canada 367
The illustrated encyclopedia of mankind 121
An illustrated guide to easier and more independent living for physically disabled people, their families and friends 39
Immigrants and their children in the United States 354
Immigration and ethnicity 355
Immigration literature 247
Incest: an annotated bibliography 450
Incest: the last taboo 451
Index of published tables of statistical data 1985-86 159
Index to international public opinion 528
Index to literature on the American Indian 272
Index to sociology readers, 1960-1965 139
The Indian city 303
Indians of North America 273
Indians of North and South America 274
Information sources in criminal justice 559
International bibliography of research in marriage and the family, 1900-1964 224
International bibliography of research in marriage and the family, volume II, 1965-1972 225
International bibliography of social and cultural anthropology 122
International bibliography of sociology 140
International bibliography of studies on alcohol 483

International dictionary of regional European ethnology and folklore 123
International directory of anthropologists 90
International directory of organizations concerned with the aging 337
International directory of population information and library resources 248
International encyclopedia of population 249
The international encyclopedia of sociology 141
International encyclopedia of the social sciences 54
International family-planning programs 226
The international foundation directory 20
International handbook of contemporary developments in criminology 197
International handbook on aging 338
International population census bibliography 250
International terrorism 489
Inventory of marriage and family literature 227
The invisible empire 395
The Irish-American experience 368
Irregular serials and annuals 37
Issues in social conflict and change 412
Issues in the sociology of religion 177
Italian Americans 369
Italians in the United States 370
The Japanese in Hawaii 371
The Jewish experience in America 372
The Jewish family 228
Juvenile delinquency 446
The Kibbutz 304
Korean and Japanese women 429
The Ku Klux Klan 396
Language in culture and society 91
The language of cities 305
Language of the underworld 490
Latin America 55
Latin America 1979-1983 56
Latin American population and urbanization analysis 251
Latin American urbanization 306
Legal, medical, economic and social aspects of sex discrimination 472
Library research guide to sociology 71
Life change events research 533
The literature of police corruption 491
Literature of the Filipino-American in the United States 373
A London bibliography of the social sciences 57
A loose-leaf encyclopedic handbook on death and dying and related subjects 202
The MacMillan dictionary of archaeology 105
Mafia 492
The male sex role 466
Marihuana 503
A marihuana dictionary 504
Marx-Engels dictionary 142
Marxist philosophy 143
Masters' theses in anthropology 92
The materials of demography 252
Mathematical sociology 178
Measuring the condition of the world's poor 511
Medical sociology 179
Men's studies 467

The methods and materials of demography 253
Methods for the social sciences 72
The Mexican American: a critical guide to research aids 386
The Mexican American: a selected and annotated bibliography 387
Mexican Americans: a research bibliography 388
Mexican Americans: an annotated bibliography of bibliographies 389
Micronesia 93
Minorities and women 406
Minorities in America 356
Minority groups and housing 307
The modern Arab woman 430
Modern British society 144
A modern dictionary of sociology 145
The multi-problem family 229
Multilingual demographic dictionary 254
Municipal year book 38
Muslim peoples 115
The national children's directory 447
The national directory of mental health 567
National directory: rape prevention and treatment resources 452
The national prison directory 560
The national senior citizens directory 339
Native American women 275
Native Americans of North America 276
The nature of woman 407
Negro almanac 293
The Negro in America 294
The Negro in the United States 295
A new dictionary of the social sciences 58
New feminist scholarship 408
1980 census of population 164
Non-Russian peoples of the USSR 366
Notes and queries on anthropology 94
One-parent children 215
The one-parent family 216
An organizational directory and reference guide for changing conditions for children and youth 447
Organized crime 493
The Oxbridge directory of ethnic periodicals 357
Parent-child separation 230
The Penguin dictionary of sociology 146
The peoples of the USSR 116
Periodical literature on United States cities 308
Perspective Canada II 165
Philippine ethnography 117
The physical quality of life index 511
The policy analysis source book for social programs 543
Polish American history and culture 374
Population: an international directory of organizations and information sources 255
Population abstract of the United States 166
Population and the population explosion 256
Population, environment and resources, and Third World development 257
Population in development planning 258
Population index 259
Population information in nineteenth century census volumes 260

Population information in twentieth century census volumes 261
Pornography 468
Poverty 512
Poverty in Canada and the United States 514
Poverty in the United States during the sixties 515
Poverty/pauvrete 513
The prison and the prisoner 561
A prison reform, organizational, and resource directory 560
Problems of early childhood 231
The process of modernization 534
A profile of America's older population 330
The progress of Afro-American women 296
The Project Share Collection 577
Protecting the interests of human subjects 67
Public Affairs Information Service Bulletin 26
The Puerto Rican community and its children on the mainland 390
The Puerto Ricans 391
Questionnaires for research 73
Race and ethnic relations 397
Race and ethnic relations in Latin America and the Caribbean 398
Rape 453
Rape and rape-related issues 454
Rape and sexual assault 455
Rape prevention and treatment resources 452
A reader in linguistics and anthropology 91
A reader's guide to the social sciences 59
Reading lists in radical social science 60
Reference encyclopedia of the American Indian 277
Reference sources in social work 578
Refugee resettlement in the United States 375
Refugees in the United States 358
Religion & aging 340
Repertoire des associations du Canada 11
Research and theory in criminology in the United States 193
Research centers directory 21
Research in ritual studies 95
Research on suicide 207
Research resources 74
Role portrayal and stereotyping on television 520
The Romanians in America and Canada 376
The rural elderly 341
Rural social welfare 579
Sage family studies abstracts 232
Sage race relations abstracts 399
Sage urban studies abstracts 309
A select bibliography on Asians in America with annotations 378
Selected and annotated bibliography of youth, youth work, and provision for youth 448
A selected bibliography of ethno-cultural groups in Canada and the provinces of Ontario 344
Selected bibliography of the anthropology and ethnology of Europe 96

Selected data on social conditions and trends in the United States 540
A selected social casework bibliography 585
Serial publications in anthropology 97
Sex research 469
Sex role stereotyping in the mass media 470
Sex roles 471
Sexual abuse of children 456
The sexual barrier 472
Sexuality and aging 473
Sixty cultures 124
Social and behavioral aspects of female alcoholism 484
The social and economic status of the black population in the United States 297
Social behavior of the mentally retarded 568
Social change and internal migration 262
Social impact assessment and management 537
Social indicators 538
Social indicators for the European Community 539
Social indicators III 540
Social networks and mental health 569
Social policy and administration in Britain 544
Social policy and its administration 545
Social research on Arabs in Israel 377
A social science bibliography 56
Social science information sources 55
Social science reference sources 61
Social science research handbook 75
Social sciences citation index 27
The social sciences in educational studies 180
Social sciences index 28
Social scientific studies of religion 181
Social service organizations 580
Social services organizations and agencies directory 581
Social stratification 147
Social welfare in America 582
Social work education 583
Social work research & abstracts 584
Sociological abstracts 148
Sociology: an international bibliography of serial publications 149
The sociology and anthropology of mental illness 570
Sociology dissertations in American universities 150
The sociology of aging 182
Sociology of America 151
Sociology of education 183
The sociology of human fertility 263
Sociology of poverty in the United States 184
Sociology of sciences 185
Sociology of the law 186
Sociology theses register 152
Source book for African anthropology 98
Source book for the disabled 39
Sourcebook of criminal justice statistics 562
Sourcebook of Hispanic culture in the United States 392
Sourcebook on aging 342
Sourcebook on death and dying 208
Sources of information in the social sciences 62

Sources of information on population/family planning 233
Sources of social statistics 167
Southern poor whites 516
Soviet sociology 153
Special adoptions 234
State and metropolitan area databook 168
Statesman's yearbook 40
Statistical abstract of the United States 169
Statistical and historical annual of the states of the world 40
A statistical portrait of women in the U.S. 409
Statistical yearbook 170
Statistics sources 171
The status of the Arab woman 431
Student anthropologist's handbook 99
The student sociologist's handbook 154
A subject guide to data on industrial, business, social, educational, financial, and other topics for the United States and internationally 171
Suburbia 310
Suicide: a guide to information sources 209
Suicide: a selective bibliography of over 2,200 items 210
Survey research on comparative social change 535
A thesaurus of British archaeology 106
The third Americans 378
Township atlas of the United States 172
Tract data for standard metropolitan statistical areas 9
The troubled family 235
Tulapai to Tokay 278
Two-career families 236
Ukrainians in Canada and the United States 379
Ulrich's international periodicals directory 41
Uniform citations to bibliographies, indexes, and review articles of the literature of crime study in the United States 188
Union list of population/family planning periodicals 264
The United Media Enterprises report on leisure in America 521
University urban research centers 311
Urban affairs abstracts 312
Urban America examined 313
Urban atlas 9
Urban community 314
Urban environments and human behavior 315
Urban indicators 541
Urban needs 316
Urban policy 546
Urbanization in developing countries 317
Urbanization in tropical Africa 318
The urbanization of American Indians 279
Use of criminology literature 198
Use of social sciences literature 63
User's guide to funding resources 22
Village studies data analysis and bibliography 319
Violence against women 457
Violence in the family 237
Vital statistics of the United States 173
Warfare in primitive societies 100
Washington information directory 42

Where does the time go? 521
Women, 1965-1975 420
Women: a bibliography of bibliographies 410
Women and ambition 411
Women and deviance 412
Women and sexuality in America 474
Women and society 413
Women and society, citations 3,601 to 6,000 414
Women and urban society 415
Women and world development 416
Women at work 417
Women helping women 418
Women in America 432
Women in China 433
Women in perspective 419
Women in popular culture 522
Women in Southeast Asia 434
Women in Spanish America 435
Women in the Caribbean 436
Women in the Middle East and North Africa 437
Women of India 438
Women of South Asia 439
Women studies abstracts 421
Women's action almanac 422
The women's movement in the seventies 423
Women's organizations & leaders directory 424
Women's studies: a checklist of bibliographies 425
Women's studies: a recommended core bibliography 426
Words, terms, events, and persons relating to cannabis 504
Work and family 238
A working bibliography on the Negro in the United States 298
A working guide to organizations engaged in social work and social welfare research 572
Working with people 585
World almanac and book of facts 43
World directory of social science institutions 23
World guide to scientific associations and learned societies 24
World guide to social work education 586
World handbook of political and social indicators 542
World list of social science periodicals 64
World population policy 265
Yearbook of international organizations 44

AUTHOR INDEX

Abel, Ernest L. 480, 497, 498, 504
Abercrombie, Nicholas 146
Abler, Thomas S. 268
Abrams, Charles 305
Abramson, Harold J. 139
Achenbaum, W. Andrew 582
Acri, Michael James 201
Adkins, Lesley 106
Adkins, Roy A. 106
Adler, Johann Anton 195
Akins, Faren R. 230
Aldous, Joan 224, 225
American Sociological Association 130, 135
Ander, O. Fritiof 361
Andrews, Theodora 494, 495
Andriot, John L. 166, 172
Astin, Helen S. 471
Astone, Nicholas A. 554
Attneave, Carolyn L. 564
August, Eugene R. 467
Austin, Gregory A. 500
Baatz, Wilmer H. 283
Baden, Clifford 238
Bahr, Howard M. 327
Balkema, John B. 322
Ballou, Patricia K. 410
Bardis, Panos 129
Barkas, Janet L. 35
Barnes, Dorothy L. 453
Barnes, Grace M. 476, 477
Barrer, Lester A. 424
Bart, Pauline 154
Beckman, Erik 549
Bell, Alan P. 461
Bell, Gwen 315
Belli, Donna 406
Belson, William A. 65
Bentley, G. Carter 110
Bergstrom, Len V. 413
Berkowitz, Morris I. 181
Bernardo, Stephanie 348
Best, Reba A. 486
Beyleveld, Deryck 187
Bickner, Mei Liang 417
Biegel, David E. 569
Bilsborrow, Richard E. 258
Binstock, Robert H. 335
Blackstone, Tessa 544
Blank, Marion S. 585
Blasi, Anthony J. 177
Bleckman, Isaac A. 202
Booth, Robert E. 508
Boulding, Elise 405
Bower, Robert T. 67
Boyce, Byrl N. 307
Brace, C. Loring 4
Branham, Vernon Carnegie 196
Branigan, Keith 2
Brantley, James R. 547
Brewer, Joan Scherer 469
Brode, John 534
Brown, Bruce W. 221
Brown, Edward J. 562
Brown, Kristi 574
Bruhn, John G. 179
Brunn, Stanley D. 317
Brye, David L. 352
Bucchioni, Eugene 390
Buenker, John D. 355
Bullough, Vern L. 458, 459

Bundy, Mary Lee 339, 447, 560
Burckel, Nicholas C. 355
Burgess, Ann Wolbert 455
Burns, Ada 389
Butler, Lois 349
Buvinic, Mayra 416
Byerly, Greg 239, 451, 468
Cabello-Argandona, Robert 382
Cabot, Phillippe Sidney de Q, 446
Cameron, Colin 505
Cashmore, E. Ellis 394
Casper, Dale E. 313
Center for Afroamerican studies 285
Chafetz, Morris 482
Chalfant, H. Paul 184, 484
Chambliss, William J. 186
Champion, Sara 104
Chang, Dae H. 189
Chekki, Dan A. 174
Chubin, Daryl E. 185
Cibulski, Ora 377
Cocozzoli, Gary 364
Cohen, Lilly 331
Cohen, Ronald 119
Cohen, Sidney 502
Cohen Stuart, Bertie A. 436
Colombo, John Robert 29
Conklin, Harold C. 118
Conrad, James H. 578
Converse, Philip E. 524
Cordasco, Francesco 183, 369, 370, 390
Cordasco, Michael Vaughn 370
Costa, Joseph J. 320, 449
Crawford, William 464
Crippen, Cynthia 420
Cruz, Gilbert R. 383
Cuellar, Jose B. 334
Cuneo, Michael W. 177
Dahl, Nancy 225
David, Ella M. 533
Davis, Bruce L. 188
Davis, Lenwood G. 284, 289, 325, 396
Davis, Nanette J. 412
de Young, Mary 450
DeGasparis, Priscilla 67
Delorme, Robert L. 55, 56
Dennis, Deborah Ellis 310
Denno, Deborah W. 565
Derrick, Deborah 448
DeSola, Ralph 487
Detlefsen, Ellen Gay 567
Diner, Hasia R. 415
Divale, William Tulio 100
Doezema, Linda Pegman 362
Domschke, Eliane 245
Douglass, William A. 380
Driver, Edwin D. 265, 570
Duchaine, Nina 491
Duncan, J.T. Skip 485
Dunmore, Charlotte 282
Eckstein, Burton J. 34
Edwards, Bernard 167
Edwards, Willie M. 332
Een, JoAnn Delores 414
Ekstrom, Brenda 537
Eldridge, Hope T. 252
Estes, Richard J. 572
Etulain, Richard W. 380
Fan, Kok Sim 434
Farberow, Norman L. 200
Farr, Sidney Saylor 428
Faunce, Patricia S. 411
Favazza, Armando R. 563
Fecher, Vincent John 340
Filipovitch, Anthony J. 314
Filler, Louis 532
Fishburn, Katherine 522
Fisher, Mary L. 294
Fisher, William H. 395
Flynn, Frances 332
Flynt, Dorothy S. 516
Fogle, Catherine 248
Folk, Karen R. 274
Foster, David William 392
Foundation Center 15, 16, 17
Frankel, Linda 154
Frantz, Charles 99
Freedman, Ronald 263
Freeman, Howard E. 175
Frey, Frederick W. 535
Friedman, Leslie 470
Fritz, Jan M. 174
Fruehling, James A. 208

Fujioka, Jerry Y. 371
Gallup, George Horace 525, 526, 527
Garoogian, Andrew 218
Garoogian, Rhoda 218
Ghosh, P.K. 257
Gilbert, Neil 576
Gilmartin, Kevin J. 538
Gilroy, Dan 60
Glenn, Norval D. 147
Gold, Robert S. 479
Gonzales, Sylvia Alicia 385
Goslin, David A. 137
Gottlieb, David 445
Gouke, Mary Noel 215
Gould, Julius 48
Goyer, Doreen S. 245
Grady, Kathleen E. 466
Green, Rayna 275
Greenberg, Martin H. 489
Greenstone, J.L. 36
Gregorovich, Andrew 344
Grimes, Ronald 95
Grodsky, Susan J. 247
Grollig, F.X. 97
Haas, Marilyn L. 273
Haines, David W. 358
Hale, Glorya 39
Hambly, Wilfrid Dyson 98
Hare, A. Paul 70
Harris, Diana K. 182
Hartman, John J. 72
Hartnett, Anthony 180
Hauser, Philip Morris 68
Hausslein, Evelyn B. 211
Hawes, Joseph M. 440
Hawkes, Jacquetta 1
Hays, Terence A. 81
Hedblom, Jack H. 72
Heiliger, William S. 46
Heizer, Robert F. 102
Henry, Louis 254
Hewitt, John D. 550
Hill, George H. 517
Hill, Reuben 224
Hill, Sylvia Saverson 517
Hiner, N. Ray 440
Hippler, Arthur E. 266
Hirsch, Elisabeth S. 231
Hirschfelder, Arlene B. 270
Hodson, H.V. 20
Hoglund, A. William 354
Holland, Janet 178
Holmes, Thomas H. 533
Honigmann, John J. 120
Hood, Roger 191
Hoover, Dwight W. 300
Hopkins, Isabella 493
Horak, Stephan M. 109, 366
Hornback, Kenneth E. 529
Hoselitz, Berthold Frank 59
Hoult, Thomas Ford 128
Hughes, Marija Matich 472
Human Resources Network 22
Hunter, David E. 88
Hunter, Edna J. 219
Hurst, Marsha 402
Hymes, Dell 91
Iiyama, Patti 501
Inge, Thomas M. 519
International Committee for Social Science Information and Documentation 64
Irving, Mary B. 101
Jacobs, Sue-Ellen 419
Jenkins, Betty Lanier 287
Jodice, David A. 542
Johnson, Alvin 51
Johnson, Elmer H. 197
Johnson, J. Edmund 181
Johnson, Tanya F. 328
Jones, Richard 6
Jones, Thomas A. 153
Joy, Jody 403
Kadish, Sanford H. 558
Kalisch, Beatrice J. 442
Kanitkar, Helen A. 79
Katz, Zev 114
Keith, Jone M. 412
Keller, Mark 481, 483
Kelso, Dianne R. 564
Kemmer, Elizabeth 237, 454
Kemper, Robert V. 89
Kendall, Katherine A. 586
Kennedy, James R. Jr. 71
Keresztesi, Michael 364
Keterman, Thomas 557
Kinloch, Graham C. 397
Kinton, Jack F. 343
Kipps, Harriet Clyde 30
Klein, Barry 277

Kline, Paula 316
Klotman, Phyllis Rauch 283
Knaster, Meri 435
Koh, Hesung Chun 429
Kolb, William L. 48
Konoshima, Sumiye 233
Kotz, Arnold 543
Kratochvil, Laura 427
Kravitz, Marjorie 547
Krichmar, Albert 423
Krout, John A. 341
Kruzas, Anthony T. 581
Kutash, Samuel B. 196
Lachs, John 143
Lagace, Robert O. 124
Land, Brian 11
Lear, Julia Graham 543
Leistritz, F. Larry 537
Leitch, Barbara A. 269
Lester, David 209
Levine, Robert M. 398
Levinson, David 124
Leviton, S. 36
Li, Hong-Chan 583
Li, Tze-chung 61
Loeb, Catherine 426
Logie, Gordon 244
Low, W. Augustus 292
Lunday, G. Albert 150
Lyle, Katherine Ch'iu 226
MacCorkle, Lyn 384
Maier, Mark 60
Mail, Patricia D. 278
Maluccio, Anthony N. 324
Mangalam, J.J. 246
Manheim, Jarol B. 159
Mann, Michael 141
Mark, Charles 151
Marshall, Mac 93
Martin, Julian A. 554
Martindale, Don 136
Martinez, Julio A. 389
Mason, John Brown 74
Mason, Mervyn L. 465
Matthews, Mervyn 153
Maurer, David W. 490
McDonald, David R. 92, 278
McEvedy, Colin 6
McIlvaine, B. 321
McInnis, Raymond G. 75
McIntosh, John L. 207
McKenney, Mary 212
McMillan, Patricia 71
Meghdessian, Samira Rafidi 431
Melton, J. Gordon 134
Metress, Seamus P. 368
Meyer, Jon K. 299
Meyer, Manfred 518
Mickiewicz, Ellen Propper 536
Miller, Albert Jay 201, 531
Miller, Delbert Charles 69
Miller, Elizabeth W. 294
Miller, P. McC. 66
Miller, Wayne Charles 345, 356
Mitchell, Geoffrey Duncan 58
Mohan, Raj P. 136
Momeni, Jamshid A. 290, 346
Monie, Joanna 545
Monroe, Margaret E. 326
Morris, Morris David 511
Morrison, Denton E. 529
Muldoon, Maureen 400
Mullins, Carolyn J. 53
Mundkur, Mohini 321
Murdock, George Peter 5, 8, 111
Murguia, Edward 329
Murphy, Thomas P. 541
Murray, Jocelyn 7
Myers, Hector F. 281
Nandan, Yash 131
Naroll, Raoul 119
Nason, James D. 93
National Center for the Prevention and Control of Rape 452
Newton, Anne 559
Newton, Frank 566
Nimkoff, Meyer F. 138
Nissen, Ursula 518
Nogales, Luis G. 387
Norell, Irene P. 373
North, Jeannette H. 247
Norton, Augustus R. 489
O'Block, Robert L. 552
O'Brien, Jacqueline 171

O'Brien, Robert 482, 502
O'Connor, Anthony Michael 318
O'Farrell, Timothy J. 475
O'Leary, Timothy J. 111, 112
Oakes, Elizabeth H. 404
Obudho, Constance E. 288
Ogawa, Dennis M. 371
Ogburn, William F. 138
Oman, Mary 563
Ondrasik, Allison 159
Oster, Sharon M. 509
Page, Penny Booth 478
Palmore, Erdman 336, 338
Paltiel, Freda L. 512
Palumbo, Dennis James 546
Pandit, Harshida 438
Pardeck, John T. 444
Parish, David W. 127
Parker, William 460, 462, 463
Pasquariella, Susan Kingsley 264
Peck, Theodore P. 235
Perkins, David 276
Petersen, William 241-243
Phillis, Susan 287
Phinney, John F.S. 89
Picquet, D. Cheryn 486
Pino, Frank 388
Place, Linna Funk 323
Ploski, Harry A. 293
Poole, Adrian 194
Poole, Dennis L. 579
Porter, Dorothy Burnett 295, 298
Porter, Jack Nusan 530
Potter, Dale R. 73
Prendergast, Michael L. 500
Prentice, Ann E. 210
Pressat, Roland 240
Preuss, Arthur 10
Public Affairs Information Service 26
al-Qazzaz, Ayad 437
Raccagni, Michelle 430
Radzinowicz, Leon 191
Rank, Richard 553
Rao, Vijaya 586
Reading, Hugo F. 49
Reeves, Earl J. 314
Research & Forecasts, Inc. 521
Richardson, John G. 176
Rihani, May 403
Ripley, William Zebina 96
Ritchie, Maureen 425
Rj Associates 360
Robbins, Maurice 101
Roberts, J.R. 286
Roberts, N. 63
Robinson, Barbara J. 386
Robinson, Joy C. 386
Rollins, Arline McClarty 215
Romanofsky, Peter 580
Rooke, M. Leigh 333
Rosenberg, Marie Barovic 413
Rosenberg-Dishman, Marie B. 414
Rosenstiel, Annette 87
Ross, John A. 249
Royal Anthropological Institute 94
Rubin, Rhea Joyce 326
Rubin, Richard E. 239
Rubin, Rick 451, 468
Rush, George Eugene 556
Russell, James 142
Sable, Martin Howard 306
Sahli, Nancy 474
Saito, Shiro 117, 363
Sakala, Carol 439
Saunders, Doris E. 291
Schlachter, Gail A. 406
Schlesinger, Benjamin 216, 228, 229, 456, 514
Schmidt, Alvin J. 18
Schulze, Suzanne 260, 261
Schwarz, Ruth M. 565
Scott, James William 75
Segal, Sheldon J. 226
Seidman, Robert B. 186
Seligman, E.R.A. 51
Sell, Betty H. 214
Sell, Irene L. 204
Sell, Kenneth D. 213, 214
Sells, Helen F. 496
Shanas, Ethel 335
Sharrock, Susan R. 108

Shaw, Shauna 427
Shearer, Barbara Smith 308
Shearer, Benjamin F. 308
Sheldon, Kathleen E. 404
Sherratt, Andrew 103
Shoup, Paul S. 162
Shryock, Henry S. 253
Shur, Shimon 304
Sifakis, Carl 488
Signorielli, Nancy 520
Sills, David L. 54
Simmons, Alan 262
Simpson, Antony E. 491
Simpson, Michael A. 205
Sims, Janet L. 296
Sims-Wood, Janet L. 396
Smooha, Sammy 377
Smythe, Mabel M. 280
Sofios, Nicholas 139
Sokolyszyn, Aleksander 379
Soliday, Gerald L. 223
Specht, Harry 576
Stanford, E. Percil 334
Statistical Office of the European Communities 539
Statistics Canada 165
Sternlicht, Manny 568
Steuer, Max D. 178
Stineman, Esther 426
Stither, Deborah J. 339
Stockwell, Edward G. 253
Straus, Murray A. 221
Strugnell, Cecile 199
Survey Research Consultants International, Inc. 528
Sussman, Marvin B. 125
Szabo, Denis 192
Szeplaki, Joseph 367
Talbot, Jane Mitchell 383
Tanis, Norman 276
Tax, Sol 97
Taylor, Charles Lewis 542
Taylor, George Albert 546
Terrell, John Upton 267
Terris, Virginia R. 432
Textor, Robert B. 85
Theodoratus, Robert J. 113
Theodorson, Achilles G. 145
Theodorson, George A. 145
Thernstrom, Stephan 353
Thompson, Beryl-Anne 65
Thornton, Russell 279
Tindale, Norman Barnett 107
Tippett, Alan Richard 84
Tolzmann, Don Heinrich 365
Tompkins, Dorothy 515, 561
Tong, Tekong 378
Trattner, Walter I. 582
Trejo, Arnulfo D. 381
Triche, Charles W. 206
Triche, Diane Samson 206
Trott, Lloyd 492
Trzyna, Thaddeus C. 255
Turoff, Sidney 307
U.S. Bureau of the Census 9, 157, 158, 161, 164, 168, 169, 297, 409
U.S. Department of Commerce 163
U.S. National Vital Statistics Division 173
van de Walle, Etienne 254
van Warmelo, N.J. 83
van Why, Elizabeth Wharton 217
Van Willigen, John 82, 303
Vivo, Paquita 391
von Furer-Haimendorf, Elizabeth 78
Wakefield, Rowan A. 222
Wakeford, Frances 152
Walford, Albert John 52
Waller, Coy W. 503
Walsh, Dermot 194
Warren, Mary Anne 407
Wass, Hannelore 203
Wasserman, Paul 171, 350
Wauchope, Robert 271
Weaver, Sally M. 268
Webb, William H. 62
Weekes, Richard V. 115
Wei, Karen T. 433
Weinberg, Martin S. 461
Weist, Katherine M. 108
Wells, Dorothy P. 441
Wertsman, Vladimir 376, 379
Westergaard, John H. 144
Whalen, William Joseph 19
Whaley, Rebecca Glenn 447
Wharton, George F. 473

Whitehouse, Ruth D. 105
Whitten, Phillip 88
Whittick, Arnold 302
Wieschhoff, Heinrich Albert 77
Wilczynski, Jozef 133
Wile, Annadel N. 126
Wilkie, Richard W. 251
Williams, James 293
Williams, Vergil L. 555
Williamson, Jane 408, 422
Wilson, Carolyn F. 457
Wilson, Christopher 240
Wilson, M.J. 66
Windholz, George 568
Wingrove, C. Ray 333
Winick, Charles 86
Winston, Eric V.A. 301
Wise, Adrienne 545
Wixman, Ronald 116
Wolf, Carolyn E. 274
Wolfgang, Marvin E. 193
Wood, John Richard 266
Woodward, Agnes 513
Wright, Martin 198
Wright, Rod W. 469
Wu, Robert 378
Wynar, Lubomyr R. 347, 349
Zadrozny, John Thomas 47
Zambrana, Ruth E. 402
Zikmund, Joseph 310
Zils, Michael 24
Zimpfer, David G. 575
Znaniecki, Helena 220
Zurawski, Joseph W. 374

THESAURUS-INDEX

ABBREVIATIONS

UF Acronyms
UF Initialisms
Crime
Dictionaries 487

ABORIGINES

SN Native inhabitants of a region
NT American Indians
Guides
Social organization 107
Tribal groups 107
Women 107

ABORTION

BT Social issues
RT Family planning
Abstracts
Women 421
Almanacs
Statistics 43
Statistics (U.S.) 169
Women 422
Asian women
Guides 439
Australia
Guides 545
Bibliographies 140, 256, 401, 412, 531
Black-Americans 290
Latin American women 435
Sex discrimination 472
Women 419, 423, 432
Black-Americans
Bibliographies 290
Directories
Organizations 255, 424
Encyclopedias 249
Women 407
Guides
Asian women 439
Australia 545
Handbooks 202
Indexes
Public opinion 523, 528
Statistics (International) 159
Statistics (U.S.) 159
Latin American women
Bibliographies 435
Organizations
Directories 255, 424
Public opinion 525-527
Indexes 523, 528
Sex discrimination
Bibliographies 472
Social characteristics
Women 400
Statistics (International)
Indexes 159
Yearbooks 160
Statistics (U.S.)
Almanacs 43, 169
Indexes 159
Women
Abstracts 421
Almanacs 422
Bibliographies 419, 423, 432
Encyclopedias 407
Social characteristics 400
Yearbooks
Statistics (Interna-

tional) 160

ABSTRACTS

UF Digests
UF Excerpts
UF Summaries
UF Synopses
RT Bibliographies
RT Indexes
Abortion
Women 421
Alcoholism
Social research 577
Anthropology 76, 190
Archaeology 76
Asians
Immigration 247
Black-Americans
Families 297
Fertility 297
Mortality 297
Population 297
Statistics (U.S.) 297
Brain drain
Immigration 247
Child abuse
Social research 577
Crime
Urban affairs 309, 312
Criminal justice 548
Criminology 190
Cultural anthropology 76, 190
Demography
Immigration 247
Urban affairs 312
Elderly 510
Social research 584
Urban affairs 312
Ethnic groups 510
Families
Black-Americans 297
Social research 577, 584
Women 421
Family planning
Women 421
Fertility
Black-Americans 297
Foster families
Social research 577
Handicapped
Urban affairs 312
Hispanics
Immigration 247
Historic archaeology 76
Illegal aliens
Immigration 247
Immigration 399
Asians 247
Brain drain 247
Demography 247
Hispanics 247
Illegal aliens 247
Social policy 247
Social research 247
Juvenile delinquency 548
Social research 577
Mental health 510
Social research 577
Women 421
Migration 510
Minority groups 510
Mortality
Black-Americans 297
Physical anthropology 76
Population
Black-Americans 297
Statistics (U.S.) 166
Poverty 510
Prisons 548
Race relations 399
Sex roles
Women 421
Sexuality
Women 421
Social change 510
Social conditions 510
Urban affairs 309
Social indicators
Social research 577
Urban affairs 312
Social policy
Immigration 247
Social relations 190
Social research
Alcoholism 577
Child abuse 577
Elderly 584
Families 577, 584
Foster families 577
Immigration 247
Juvenile delinquency 577
Mental health 577
Social indicators 577
Social services 577
Social systems 577

Social work 584
Youth 584
Social services
Social research 577
Urban affairs 309, 312
Social structures 190
Social systems
Social research 577
Social welfare 510
Social work 190
Social research 584
Socialization 190
Women 421
Sociology 190
Urban affairs 312
Statistics (U.S.)
Black-Americans 297
Population 166
Urban affairs
Crime 309, 312
Demography 312
Elderly 312
Handicapped 312
Social conditions 309
Social indicators 312
Social services 309, 312
Sociology 312
Women 312
Youth 312
Women
Abortion 421
Families 421
Family planning 421
Mental health 421
Sex roles 421
Sexuality 421
Socialization 421
Urban affairs 312
Youth
Social research 584
Urban affairs 312

ABUSED CHILDREN

See Child abuse

ACCULTURATION

SN Acquisition of the culture of one group from another
UF Biculturalism
UF Cultural adaption
UF Cultural assimilation
RT Assimilation
RT Socialization
Adoptions
Bibliographies 234
American Indians
Bibliographies 278, 564
Indexes 272
Anthropology
Bibliographies 87
Asian-Americans
Guides 360
Basque-Americans
Bibliographies 380
Bibliographies
Adoptions 234
American Indians 278, 564
Anthropology 87
Basque-Americans 380
Cross-cultural studies 84
Ethnicity 355
German-Americans 365
Hispanics 566
Immigration 355
Italian-Americans 369
Jewish-Americans 372
Mental health 563
Mexican-Americans 383, 387
Refugees 375
Theses 92
Vietnamese-Americans 378
Cross-cultural studies
Bibliographies 84
Ethnicity
Bibliographies 355
German-Americans
Bibliographies 365
Guides
Asian-Americans 360
Puerto Ricans 390
Handbooks
Social research 68
Hispanics
Bibliographies 566
Immigration
Bibliographies 355
Indexes
American Indians 272
Italian-Americans
Bibliographies 369
Theses 370
Jewish-Americans

Bibliographies 372
Mental health
Bibliographies 563
Mexican-Americans
Bibliographies 383, 387
Puerto Ricans
Guides 390
Refugees
Bibliographies 375
Social research
Handbooks 68
Theses
Bibliographies 92
Italian-Americans 370
Vietnamese-Americans
Bibliographies 378

ACRONYMS

See Abbreviations

ADOLESCENTS

See Youth

ADOPTION

NT Transracial adoption
RT Foster care
RT Foster families
Acculturation
Bibliographies 234
American Indians
Bibliographies 217, 234
Asian-Americans
Bibliographies 217
Asian women
Bibliographies 429
Bibliographies 224, 225, 227
Acculturation 234
American Indians 217, 234
Asian-Americans 217
Asian women 429
Black-Americans 217, 234, 282
Child welfare 444
Chinese-Americans 217, 234
Filipino-Americans 234
Japanese-Americans 217, 234
Korean-Americans 217, 234
Mexican-Americans 234
Minority groups 234
Puerto Ricans 217
Social classes 234
Socialization 234
Vietnamese-Americans 217
Black-Americans
Bibliographies 217, 234, 282
Child welfare
Bibliographies 444
Chinese-Americans
Bibliographies 217, 234
Directories
Organizations 13, 581
Encyclopedias
Organizations 14
Filipino-Americans
Bibliographies 234
Guides
Organizations 35
Indexes 551
Japanese-Americans
Bibliographies 217, 234
Korean-Americans
Bibliographies 217, 234
Mexican-Americans
Bibliographies 234
Minority groups
Bibliographies 234
Organizations
Directories 13, 581
Encyclopedias 14
Guides 35
Puerto Ricans
Bibliographies 217
Social classes
Bibliographies 234
Socialization
Bibliographies 234
Vietnamese-Americans
Bibliographies 217

ADULTS

BT Social groups
RT College students
RT Parents
RT Youth
Socialization

Handbooks 137

AFRICA

NT South Africa
RT Asia
RT Australia
RT Europe
Bibliographies
Demography 318
Sociology 318
Urbanization 318
Women 404
Handbooks
Sociological research 136

AFRICAN CULTURES

BT Cultures
RT Blacks (African)
RT Tribal groups
Atlases 7

AFRICAN WOMEN

BT Women
RT Arab women
RT Asian women
RT Caribbean women
RT Chinese women
RT Indian women
RT Latin American women
Bibliographies
Child care 427
Divorce 427
Families 427
Fertility 427
Marriage 427
Sexual relations 427
Urban studies 427

AGE COMPOSITION

SN Relative age distribution in society
BT Demography
Statistics (U.S.)
Counties 3

AGING

See Elderly

ALCOHOL

BT Depressants
NT Beer
NT Wine
Bibliographies 494, 495
Dictionaries 481
Encyclopedias 482

ALCOHOL ABUSE

See Alcoholism

ALCOHOLISM

BT Drug abuse
RT Drinking patterns
Abstracts
Social research 577
American Indians
Bibliographies 278, 279, 477, 564
Indexes 272
Bibliographies
American Indians 278, 279, 477, 564
Black-Americans 477
Child abuse 475
College students 477
Crime 475, 477, 483
Driving 477
Elderly 327, 341, 476
Families 477, 574
Hispanics 566
Homosexuality 460, 461, 475
Information sources 316
Juvenile delinquency 477
Marihuana 477
Mental health 563
Prevention 477
Sexuality 475
Social casework 585
Social characteristics 483
Social correlates 477
Social research 479
Social work 483
Sociology 496
Suicide 200, 209
Treatment 477, 496
Women 412, 477, 484
Youth 477, 483
Black-Americans
Bibliographies 477
Canadian organizations

Directories 11
Child abuse
Bibliographies 475
College students
Bibliographies 477
Crime
Bibliographies 475, 477, 483
Criminal justice
Encyclopedias 558
Dictionaries 481
Slang 480
Directories 316
Canadian organizations 11
Grants 15
Organizations 30, 581
Publications 37, 41
Drinking patterns
Encyclopedias 482
Driving
Bibliographies 477
Education
Guides 478
Elderly
Bibliographies 327, 341, 476
Encyclopedias 482, 502
Criminal justice 558
Drinking patterns 482
Organizations 14
Treatment 482, 502
Families
Bibliographies 477, 574
Guides 222, 478
Grants
Directories 15
Guides 22
Guides 22
Education 478
Families 222, 478
Grants 22
Institutions 324
Organizations 35
Treatment 478
Youth 478
Handbooks
Social services 576
Hispanics
Bibliographies 566
Homosexuality
Bibliographies 460, 461, 475
Indexes
American Indians 272
Information sources
Bibliographies 316
Institutions
Guides 324
Juvenile delinquency
Bibliographies 477
Marihuana
Bibliographies 477
Mental health
Bibliographies 563
Organizations
Directories 30, 581
Encyclopedias 14
Guides 35
Prevention
Bibliographies 477
Publications
Directories 37, 41
Research guides 198
Sexuality
Bibliographies 475
Slang
Dictionaries 480
Social casework
Bibliographies 585
Social characteristics
Bibliographies 483
Social correlates
Bibliographies 477
Social groups
Treatment 482
Social research
Abstracts 577
Bibliographies 479
Social services
Handbooks 576
Social work
Bibliographies 483
Sociology
Bibliographies 496
Suicide
Bibliographies 200, 209
Treatment
Bibliographies 477, 496
Encyclopedias 482, 502
Guides 478
Social groups 482
Women
Bibliographies 412, 477, 484
Youth
Bibliographies 477, 483

Guides 478

ALIENATION

SN Estrangement from individuals or society
RT Anomie
RT Social isolation
RT Social role loss
Bibliographies 531
Indexes 139

ALMANACS

RT Encyclopedias
RT Handbooks
Abortion
Statistics (U.S.) 43, 169
Women 422
American Indians
Anthropology 267
Archaeology 267
Customs 267
Marriage 267
Population 267
Tribal groups 267
Anthropology
American Indians 267
Archaeology
American Indians 267
Austrian-Americans 348
Births
Statistics (Great Britain) 155
Statistics (U.S.) 43, 168, 169
Black-Americans
Families 293
Intermarriage 293
Population 293
Poverty 293
Statistics 293
Canadian-Americans 348
Child abuse 220
Crime
Statistics (Great Britain) 155
Statistics (U.S.) 43, 168
Criminal justice
Women 422
Customs
American Indians 267
Day care 220
Deaths
Statistics (Great Britain) 155
Statistics (U.S.) 43, 168, 169
Discrimination
Ethnic groups 348
Divorce
Statistics (Great Britain) 155
Statistics (U.S.) 43, 168, 169
Women 422
Drug abuse
Statistics (U.S.) 43
Ethnic groups
Discrimination 348
Families
Black-Americans 293
Statistics (Great Britain) 155
Statistics (U.S.) 43, 220
Women 422
Family planning
Women 422
German-Americans 348
Homosexuality
Women 422
Immigration
Statistics (U.S.) 43
Incest
Women 422
Intermarriage
Black-Americans 293
Irish-Americans 348
Italian-Americans 348
Marriage 220
American Indians 267
Statistics (Great Britain) 155
Statistics (U.S.) 43, 168, 169
Women 422
Mexican-Americans 348
Migration
Statistics (Great Britain) 155
Statistics (U.S.) 169
Polish-Americans 348
Population
American Indians 267
Black-Americans 293
Statistics (Great Britain) 155
Statistics (Interna-

tional) 43
Statistics (U.S.) 43, 168, 169
Pornography
Women 422
Poverty
Black-Americans 293
Women 422
Prostitution
Women 422
Rape
Women 422
Russian-Americans 348
Sex discrimination
Women 422
Sex roles
Women 422
Sexuality
Women 422
Social services
Statistics (Great Britain) 155
Social welfare
Women 422
Spouse abuse
Women 422
Statistics
Black-Americans 293
Statistics (Canada)
Population 29
Statistics (Great Britain)
Births 155
Crime 155
Deaths 155
Divorce 155
Families 155
Marriage 155
Migration 155
Population 155
Social services 155
Statistics (International)
Population 43
Statistics (U.S.)
Abortion 43, 169
Births 43, 168, 169
Crime 43, 168
Deaths 43, 168, 169
Divorce 43, 168, 169
Drug abuse 43
Families 43, 220
Immigration 43
Marriage 43, 168, 169
Migration 169
Population 43, 168, 169
Swedish-Americans 348
Tribal groups
American Indians 267
Women 220
Abortion 422
Criminal justice 422
Divorce 422
Families 422
Family planning 422
Homosexuality 422
Incest 422
Marriage 422
Pornography 422
Poverty 422
Prostitution 422
Rape 422
Sex discrimination 422
Sex roles 422
Sexuality 422
Social welfare 422
Spouse abuse 422
Youth 220

AMBITION

SN Desire for success
UF Aspiration
Bibliographies
Families 411
Minorities 411
Role models 411
Sex roles 411

AMERICAN INDIANS

UF Indians (North American)
UF Native Americans
BT Aborigines
RT Tribal groups
Acculturation
Bibliographies 278, 564
Indexes 272
Adoption
Bibliographies 217, 234
Alcoholism
Bibliographies 278, 279, 477, 564
Indexes 272
Almanacs
Anthropology 267
Archaeology 267

Customs 267
Marriage 267
Population 267
Tribal groups 267
Anomie
Bibliographies 564
Anthropology
Almanacs 267
Bibliographies 276
Indexes 272
Antiquities
Bibliographies 274
Archaeology
Almanacs 267
Bibliographies 274, 276
Encyclopedias 277
Guides 270
Handbooks 271
Indexes 272
Audio-visual sources
Guides 349
Bibliographies 345
Acculturation 278, 564
Adoptions 217, 234
Alcoholism 278, 279, 477, 564
Anomie 564
Anthropology 276
Antiquities 274
Archaeology 274, 276
Child welfare 444
Crime 279
Cultural continuity 564
Cultures 274, 275
Demography 268, 279
Deviant behavior 564
Discrimination 564
Drug abuse 501, 564
Elderly 329
Ethnicity 329, 564
Ethnography 108, 111
Ethnohistory 108
Family structures 564
Kinship 279
Mental health 279, 563, 564
Northern plains 108
Poverty 505
Sex differences 564
Sex roles 275
Social life 274
Social organization 268
Social relations 275
Social status 564
Social stratification 275
Suicide 278
Tribal groups 274
Urban affairs 564
Urbanization 278, 279, 564
Women 275, 406, 410
Child welfare
Bibliographies 444
Crime
Bibliographies 279
Cultural continuity
Bibliographies 564
Cultures
Bibliographies 274, 275
Encyclopedias 277
Handbooks 271
Indexes 272
Customs
Almanacs 267
Dictionaries 269
Encyclopedias 277
Demography
Bibliographies 268, 279
Deviant behavior
Bibliographies 564
Dictionaries
Customs 269
Marriage 269
Social life 269
Tribal groups 269
Directories
Statistics (U.S.) 161
Discrimination
Bibliographies 564
Drug abuse
Bibliographies 501, 564
Elderly
Bibliographies 329
Guides 334
Encyclopedias
Archaeology 277
Cultures 277
Customs 277
Ethnology 277
Social life 277
Ethnicity
Bibliographies 329, 564
Ethnography

Bibliographies 108, 111
Ethnology
Encyclopedias 277
Handbooks 271
Families
Guides 222
Family structures
Bibliographies 564
Guides
Archaeology 270
Audio-visual sources 349
Elderly 334
Families 222
Population 270
Social life 270
Social organization 270
Handbooks
Archaeology 271
Cultures 271
Ethnology 271
Linguistics 271
Physical anthropology 271
Social anthropology 271
Youth 440
Indexes
Acculturation 272
Alcoholism 272
Anthropology 272
Archaeology 272
Cultures 272
Linguistics 272
Sociology 272
Urban affairs 272
Women 272
Kinship
Bibliographies 279
Linguistics
Handbooks 271
Indexes 272
Marriage
Almanacs 267
Dictionaries 269
Mental health
Bibliographies 279, 563, 564
Northern plains
Bibliographies 108
Physical anthropology
Handbooks 271
Population
Almanacs 267
Guides 270
Poverty
Bibliographies 505
Race relations
Bibliographies 393
Research guides 273
Youth 440
Sex differences
Bibliographies 564
Sex roles
Bibliographies 275
Social anthropology
Handbooks 271
Social life
Bibliographies 274
Dictionaries 269
Encyclopedias 277
Guides 270
Social organization
Bibliographies 268
Guides 270
Social relations
Bibliographies 275
Social status
Bibliographies 275, 564
Sociology
Indexes 272
Statistics (U.S.)
Directories 161
Women 409
Suicide
Bibliographies 278
Tribal groups
Almanacs 267
Bibliographies 274
Dictionaries 269
Urban affairs
Bibliographies 564
Indexes 272
Urbanization
Bibliographies 278, 279, 564
Women
Bibliographies 275, 406, 410
Indexes 272
Statistics (U.S.) 409
Youth
Handbooks 440
Research guides 440

AMPHETAMINES

BT Stimulants
Encyclopedias 502

ANCIENT ARCHAEOLOGY

BT Archaeology
RT Historic archaeology
Atlases 1

ANOMIE

SN Normlessness or absence of values
UF Powerlessness
RT Alienation
RT Social isolation
RT Social role loss
Bibliographies
American Indians 564
Elderly 327

ANTHROPOLOGISTS

BT Social scientists
NT Archaeologists
NT Cultural anthropologists
NT Physical anthropologists
NT Population anthropologists
RT Sociologists
Biographies 51, 54
Directories 90
Encyclopedias 88

ANTHROPOLOGY

SN Study of the origin, development and behavior of man
BT Social sciences
NT Anthropology of war
NT Applied anthropology
NT Archaeology
NT Cognitive anthropology
NT Cultural anthropology
NT Ecological anthropology
NT Economic anthropology
NT Folklore
NT Linguistics
NT Mathematical anthropology
NT Medical anthropology
NT Paleoanthropology
NT Physical anthropology
NT Political anthropology
NT Psychological anthropology
NT Social anthropology
NT Structural anthropology
NT Urban anthropology
Abstracts 76, 190
Acculturation
Bibliographies 87
Almanacs
American Indians 267
American Indians
Almanacs 267
Bibliographies 276
Indexes 272
Bibliographies 122
Acculturation 87
American Indians 276
Cross-cultural studies 84
Cultures 87
Education 87
Ethnicity 110
Europe 96
Filipino-Americans 117
Folklore 118
History 89
Homosexuality 458, 460, 461
Incest 451
Italian-Americans 369
Latin America 55, 56
Mental health 563
Micronesia 93
Prostitution 459
Social change 87
Socialization 87
Theses 92
Urban affairs 303
Women 404, 406, 408, 410, 413, 414, 425, 426
Black-Americans
Encyclopedias 292
Blacks (African)
Guides 98
Citations
Indexes 27
Cross-cultural studies
Bibliographies 84
Cultural areas
Handbooks 99
Cultures
Bibliographies 87

Dictionaries 48, 86, 142
Directories
Grants 15
International organizations 24
Organizations 12
Publications 37, 41, 97
Research centers 21
Education
Bibliographies 87
Elderly
Handbooks 335
Encyclopedias 51, 54, 88
Black-Americans 292
Organizations 14
Women 407
Ethnic groups (Soviet Union)
Guides 366
Ethnicity
Bibliographies 110
Europe
Bibliographies 96
Field research
Handbooks 99
Filipino-Americans
Bibliographies 117
Folklore
Bibliographies 118
Grant recipients
Indexes 16
Grants
Directories 15
Guides 17
Guides 52, 59, 62, 91
Blacks (African) 98
Ethnic groups (Soviet Union) 366
Grants 17
Mexican-Americans 392
Puerto Ricans 392
Social research 74
Handbooks 197
Cultural areas 99
Elderly 335
Field research 99
Library research 99
Regional studies 99
Research methods 75
History
Bibliographies 89
Homosexuality
Bibliographies 458, 460, 461
Incest
Bibliographies 451
Indexes 28, 80, 126
American Indians 272
Citations 27
Grant recipients 16
South Africa 83
Women 420
International organizations
Directories 24
Italian-Americans
Bibliographies 369
Latin America
Bibliographies 55, 56
Library research
Handbooks 99
Mental health
Bibliographies 563
Mexican-Americans
Guides 392
Micronesia
Bibliographies 93
Organizations
Directories 12
Encyclopedias 14
Yearbooks 44
Prostitution
Bibliographies 459
Publications
Directories 37, 41, 97
Puerto Ricans
Guides 392
Regional studies
Handbooks 99
Research centers
Directories 21
Research methods
Handbooks 75
Social change
Bibliographies 87
Social research
Guides 74
Socialization
Bibliographies 87
South Africa
Indexes 83
Theses
Bibliographies 92
Urban affairs
Bibliographies 303
Women
Bibliographies 404, 406, 408, 410, 413,

414, 425, 426
Encyclopedias 407
Indexes 420
Yearbooks
Organizations 44

ANTHROPOLOGY, APPLIED

See Applied anthropology

ANTHROPOLOGY, COGNITIVE

See Cognitive anthropology

ANTHROPOLOGY, CULTURAL

See Cultural anthropology

ANTHROPOLOGY, ECOLOGICAL

See Ecological anthropology

ANTHROPOLOGY, ECONOMIC

See Economic anthropology

ANTHROPOLOGY, MATHEMATICAL

See Mathematical anthropology

ANTHROPOLOGY, MEDICAL

See Medical anthropology

ANTHROPOLOGY OF WAR

BT Anthropology
RT Warfare
Handbooks 120

ANTHROPOLOGY, PHYSICAL

See Physical anthropology

ANTHROPOLOGY, POLITICAL

See Political anthropology

ANTHROPOLOGY, PSYCHOLOGICAL

See Psychological anthropology

ANTHROPOLOGY, SOCIAL

See Social anthropology

ANTHROPOLOGY, STRUCTURAL

See Structural anthropology

ANTHROPOLOGY, URBAN

See Urban anthropology

ANTHROPOMETRY

SN Measurement and classification of human body types
BT Physical anthropology
Bibliographies 122
Theses 92

ANTIQUITIES

SN Ancient times
American Indians
Bibliographies 274

ANTISOCIAL BEHAVIOR

SN Behavior that violates accepted social norms and values
UF Behavior, antisocial
BT Social issues
NT Juvenile delinquency
NT Rape
NT Sexual abuse
NT Social aggression
NT Terrorism
NT Violence
RT Collective behavior
RT Deviant behavior
RT Group behavior
RT Social behavior
RT Sociopathy
RT Urban behavior
Sex roles
Bibliographies 466

APPALACHIA

Poverty
Bibliographies 505
Women

Child abuse 428
Folklore 428
Social life 428
Spouse abuse 428

APPLIED ANTHROPOLOGY

UF Anthropology, applied
BT Anthropology
Cross-cultural studies
Bibliographies 84
Encyclopedias 54
Guides 62, 82
Indexes 28, 126

APPLIED SOCIOLOGY

UF Clinical sociology
BT Sociology
Handbooks 174
Indexes 148

ARAB WOMEN

BT Women
RT African women
RT Asian women
RT Caribbean women
RT Chinese women
RT Indian women
RT Latin American women
Bibliographies
Divorce 431
Ethnology 437
Families 430, 431, 437
Family planning 431
Fertility 437
Marriage 430, 431, 437
Polygamy 430, 437
Sex roles 437
Social research 437
Social roles 431
Social status 431, 437

ARAB-AMERICANS

BT Ethnic groups
Bibliographies 345
Mental health 563
Social life 378

ARABS

RT Asians
Bibliographies
Discrimination 377
Families 377
Population 377
Social research 377
Urbanization 377
Women 377

ARCHAEOLOGISTS

BT Anthropologists
Dictionaries 105
Directories 90

ARCHAEOLOGY

BT Anthropology
NT Ancient archaeology
NT Historic archaeology
NT Public archaeology
Abstracts 76
Almanacs
American Indians 267
American Indians
Almanacs 267
Bibliographies 274, 276
Encyclopedias 277
Guides 270
Handbooks 271
Indexes 272
Atlases 2
Burial practices 1
Customs 1
Bibliographies 122
American Indians 274, 276
Europe 96
Field research 102
Folklore 118
History 89
Latin America 55, 56
Micronesia 93
Research methods 102
South Asia 78
Theses 92
Women 406
Burial practices
Atlases 1
Customs
Atlases 1
Dictionaries 86, 103-106
Directories
Grants 15

International organizations 24
Organizations 101
Proceedings 50
Publications 37, 41, 97
Encyclopedias 54, 103
American Indians 277
Research methods 103
Europe
Bibliographies 96
Field research
Bibliographies 102
Folklore
Bibliographies 118
Gazetteers 2
Glossaries 2, 106
Grants
Directories 15
Guides 52
American Indians 270
Publications 64
Handbooks 101
American Indians 271
History
Bibliographies 89
Indexes 28, 80
American Indians 272
Women 420
International organizations
Directories 24
Latin America
Bibliographies 55, 56
Micronesia
Bibliographies 93
Organizations
Directories 101
Yearbooks 44
Proceedings
Directories 50
Publications
Directories 37, 41, 97
Guides 64
Research methods
Bibliographies 102
Encyclopedias 103
South Asia
Bibliographies 78
Thesauri 106
Theses
Bibliographies 92
Women
Bibliographies 406
Indexes 420

Yearbooks
Organizations 44

ARGOT

See Slang

ARSON

BT Crime
Bibliographies 485

ASIA

NT South Asia
RT Africa
RT Australia
RT Europe
Handbooks
Family planning 233
Population 233
Sociological research 136

ASIAN-AMERICANS

BT Ethnic groups
Acculturation
Guides 360
Adoption
Bibliographies 217
Bibliographies 345
Adoption 217
Drug abuse 501
Elderly 329
Ethnicity 329
Immigrants 375
Women 406
Demography
Guides 360
Discrimination
Guides 360
Drug abuse
Bibliographies 501
Elderly
Bibliographies 329
Guides 334, 360
Ethnicity
Bibliographies 329
Family structures
Guides 360
Guides
Acculturation 360
Demography 360
Discrimination 360

Elderly 334, 360
Family structures 360
Immigrants 360
Immigration 360
Mental health 360
Population 360
Poverty 360
Social organization 360
Social services 360
Social structures 360
Social welfare 360
Immigrants
Bibliographies 375
Guides 360
Immigration
Guides 360
Mental health
Guides 360
Population
Guides 360
Poverty
Guides 360
Social organization
Guides 360
Social services
Guides 360
Social structures
Guides 360
Social welfare
Guides 360
Statistics (U.S.)
Women 409
Women
Bibliographies 406
Statistics (U.S.) 409

ASIAN WOMEN

BT Women
RT African women
RT Arab women
RT Caribbean women
RT Chinese women
RT Indian women
RT Latin American women
Bibliographies
Adoption 429
Crime 434
Divorce 429, 434
Families 429
Family planning 434
Fertility 429, 434
Kinship 429
Marriage 429, 434
Sex roles 429
Social conditions 434
Social roles 429, 434
Social status 429, 434
Social stratification 429
Social structures 429
Social welfare 434
Guides
Abortion 439
Kinship 439
Marriage 439
Population 439
Sexuality 439
Social change 439

ASIANS

RT Arabs
Immigration
Abstracts 247

ASPIRATION

See Ambition

ASSIMILATION

SN Complete merging of the culture of one group into another
RT Acculturation
RT Socialization
Basque-Americans
Bibliographies 380
Bibliographies
Basque-Americans 380
Dutch-Americans 362
Ethnicity 355
Immigration 355
Japanese-Americans 371
Jewish-Americans 372
Mexican-Americans 387
Polish-Americans 374
Dutch-Americans
Bibliographies 362
Encyclopedias
Ethnic groups 353
Ethnic groups
Encyclopedias 353
Ethnicity
Bibliographies 355
Guides

    Migration 246
  Immigration
    Bibliographies 355
  Italian-Americans
    Theses 370
  Japanese-Americans
    Bibliographies 371
  Jewish-Americans
    Bibliographies 372
  Mexican-Americans
    Bibliographies 387
  Migration
    Guides 246
  Polish-Americans
    Bibliographies 374
  Theses
    Italian-Americans 370

ASSISTANCE PROGRAMS

 RT Social services
 RT Social welfare
  Families 219

ASSOCIATIONS

 See Organizations

ATLASES

  African cultures 7
  Ancient archaeology 1
  Archaeology 2
    Burial practices 1
    Customs 1
  Black-Americans
    Urban affairs 9
  Burial practices
    Archaeology 1
  Counties 172
    Demography 3
    Population density 3
  Cross-cultural studies
    Ethnography 8
  Customs
    Archaeology 1
  Demography
    Counties 3
  Elderly
    Urban affairs 9
  Ethnography 5
    Cross-cultural studies 8
    Kinship 5
    Marriage customs 5
    Social organization 5
  History
    Population 6
  Human evolution
    Physical anthropology 4
  Kinship
    Ethnography 5
  Marriage customs
    Ethnography 5
  Minor Civil Divisions 172
  Physical anthropology
    Human evolution 4
  Population
    History 6
    Urban affairs 9
  Population density
    Counties 3
  Social organization
    Ethnography 5
  Townships 172
  Urban affairs
    Black-Americans 9
    Elderly 9
    Population 9
    Youth 9
  Youth
    Urban affairs 9

AUDIO-VISUAL SOURCES

 SN Nonprint materials
  Guides
    American Indians 349
    Black-Americans 349
    Chinese-Americans 349
    Cuban-Americans 349
    Ethnic groups 349
    Japanese-Americans 349
    Jewish-Americans 349
    Mexican-Americans 349
    Puerto Ricans 349

AUSTRALIA

 RT Africa
 RT Asia
 RT Europe
  Guides
    Aborigines 545
    Demography 545
    Social policy 545
    Social services 545
    Social welfare 545

Urban affairs 545

AUSTRIAN-AMERICANS

BT Ethnic groups
Almanacs 348

BABY BOOM

SN The sudden increase in births from 1946 to 1961
BT Social trends
RT Fertility
Bibliographies
Demographic factors 239
Social factors 239

BARBITURATES

BT Sedatives
Encyclopedias 502

BASQUE-AMERICANS

BT Ethnic groups
Bibliographies
Acculturation 380
Assimilation 380
Ethnicity 380
Physical anthropology 380

BATTERED WOMEN

See Spouse abuse

BEER

BT Alcohol
RT Wine
Encyclopedias 482

BEHAVIOR, ANTISOCIAL

See Antisocial behavior

BEHAVIORS, SEX-TYPED

See Sex-typed behaviors

BELIEF SYSTEMS

SN Statements accepted as true
NT Religion
RT Cultural values
RT Social values
Handbooks 120

BEREAVEMENT

SN Feelings of desolation following the death of a loved one
RT Death and dying
RT Widowhood
Bibliographies 205
Death and dying 201, 204
Social change 533
Widowhood 199
Death and dying
Bibliographies 201, 204
Guides 208
Handbooks 202
Guides
Death and dying 208
Handbooks
Death and dying 202
Social change
Bibliographies 533
Widowhood
Bibliographies 199

BIAS

See Prejudice

BIBLIOGRAPHIES

RT Abstracts
RT Indexes
RT Information sources
RT Citations
Abortion 140, 256, 401, 412, 531
Black-Americans 290
Latin American women 435
Sex discrimination 472
Women 419, 423, 432
Acculturation
Adoption 234
American Indians 278, 564
Anthropology 87
Basque-Americans 380
Cross-cultural studies

84
Ethnicity 355
German-Americans 365
Hispanics 566
Immigration 355
Italian-Americans 369
Jewish-Americans 372
Mental health 563
Mexican-Americans 383, 387
Refugees 375
Theses 92
Vietnamese-Americans 378
Adoption 224, 225, 227
Acculturation 234
American Indians 217, 234
Asian-Americans 217
Asian women 429
Black-Americans 217, 234, 282
Child welfare 444
Chinese-Americans 217, 234
Filipino-Americans 234
Japanese-Americans 217, 234
Korean-Americans 217, 234
Mexican-Americans 234
Minority groups 234
Puerto Ricans 217
Social classes 234
Socialization 234
Vietnamese-Americans 217
Africa
Demography 318
Sociology 318
Urbanization 318
Women 404
African women
Child care 427
Divorce 427
Families 427
Fertility 427
Marriage 427
Sexual relations 427
Urban studies 427
Alcohol 494, 495
Alcoholism
American Indians 278, 279, 477, 564
Black-Americans 477
Child abuse 475
College students 477
Crime 475, 477, 483
Driving 477
Elderly 327, 341, 476
Families 477, 574
Hispanics 566
Homosexuality 460, 461, 475
Information sources 316
Juvenile delinquency 477
Marihuana 477
Mental health 563
Prevention 477
Sexuality 475
Social casework 585
Social characteristics 483
Social correlates 477
Social research 479
Social work 483
Sociology 496
Suicide 200, 209
Treatment 477, 496
Women 412, 477, 484
Youth 477, 483
Alienation 531
Ambition
Families 411
Minority groups 411
Role models 411
Sex roles 411
Women 411
American Indians 345
Acculturation 278, 564
Adoption 217, 234
Alcoholism 278, 279, 477, 564
Anomie 564
Anthropology 276
Antiquities 274
Archaeology 274, 276
Child welfare 444
Crime 279
Cultural continuity 564
Cultures 274, 275
Demography 268, 279
Deviant behavior 564
Discrimination 564
Drug abuse 501, 564
Elderly 329
Ethnicity 329, 564

Ethnography 108, 111
Ethnohistory 108
Family structures 564
Kinship 279
Mental health 279, 563, 564
Northern plains 108
Poverty 505
Race relations 393
Sex differences 564
Sex roles 275
Social life 274
Social organization 268
Social relations 275
Social status 275, 564
Suicide 278
Tribal groups 274
Urban affairs 564
Urbanization 278, 279, 564
Women 275, 406, 410
Anomie
American Indians 564
Elderly 327
Anthropology 122
Acculturation 87
American Indians 276
Cross-cultural studies 84
Cultures 87
Education 87
Ethnicity 110
Europe 96
Filipino-Americans 117
Folklore 118
History 89
Homosexuality 458, 460, 461
Incest 451
Italian-Americans 369
Latin America 55, 56
Mental health 563
Micronesia 93
Prostitution 459
Social change 87
Socialization 87
Theses 92
Urban affairs 303
Women 404, 406, 408, 410, 413, 414, 425, 426
Anthropometry
Bibliographies 122
Theses 92
Antiquities
American Indians 274
Antisocial behavior
Sex roles 466
Appalachia
Poverty 505
Applied anthropology
Cross-cultural studies 84
Arab-Americans 345
Mental health 563
Social life 378
Arab women
Divorce 431
Ethnology 437
Families 430, 431, 437
Family planning 431
Fertility 437
Marriage 430, 431, 437
Polygamy 430, 437
Sex roles 437
Social research 437
Social roles 431
Social status 431, 437
Arabs
Discrimination 377
Families 377
Population 377
Social research 377
Urbanization 377
Women 377
Archaeology
American Indians 274, 276
Bibliographies 122
Europe 96
Field research 102
Folklore 118
History 89
Latin America 55, 56
Micronesia 93
Research methods 102
South Asia 78
Theses 92
Women 406
Arson 485
Asian-Americans 345
Adoption 217
Drug abuse 501
Elderly 329
Ethnicity 329
Immigrants 375

Women 406
Asian women
Adoption 429
Crime 434
Divorce 429, 434
Families 429
Family planning 434
Fertility 429, 434
Kinship 429
Marriage 429, 434
Sex roles 429
Social conditions 434
Social roles 429, 434
Social status 429, 434
Social stratification 429
Social structures 429
Social welfare 434
Assimilation
Basque-Americans 380
Dutch-Americans 362
Ethnicity 355
Immigration 355
Japanese-Americans 371
Jewish-Americans 372
Mexican-Americans 387
Polish-Americans 374
Baby boom
Demographic factors 239
Social factors 239
Basque-Americans
Acculturation 380
Assimilation 380
Ethnicity 380
Physical anthropology 380
Bereavement 205
Death and dying 201, 204
Social change 533
Widowhood 199
Births
Family planning 226
Black-Americans 151, 345
Abortion 290
Adoption 217, 234, 282
Alcoholism 477
Crime 295, 298
Demography 290
Desegregation 287
Divorce 213
Drug abuse 501
Elderly 325, 329
Ethnic groups 288
Ethnicity 285, 329
Families 238, 282-284, 290, 296
Family planning 282, 290
Folklore 294
Homosexuality 286
Immigration 285
Juvenile delinquency 281, 295
Lesbianism 286
Marriage 294
Mental health 282, 296
Migration 294
Minority groups 307
Population 256, 290, 294
Poverty 284, 325, 505
Prejudice 288
Race relations 288, 295, 298, 393
Racism 286, 288
Riots 295
Segregation 287
Sex roles 284, 466
Social change 127
Social classes 294
Social conditions 294-296, 298
Social identity 287
Social institutions 294
Social life 282, 296
Social relations 294
Social welfare 582
Socialization 281
Sociology 283
Sociology of education 183
Television 517
Urban affairs 299, 300, 308, 541, 546
Urban communities 314
Urbanization 290
Women 283, 289, 296, 404, 406, 410, 423, 426, 432
Youth 281, 282, 284
Blacks (African)
Ethnography 77
Tribal groups 77
Canada

Homosexuality 464
Caribbean
Ethnic relations 398
Race relations 398
Caribbean women
Ethnicity 436
Social norms 436
Social status 436
Social values 436
Case studies
Child abuse 441
Incest 450
Censuses
Population 250
Central America
Criminal justice 553
Child abuse
Alcoholism 475
Case studies 441
Child welfare 444
Demographic factors 442
Families 235, 574
Family dysfunction 442
Social factors 237, 441, 442
Social research 441
Social work 578
Treatment 237, 442
Women 457
Youth 218
Child care
African women 427
Women 408, 417, 432
Child molesting 456
Child welfare
Adoption 444
American Indians 444
Child abuse 444
Foster care 444
Mexican-Americans 444
Minority groups 444
Chinese-Americans 371
Adoption 217, 234
Mental health 563
Race relations 378
Social life 378
Chinese women
Customs 433
Families 433
Family planning 433
Fertility 433
Marriage 433
Sex roles 433
Social status 433
Citation research 185
Classifications
Folklore 118
Cocaine 499
Collective behavior 529
College students
Alcoholism 477
Drug abuse 499
Communal living
Families 304
Mental health 304
Sex roles 304
Social change 304
Socialization 304
Women 304
Community-based corrections 547
Community development
Great Britain 544
Information sources 316
Youth 448
Computer crime 486
Conflict resolution 530
Corrections
Criminal justice 550
Social casework 585
Social group work 575
Countries of the world
Families 223
Kinship 223
Social research 535
Social work education 583
Courts
Criminal justice 550
Crime 151, 188
Alcoholism 475, 477, 483
American Indians 279
Asian women 434
Black-Americans 295, 298
Drug abuse 499
Elderly 341
Ethnic groups 352
Great Britain 144
Homosexuality 461
Italian-Americans 369
Juvenile delinquency 446
Latin America 56
Mental health 565
Mental retardation 568

Poverty 515
Social change 127
Social indicators 538
Urban affairs 299, 300, 308, 541, 546
Urban communities 314
Women 408, 432
Crime control policies 187
Crime prevention 187
Criminal deterrence 187
Criminal justice 191
Central America 553
Corrections 550
Courts 550
Cuba 553
Dominican Republic 553
Haiti 553
Latin America 553
Law enforcement 550
Puerto Rico 553
Rape 454
South America 553
Criminal organizations 493
Criminology 186, 188, 191
Theses 150
Women 425
Cross-cultural studies
Acculturation 84
Anthropology 84
Applied anthropology 84
Economic anthropology 84
Social anthropology 84
Urban anthropology 84
Women 419
Cuba
Criminal justice 553
Cuban-Americans 346, 384
Immigrants 375
Cultural anthropology 122
History 89
New Guinea 81
South Asia 78, 79
Theses 92
Cultural change
Hispanics 566
Cultural continuity
American Indians 564
Cultural life
Polish-Americans 374
Urbanization 317
Cultural pluralism
Ethnic groups (Canadian) 344
Hispanics 566
Cultural values
Mexican-Americans 387
Culturally disadvantaged 508
Cultures 140
American Indians 274, 275
Anthropology 87
Ethnic groups 352
German-Americans 364, 365
Homosexuality 461
Latin America 55, 56
Mexican-Americans 382
Romanian-Americans 376
Southern whites 516
Ukrainian-Americans 379
Urban communities 314
Customs
Chinese women 433
Dutch-Americans 362
German-Americans 364, 365
Jewish-Americans 372
Dating 224, 225, 227
Day care
Youth 218
Death and dying 202, 205
Bereavement 201, 204
Elderly 201, 321, 323, 326
Families 201, 204
Gerontology 332
Jews 228
Social attitudes 201
Social behavior 204
Social problems 204
Social sciences 201
Social welfare 204
Youth 201, 205
Deaths
Elderly 341
Women 484
Youth 231
Demographic factors

Baby boom 239
Child abuse 442
Warfare 100
Demography 252
Africa 318
American Indians 268, 279
Black-Americans 290
Elderly 323, 341
Ethnic groups (Canadian) 344
Ethnicity 110
Family planning 226, 238
Fertility 263
Filipino-Americans 363
Gerontology 332
Italian-Americans 369
Japanese-Americans 371
Latin America 55, 56
Minority groups 307, 346
Social research 535
Theses 150
Urbanization 303
Women 406
Desegregation
Black-Americans 287
Ethnic groups 343, 351
Sociology of education 183
Urban affairs 308
Development planning
Migration 258
Population 258
Deviant behavior 153, 191, 485
American Indians 564
Latin American women 435
Mental health 565
Social mobility 147
Women 484
Dialectics 143
Discrimination 531
American Indians 564
Arabs 377
Hispanics 566
Immigration 355
Mexican-Americans 387
Minority groups 307
Poverty 505
Urban affairs 308
Women 417
Divorce 224, 225, 227
African women 427
Arab women 431
Asian women 429, 434
Black-Americans 213
Families 235
Homosexuality 460
Jews 228
One-parent families 212, 213, 216
Religion 181
Sociology 212
Statistics (U.S.) 212
Women 212, 413, 414, 419, 432
Youth 211-213, 215, 231
Dominican Republic
Criminal justice 553
Driving
Alcoholism 477
Drug abuse 188, 494, 495, 531
American Indians 501, 564
Asian-Americans 501
Black-Americans 501
College students 499
Crime 499
Elderly 476, 499
Families 235, 499, 574
Hispanics 501
Information sources 316
Mexican-Americans 501
Minority groups 501
Puerto Ricans 501
Social casework 585
Social work 578
Social change 127
Social policy 543
Social research 499
Sociology 496, 499
Suicide 200, 210
Treatment 494, 495, 496, 501
Women 408, 412, 499
Youth 448, 494, 495, 499, 501
Durkheimian school
Sociological theory 131
Dutch-Americans
Assimilation 362

Customs 362
Immigration 362
Population 362
Social conditions 362
Social life 362
Economic anthropology
Cross-cultural studies 84
Education
Anthropology 87
Urban affairs 313
Elderly
Alcoholism 327, 341, 476
American Indians 329
Anomie 327
Asian-Americans 329
Black-Americans 325, 329
Crime 341
Death and dying 201, 321, 323, 326
Deaths 341
Demography 323, 341
Drug abuse 476, 499
Ethnicity 323, 329
Families 323, 326, 341, 473
Family relations 328
Family violence 328
Fertility 473
Hispanics 329
Homelessness 327
Homosexuality 473
Marriage 473
Mental health 321, 326, 341
Minority groups 341
Mortality 476
Physical abuse 328
Polish-Americans 374
Population 256
Poverty 325, 505
Religion 340
Retirement 321, 323, 326, 340
Rural areas 341
Sex roles 470, 473
Sexuality 323, 326, 473
Social casework 585
Social change 127, 341
Social isolation 326, 327
Social life 326
Social participation 341
Social policy 543
Social role loss 326
Social sciences 321
Social welfare 340, 582
Social work 512, 513
Sociology 321
Suicide 210
Urban communities 314
Widowhood 326, 341
Women 341, 426
Emigration
German-Americans 365
Italian-Americans 369
Eskimos
Linguistics 266
Ethics
Social group work 575
Ethnic groups 151
Black-Americans 288
Crime 352
Cultures 352
Desegregation 343, 351
Europe 113
Families 351, 352
Immigration 343
Latin America 55, 56
Population 351
Poverty 505
Race relations 343
Social conditions 352
Social organization 351, 352
Social policy 351
Social relations 343
Social roles 351
Social status 352
Social theory 351
Social welfare 351
Social work 578
Urban affairs 300, 308, 546
Women 408, 410, 417
Ethnic groups (Canadian)
Demography 344
Ethnicity 344
Immigration 344
Social structures 344
Ethnic relations
Caribbean 398
Latin America 398
Research methods 397
Social theory 397

Ethnicity
Acculturation 355
American Indians 329, 564
Anthropology 110
Asian-Americans 329
Assimilation 355
Basque-Americans 380
Black-Americans 285, 329
Caribbean women 436
Demography 110
Elderly 323, 329
Ethnic groups (Canadian) 344
Families 110
German-Americans 365
Hispanics 329
Italian-Americans 369
Jewish-Americans 372
Migration 110
Romanian-Americans 376
Social identity 110
Social stratification 110
Social work 512, 513
Sociology 110
Ukrainian-Americans 379
Urban affairs 313
Urban communities 314
Women 406
Ethnography 113
American Indians 108, 111
Blacks (African) 77
Filipino-Americans 117
Latin American women 435
South America 112
Theses 92
Tribal groups 111, 112
Ethnohistory
American Indians 108
Ethnology
Arab women 437
Europe 96
Theses 92
Women 406
Europe
Anthropology 96
Archaeology 96
Ethnic groups 113
Ethnology 96
Euthanasia 205, 206
Statistics (International) 206
Families 140, 151, 224, 225, 227
African women 427
Alcoholism 477, 574
Ambition 411
Arab women 430, 431, 437
Arabs 377
Asian women 429
Black-Americans 238, 282-284, 290, 296
Child abuse 235, 574
Chinese women 433
Communal living 304
Countries of the world 223
Death and dying 201, 204
Demography 238
Divorce 235
Drug abuse 235, 499, 574
Elderly 323, 326, 341, 473
Ethnic groups 351, 352
Ethnicity 110
History 223
Homosexuality 460, 461
Incest 451
Jews 228
Juvenile delinquency 446, 574
Latin America 56
Latin American women 435
Marriage 235, 574
Maternal employment 402
Mental health 235, 563
Mental retardation 568
Mexican-Americans 382, 383
Minority groups 346
Parents 574
Polish-Americans 374
Poverty 505, 509, 514, 515

Publications 149
Religion 181
Research methods 221
Sex roles 232
Single parents 235
Social change 127, 574
Social indicators 538
Social life 235
Social mobility 147
Social policy 238
Social problems 235
Social roles 232, 238
Social research 535
Social trends 232
Social welfare 582
Social work 512, 513, 578
Socialization 235
Suicide 200
Television 518
Treatment 574
Urban affairs 315, 534
Violence 574
Women 238, 404, 408, 410, 413-415, 417, 419, 423, 426
Work roles 238
Working women 402
Youth 211, 218
Family dysfunction
Child abuse 442
Family planning 140, 224, 225, 227, 256, 401
Arab women 431
Asian women 434
Births 226
Black-Americans 282, 290
Chinese women 433
Demography 226
Information sources 316
Latin American women 435
Population policy 226
Poverty 514
Sex discrimination 472
Social casework 585
Social programs 226
Women 403, 413, 414, 432
Family relations
Elderly 328
Sex discrimination 472
Family roles
Hispanics 566
Family structures
American Indians 564
Hispanics 566
Family violence 235, 237
Elderly 328
Women 457
Fatherhood
Sex roles 466
Fertility 252
African women 427
Arab women 437
Asian women 429, 434
Chinese women 433
Demography 263
Elderly 473
Latin America 55
Research methods 263
Social mobility 147
Social norms 263
Social stratification 263
Social structures 263
Urbanization 317
Women 403, 415, 423
Field instruction
Social work education 583
Field research
Archaeology 102
Filipino-Americans 371
Adoption 234
Anthropology 117
Demography 363
Ethnography 117
Immigration 373
Mental health 563
Migration 363
Race relations 378
Racism 373
Social conditions 363, 373
Social life 378
Sociology 117
Folklore
Anthropology 118
Archaeology 118
Black-Americans 294
Classifications 118
History 89
Puerto Ricans 391

Southern whites 516
Foster care
Child welfare 444
French-Americans 345
Mental health 563
German-Americans 345
Acculturation 365
Cultures 364, 365
Customs 364, 365
Emigration 365
Ethnicity 365
Immigration 364, 365
Mental health 563
Social conditions 364
Social life 364
Gerontology 333
Death and dying 332
Demography 332
Hospices 332
Retirement 332
Social research 535
Social services 332
Theses 150
Great Britain
Community development 544
Crime 144
Leisure 144
Migration 144
Minority groups 144
Population 144
Poverty 544
Sex roles 144
Social classes 144
Social policy 144, 544
Social work 544
Urbanization 144
Greek-Americans 345
Mental health 563
Group dynamics
Social group work 575
Haiti
Criminal justice 553
Halfway houses 547
Hallucinogens 494, 495
Handicapped
Social work 578
Youth 448
Heroin 501
Hispanics 345
Acculturation 566
Alcoholism 566
Cultural change 566
Cultural pluralism 566
Discrimination 566
Drug abuse 501
Elderly 329
Ethnicity 329
Family roles 566
Family structures 566
Interpersonal relations 566
Mental health 566
Poverty 566
Prejudice 566
Race relations 393
Sex roles 466, 566
Women 406, 410
History
Anthropology 89
Archaeology 89
Cultural anthropology 89
Families 223
Folklore 89
Kinship 223
Linguistics 89
Physical anthropology 89
Social anthropology 89
Social welfare 582
Homelessness
Elderly 327
Homosexuality 462, 463, 469
Alcoholism 460, 461, 475
Anthropology 458, 460, 461
Black-Americans 286
Canada 464
Crime 461
Cultures 461
Divorce 460
Elderly 473
Families 460, 461
Juvenile delinquency 461
Marriage 460, 461
Prisons 561
Sex roles 461
Sexuality 465
Social life 460, 461
Sociology 458, 460
Women 404, 408, 419, 425, 426
Youth 460, 461
Hospices
Gerontology 332

Hungarian-Americans 367
  Mental health 563
Illegitimacy 224, 225, 227
Immigrants 354
  Asian-Americans 375
  Cuban-Americans 375
  Russian-Americans 375
  Women 432
Immigration
  Acculturation 355
  Assimilation 355
  Black-Americans 285
  Discrimination 355
  Dutch-Americans 362
  Ethnic groups 343
  Ethnic groups (Canadian) 344
  Filipino-Americans 373
  German-Americans 364, 365
  Italian-Americans 369
  Jewish-Americans 372
  Mexican-Americans 388
  Minority groups 346
  Romanian-Americans 376
  Social life 355
  Ukrainian-Americans 379
Incest 224, 225, 227, 456
  Anthropology 451
  Case studies 450
  Families 451
  Sociology 451
  Treatment 450
  Women 457
  Youth 451
Indian-Americans
  Race relations 378
  Social life 378
Indian women 438
Industrialization
  Urban affairs 534
Information sources
  Alcoholism 316
  Community development 316
  Drug abuse 316
  Family planning 316
  Social services 316
Institutionalization
  Juvenile delinquency 547
  Parole 547
  Probation 547
  Rehabilitation 547
  Work release 547
Intermarriage 224, 225, 227
  Jews 228
Interpersonal relations
  Hispanics 566
  Social research 535
  Suicide 210
  Urban affairs 299
Invisible colleges 185
Irish-Americans 345
  Mental health 563
  Migration 368
  Social mobility 368
  Social status 368
Italian-Americans 345
  Acculturation 369
  Anthropology 369
  Crime 369
  Demography 369
  Emigration 369
  Ethnicity 369
  Immigration 369
  Mental health 563
  Social life 369
  Social structures 369
Japanese-Americans
  Adoption 217, 234
  Assimilation 371
  Demography 371
  Mental health 371, 563
  Race relations 371, 378
  Social life 378
Jewish-Americans 345, 346
  Acculturation 372
  Assimilation 372
  Customs 372
  Ethnicity 372
  Immigration 372
  Mental health 563
  Race relations 372
  Social change 372
  Social conditions 372
  Social mobility 372
  Social organization 372
Jews
  Death and dying 228
  Divorce 228
  Families 228

Intermarriage 228
Marriage 228
Sexuality 228
Social life 228
Social welfare 228
Juvenile delinquency 140, 151, 188, 531
Alcoholism 477
Black-Americans 281, 295
Crime 446
Families 446, 574
Homosexuality 461
Institutionalization 547
Leisure 446
Mental health 565
Mental retardation 568
Parent-child separation 230
Poverty 515
Social behavior 446
Social change 127
Social institutions 446
Social issues 446
Social welfare 582
Theses 150
Youth 448
Kinship
American Indians 279
Asian women 429
Countries of the world 223
History 223
Korean-Americans
Adoption 217, 234
Mental health 563
Ku Klux Klan 395, 396
LSD 494, 495
Latin America
Anthropology 55, 56
Archaeology 55, 56
Crime 56
Criminal justice 553
Cultures 55, 56
Demography 55, 56
Ethnic groups 55, 56
Ethnic relations 398
Families 56
Fertility 55
Migration 55, 56
Population 55, 56
Poverty 56
Race relations 55, 398
Social change 55, 56
Social classes 55, 56
Social conflict 55
Social organization 55, 56
Social structures 56
Latin American women
Abortion 435
Deviant behavior 435
Ethnography 435
Families 435
Family planning 435
Marriage 435
Prostitution 435
Sex roles 435
Sexuality 435
Socialization 435
Statistics 435
Law enforcement
Criminal justice 550
Leisure
Great Britain 144
Juvenile delinquency 446
Mental retardation 568
Social indicators 538
Social mobility 147
Television 518
Youth 448
Lesbianism
Black-Americans 286
Women 412
Lesbians
Sexuality 474
Life events 533
Linguistics
Eskimos 266
History 89
Micronesia 93
New Guinea 81
Mafia 492
Marihuana 494, 495, 499, 501
Alcoholism 477
Social behavior 503
Social interaction 503
Sociology 503
Youth 503
Marital separation 224, 225, 227
Marital status
Women 417
Marriage 151, 224, 225,

227
African women 427
Arab women 430, 431, 437
Asian women 429, 434
Black-Americans 294
Chinese women 433
Elderly 473
Families 235, 574
Homosexuality 460, 461
Jews 228
Latin American women 435
Mexican-Americans 382, 383
Religion 181
Research methods 221
Sex roles 466
Women 404, 408, 410, 413, 414, 419, 423, 432
Marxism 143
Maternal employment
Families 402
Mathematical sociology 178
Medical sociology 179
Men
Sex roles 466, 467
Social roles 467
Mental health
Acculturation 563
Alcoholism 563
American Indians 279, 563, 564
Anthropology 563
Arab-Americans 563
Black-Americans 282, 296
Chinese-Americans 563
Communal living 304
Crime 565
Danish-Americans 563
Deviant behavior 565
Elderly 321, 326, 341
Families 235, 563
Filipino-Americans 563
French-Americans 563
German-Americans 563
Greek-Americans 563
Hispanics 566
Hungarian-Americans 563
Irish-Americans 563
Italian-Americans 563
Japanese-Americans 371, 563
Jewish-Americans 563
Juvenile delinquency 565
Korean-Americans 563
Mexican-Americans 383, 387, 563
Norwegian-Americans 563
Polish-Americans 563
Portuguese-Americans 563
Poverty 514, 515
Puerto Ricans 563
Refugees 375
Russian-Americans 563
Scandinavian-Americans 563
Sex roles 466
Social casework 585
Social classes 563
Social mobility 147
Social networks 569
Social research 563
Social work 578
Socialization 563
Suicide 209, 563
Support groups 569
Swedish-Americans 563
Swiss-Americans 563
Women 412
Youth 218
Mental retardation
Crime 568
Families 568
Juvenile delinquency 568
Leisure 568
Social adjustment 568
Social life 568
Socialization 568
Methadone 501
Mexican-Americans 389
Acculturation 383, 387
Adoption 234
Assimilation 387
Child welfare 444
Cultural values 387
Cultures 382
Discrimination 387
Drug abuse 501
Families 382, 383
Immigration 388

Marriage 382, 383
Mental health 383, 387, 563
Migrants 383
Migration 388
Occupations 383
Poverty 387, 505
Race relations 388
Racism 383
Segregation 387
Sex roles 382
Social conditions 382, 388
Social life 388
Social status 387
Statistics 381, 383
Urbanization 387
Women 382, 383
Micronesia
Anthropology 93
Archaeology 93
Linguistics 93
Social organization 93
Migrants
Mexican-Americans 383
Migration 252, 256
Black-Americans 294
Development planning 258
Ethnicity 110
Filipino-Americans 363
Great Britain 144
Irish-Americans 368
Latin America 55, 56
Mexican-Americans 388
Poverty 505
Publications 149
Puerto Ricans 391
Social policy 543
Southern whites 516
Suburbs 310
Urban affairs 541
Urbanization 303, 317
Women 403
Minority groups 356
Adoption 234
Ambition 411
Black-Americans 307
Child welfare 444
Demography 307, 346
Discrimination 307
Drug abuse 501
Elderly 341
Families 346
Great Britain 144
Immigration 346
Population 256, 346
Poverty 505, 515
Segregation 307
Sex discrimination 472
Slums 307
Social casework 585
Social stratification 147
Social work 512, 513
Social work education 583
Sociology of education 183
Urban affairs 308, 546
Urbanization 346
Women 406
Modernization
Urban affairs 534
Mortality 252
Elderly 476
Urbanization 317
Motherhood 432
New Guinea
Cultural anthropology 81
Linguistics 81
Physical anthropology 81
Social anthropology 81
Northern plains
American Indians 108
Norwegian-Americans
Mental health 563
Occupations
Mexican-Americans 383
Women 417
One-parent families 215
Divorce 212, 213, 216
Remarriage 216
Widowhood 216
Youth 231
Organized crime 493
Paleoanthropology 122
Parent-child separation
Juvenile delinquency 230
Suicide 230
Parental absence 219
Parents
Families 574
Parole 191

Institutionalization 547
Physical abuse
Elderly 328
Physical anthropology 122
Basque-Americans 380
History 89
New Guinea 81
South Asia 78
Theses 92
Polish-Americans
Assimilation 374
Cultural life 374
Elderly 374
Families 374
Mental health 563
Youth 374
Polygamy
Arab women 430, 437
Popular culture 151
Population 151
Arabs 377
Black-Americans 256, 290, 294
Censuses 250
Development planning 258
Dutch-Americans 362
Elderly 256
Ethnic groups 351
Great Britain 144
Latin America 55, 56
Minority groups 256, 346
Publications 149
Puerto Ricans 391
Social change 127
Social indicators 538
Social policy 543
Urban affairs 256, 541, 546
Urban communities 314
Urbanization 303, 317
Women 256
Population distribution 252
Population policy 140, 265
Family planning 226
Population studies 252
Pornography 412, 468, 531
Sex roles 470
Women 457
Portuguese-Americans 345
Mental health 563
Poverty
American Indians 505
Appalachia 505
Black-Americans 284, 325, 505
Crime 515
Discrimination 505
Elderly 325, 505
Ethnic groups 505
Families 505, 509, 514, 515
Family planning 514
Great Britain 544
Hispanics 566
Juvenile delinquency 515
Latin America 56
Mental health 514, 515
Mexican-Americans 387, 505
Migration 505
Minority groups 505, 515
Religion 515
Riots 505
Rural America 505, 515
Social change 127
Social classes 514
Social indicators 509, 538
Social organization 515
Social research 509, 535
Social services 514
Social status 505
Social welfare 582
Social work 512, 513
Southern whites 516
Urban affairs 299, 300, 514, 515
Urban communities 314
Women 412, 417, 432
Youth 514
Prejudice
Black-Americans 288
Hispanics 566
Prevention
Alcoholism 477
Suicide 210
Prisons
Homosexuality 561

Social life 561
Social research 561
Privacy
Urban affairs 315
Probation
Institutionalization 547
Prostitution 412
Anthropology 459
Latin American women 435
Sociology 459
Women 419, 425, 432
Publications
Families 149
Migration 149
Social change 149
Social conditions 149
Social sciences 149
Sociology 149
Urban communities 149
Puerto Ricans
Adoption 217
Drug abuse 501
Folklore 391
Mental health 563
Migration 391
Population 391
Social conditions 391
Social life 391
Puerto Rico
Criminal justice 553
Quality of life
Social indicators 538
Quantitative methods
Social research 178
Questionnaire design 73
Race relations 531
Black-Americans 288, 295, 298, 393
Caribbean 398
Chinese-Americans 378
Ethnic groups 343
Filipino-Americans 378
Hispanics 393
Indian-Americans 378
Japanese-Americans 371, 378
Jewish-Americans 372
Latin America 55, 398
Mexican-Americans 388
Research methods 397
Social groups 393
Social policy 543
Social theory 397
Socialization 393
Southern whites 516
Urban affairs 308
Urban communities 393
Youth 393
Racial groups
Women 410
Racial segregation
Urban communities 314
Racism 396
Black-Americans 286, 288
Filipino-Americans 373
Mexican-Americans 383
Urban affairs 299
Rape 412
Criminal justice 454
Sex roles 454, 470
Social attitudes 453
Victims 453
Women 408, 425, 432, 457
Refugees
Acculturation 375
Mental health 375
Social services 375
Rehabilitation
Institutionalization 547
Religion
Divorce 181
Elderly 340
Families 181
Marriage 181
Poverty 515
Social change 181
Social issues 181
Urban affairs 313
Remarriage
One-parent families 216
Research methods 65
Archaeology 102
Ethnic relations 397
Families 221
Fertility 263
Marriage 221
Race relations 397
Social conflict 221
Social research 535
Social control 221
Social roles 221
Social stratification 147

Retirement
  Elderly 321, 323, 326, 340
  Gerontology 332
  Social change 533
Riots 531
  Black-Americans 295
  Poverty 505
  Urban affairs 299, 308
Rituals
  Social research 95
Role models
  Ambition 411
  Women 411
Romanian-Americans
  Cultures 376
  Ethnicity 376
  Immigration 376
Rural areas
  Elderly 341
  Poverty 505, 515
Rural poverty
  Social work 512, 513
Russian-Americans
  Immigrants 375
  Mental health 563
Scandinavian-Americans 345
  Mental health 563
Segregation
  Black-Americans 287
  Mexican-Americans 387
  Minority groups 307
Sex crimes 468
Sex differences 471
  American Indians 564
  Sex research 469
Sex discrimination 471
  Abortion 472
  Family planning 472
  Family relations 472
  Minority groups 472
  Sex roles 472
  Sex differences 469
  Women 412
Sex research
  Social classes 469
  Social conditions 469
  Social sciences 469
  Socialization 469
  Sociology 469
Sex roles 224, 225, 227, 471
  Ambition 411
  American Indians 275
  Antisocial behavior 466
  Arab women 437
  Asian women 429
  Black-Americans 284, 466
  Chinese women 433
  Communal living 304
  Elderly 470, 473
  Families 232
  Fatherhood 466
  Great Britain 144
  Hispanics 466, 566
  Homosexuality 461
  Latin American women 435
  Marriage 466
  Men 466, 467
  Mental health 466
  Mexican-Americans 382
  Pornography 470
  Rape 454, 470
  Sex discrimination 472
  Socialization 466
  Stereotypes 470
  Television 518
  Widowhood 199
  Women 404, 408, 410-414, 417, 423, 425, 426, 432, 457, 470
Sex-typed behaviors 471
Sex-typed occupations 471
Sexual abuse 456
  Youth 442
Sexual deviance
  Social casework 585
Sexual relations
  African women 427
Sexual stereotypes 470
  Women 423
Sexuality
  Alcoholism 475
  Elderly 323, 326, 473
  Homosexuality 465
  Jews 228
  Latin American women 435
  Lesbians 474
  Social research 465
  Sociology 465
  Women 404, 413, 414, 426, 474

Youth 474
Single parents
Families 235
Slavic-Americans 345
Slums
Minority groups 307
Urbanization 317
Social adjustment
Mental retardation 568
Social aggression
Suicide 209
Social anthropology 122
Cross-cultural studies 84
History 89
New Guinea 81
South Asia 78, 79
Theses 92
Social attitudes
Death and dying 201
Rape 453
Social behavior
Death and dying 204
Juvenile delinquency 446
Marihuana 503
Urban affairs 315
Social casework
Alcoholism 585
Corrections 585
Drug abuse 585
Elderly 585
Family planning 585
Mental health 585
Minority groups 585
Sexual deviance 585
Women 585
Youth 585
Social change 57, 153, 529, 531,
Anthropology 87
Bereavement 533
Black-Americans 127
Communal living 304
Crime 127
Drug abuse 127
Elderly 127, 341
Families 127, 574
Jewish-Americans 372
Juvenile delinquency 127
Latin America 55, 56
Population 127
Poverty 127
Publications 149
Religion 181
Retirement 533
Social classes 533
Social life 127
Social research 535
Social support 533
Social work 512, 513
Unemployment 533
Urban communities 314
Women 127, 412
Youth 533
Social characteristics
Alcoholism 483
Women 406
Social classes 57, 151, 153
Adoption 234
Black-Americans 294
Great Britain 144
Latin America 55, 56
Mental health 563
Poverty 514
Sex research 469
Social change 533
Social mobility 147
Urban affairs 315
Urban communities 314
Women 404, 413, 414
Social conditions
Asian women 434
Black-Americans 294-296, 298
Dutch-Americans 362
Ethnic groups 352
Filipino-Americans 363, 373
German-Americans 364
Jewish-Americans 372
Mexican-Americans 382, 388
Publications 149
Puerto Ricans 391
Sex research 469
Social conflict 530, 531
Latin America 55
Research methods 221
Social stratification 147
Women 412
Social control
Research methods 221
Television 518
Social correlates
Alcoholism 477

Social demography
  Suburbs 310
Social discrimination 508
Social disorders
  Urban affairs 299
Social factors
  Baby boom 239
  Child abuse 237, 441, 442
  Suburbs 310
  Television 518
  Warfare 100
Social group work
  Corrections 575
  Ethics 575
  Group dynamics 575
  Treatment 575
Social groups
  Race relations 393
  Women 417
Social identity
  Black-Americans 287
  Ethnicity 110
Social impact assessment 537
Social indicators 537
  Crime 538
  Families 538
  Leisure 538
  Population 538
  Poverty 509, 538
  Quality of life 538
  Social mobility 538
  Social policy 543
  Socialization 538
  Urban affairs 541
  Urban communities 314
  Youth 538
Social institutions
  Black-Americans 294
  Juvenile delinquency 446
Social interaction
  Urban affairs 315
Social isolation
  Elderly 326, 327
Social issues 57, 188, 485
  Death and dying 204
  Families 235
  Juvenile delinquency 446
  Religion 181
  Urban affairs 534
  Urban communities 314
  Youth 231
Social life
  American Indians 274
  Arab-Americans 378
  Black-Americans 282, 296
  Chinese-Americans 378
  Dutch-Americans 362
  Elderly 326
  Families 235
  Filipino-Americans 378
  German-Americans 364
  Homosexuality 460, 461
  Immigration 355
  Indian-Americans 378
  Italian-Americans 369
  Japanese-Americans 378
  Jews 228
  Mental retardation 568
  Mexican-Americans 388
  Prisons 561
  Puerto Ricans 391
  Social change 127
  Urban affairs 308
  Urbanization 317
  Women 413, 414, 432, 484
Social mobility 57, 153
  Deviant behavior 147
  Families 147
  Fertility 147
  Irish-Americans 368
  Jewish-Americans 372
  Leisure 147
  Mental health 147
  Social classes 147
  Social indicators 538
  Social values 147
  Suicide 147
  Ukrainian-Americans 379
Social movements 529
Social networks
  Mental health 569
Social norms
  Caribbean women 436
  Fertility 263
Social organization
  American Indians 268
  Ethnic groups 351, 352
  Jewish-Americans 372

Latin America 55, 56
Micronesia 93
Poverty 515
Theses 92
Social participation
Elderly 341
Social patterns
Suicide 200
Social planning
Social work 512, 513
Social policy 57, 265
Drug abuse 543
Elderly 543
Ethnic groups 351
Families 238
Great Britain 144, 544
Migration 543
Population 543
Race relations 543
Social indicators 543
Social programs 543
Social welfare 543
Urban affairs 546
Women 412
Social programs
Family planning 226
Social policy 543
Social psychology
Theses 150
Social relations
American Indians 275
Black-Americans 294
Ethnic groups 343
Suicide 209
Youth 231
Social research 65
Alcoholism 479
Arab women 437
Arabs 377
Child abuse 441
Countries of the world 535
Demography 535
Drug abuse 499
Families 535
Gerontology 535
Interpersonal relations 535
Mental health 563
Poverty 509, 535
Prisons 561
Quantitative methods 178
Research methods 535
Rituals 95
Sexuality 465
Social change 535
Social work 578
Suicide 207
Survey methods 535
Television 518
Social role loss
Elderly 326
Social roles
Arab women 431
Asian women 429, 434
Ethnic groups 351
Families 232, 238
Men 467
Research methods 221
Social sciences 57
Death and dying 201
Elderly 321
Publications 149
Sex research 469
Soviet Union 46
Social services
Gerontology 332
Information sources 316
Poverty 514
Refugees 375
Youth 448
Social status
American Indians 564
Arab women 431, 437
Asian women 429, 434
Caribbean women 436
Chinese women 433
Ethnic groups 352
Irish-Americans 368
Mexican-Americans 387
Poverty 505
Urban affairs 546
Women 404, 413, 414, 417, 432
Social stratification 151, 529
American Indians 275
Asian women 429
Ethnicity 110
Fertility 263
Minority groups 147
Research methods 147
Social conflict 147
Social structures 140, 153
Asian women 429
Ethnic groups (Canadian) 344
Fertility 263

Italian-Americans 369
Latin America 56
Social support
Social change 533
Social theory
Ethnic groups 351
Ethnic relations 397
Race relations 397
Social trends
Families 232
Social values
Caribbean women 436
Social mobility 147
Social welfare 186
Asian women 434
Black-Americans 582
Death and dying 204
Elderly 340, 582
Ethnic groups 351
Families 582
History 582
Jews 228
Juvenile delinquency 582
Poverty 582
Social policy 543
South Asia 79
Theses 150
Youth 582
Social work 57
Alcoholism 483
Child abuse 578
Drug abuse 578
Elderly 512, 513
Ethnic groups 578
Ethnicity 512, 513
Families 512, 513, 578
Great Britain 544
Handicapped 578
Mental health 578
Minority groups 512, 513
Poverty 512, 513
Rural poverty 512, 513
Social change 512, 513
Social planning 512, 513
Social research 578
Urban poverty 512, 513
Social work education
Countries of the world 583
Field instruction 583
Minority groups 583
Socialization 224, 225, 227
Adoption 234
Anthropology 87
Black-Americans 281
Communal living 304
Families 235
Latin American women 435
Mental health 563
Mental retardation 568
Race relations 393
Sex research 469
Sex roles 466
Social indicators 538
Television 518
Urban affairs 313
Women 403, 404, 413, 414, 417, 419, 426, 457
Youth 218
Socially disadvantaged 508
Sociolinguistics
South Asia 79
Sociological theorists 530
Sociological theory 143
Durkheimian school 131
Soviet Union 46
Suicide 209
Sociology
Africa 318
Alcoholism 496
Black-Americans 283
Divorce 212
Drug abuse 496, 499
Elderly 321
Ethnicity 110
Filipino-Americans 117
Homosexuality 458, 460
Incest 451
Marihuana 503
Prostitution 459
Publications 149
Sex research 469
Sexuality 465
Soviet Union 46, 153
Suicide 210
Theses 150

Urban affairs 303
Women 404, 406, 408, 410, 413, 414, 425, 426
Sociology of death 205
Sociology of education 180
Black-Americans 183
Desegregation 183
Minority groups 183
Sociology of human fertility 263
Sociology of law 186
Sociology of poverty 184
Sociology of religion 177, 181
Sociology of sciences 185
South America
Criminal justice 553
Ethnography 112
South Asia
Archaeology 78
Cultural anthropology 78, 79
Physical anthropology 78
Social anthropology 78, 79
Social welfare 79
Sociolinguistics 79
Urbanization 79
Southern whites
Cultures 516
Folklore 516
Migration 516
Poverty 516
Race relations 516
Urbanization 516
Women 516
Soviet Union
Social sciences 46
Sociological theory 46
Sociology 46, 153
Spanish-Americans 345
Spouse abuse 237
Women 412, 457
Statistics
Latin American women 435
Mexican-Americans 381, 383
Statistics (International)
Euthanasia 206
Suicide 210
Statistics (U.S.)
Divorce 212, 213
Suicide 209
Stepfamilies
Youth 211
Stereotypes
Sex roles 470
Stimulants 494, 495
Suburbs
Migration 310
Social demography 310
Social factors 310
Urban affairs 300, 546
Suicide 201, 205, 206
Alcoholism 200, 209
American Indians 278
Drug abuse 200, 210
Elderly 210
Families 200
Interpersonal relations 210
Mental health 209, 563
Parent-child separation 230
Prevention 210
Social aggression 209
Social mobility 147
Social relations 209
Social research 207
Sociological theory 200, 209
Sociology 210
Statistics (International) 210
Statistics (U.S.) 209
Treatment 210
Women 412, 484
Youth 210
Support groups
Mental health 569
Survey methods
Social research 535
Swedish-Americans 361
Mental health 563
Swiss-Americans
Mental health 563
Television
Black-Americans 517
Families 518
Leisure 518
Sex roles 518
Social control 518

Social factors 518
Social research 518
Socialization 518
Violence 518
Youth 518
Terrorism 489
Theses
Acculturation 92
Anthropology 92
Anthropometry 92
Archaeology 92
Criminology 150
Cultural anthropology 92
Demography 150
Ethnography 92
Ethnology 92
Gerontology 150
Juvenile delinquency 150
Physical anthropology 92
Social anthropology 92
Social organization 92
Social psychology 150
Social welfare 150
Sociology 150
Tobacco 494, 495
Transportation
Urban affairs 313
Transracial adoptions 217, 234
Transsexualism 458
Transvestism 458
Treatment
Alcoholism 477, 496
Child abuse 237, 442
Drug abuse 494, 495, 496, 501
Families 574
Incest 450
Social group work 575
Suicide 210
Tribal groups
American Indians 274
Blacks (African) 77
Ethnography 111, 112
Two-career families 236
Ukrainian-Americans
Cultures 379
Ethnicity 379
Immigration 379
Social mobility 379
Unemployment
Social change 533
Urban affairs
American Indians 564
Anthropology 303
Black-Americans 299, 300, 308, 541, 546
Crime 299, 300, 308, 541, 546
Desegregation 308
Discrimination 308
Education 313
Ethnic groups 300, 308, 546
Ethnicity 313
Families 315, 534
Industrialization 534
Interpersonal relations 299
Migration 541
Minority groups 308, 546
Modernization 534
Population 256, 541, 546
Poverty 299, 300, 514, 515
Privacy 315
Race relations 308
Racism 299
Religion 313
Riots 299, 308
Social behavior 315
Social classes 315
Social disorders 299
Social indicators 541
Social interaction 315
Social issues 534
Social life 308
Social policy 546
Social status 546
Socialization 313
Sociology 303
Suburbs 300, 546
Transportation 313
Urban sociology 300
Urbanization 300
Women 541
Youth 315
Urban anthropology
Cross-cultural studies 84
Urban communities
Black-Americans 314
Crime 314
Cultures 314

Elderly 314
Ethnicity 314
Population 314
Poverty 314
Publications 149
Race relations 393
Racial segregation 314
Social change 314
Social classes 314
Social indicators 314
Social issues 314
Urban environment 313
Urban poverty
Social work 512, 513
Urban sociology
Urban affairs 300
Urban studies
African women 427
Urbanization 534
Africa 318
American Indians 278, 279, 564
Arabs 377
Black-Americans 290
Cultural life 317
Demography 303
Fertility 317
Great Britain 144
Mexican-Americans 387
Migration 303, 317
Minority groups 346
Mortality 317
Population 303, 317
Slums 317
Social life 317
South Asia 79
Southern whites 516
Women 415
Victims
Rape 453
Vietnamese-Americans
Acculturation 378
Adoption 217
Violence
Families 574
Television 518
Warfare
Demographic factors 100
Social factors 100
White collar crime 191
Widowhood 432
Bereavement 199
Elderly 326, 341
One-parent families 216
Sex roles 199
Women 151
Abortion 419, 423, 432
Africa 404
Alcoholism 412, 477, 484
Ambition 411
American Indians 275, 406, 410
Anthropology 404, 406, 408, 410, 413, 414, 425, 426
Arabs 377
Archaeology 406
Asian-Americans 406
Black-Americans 283, 289, 296, 404, 406, 410, 423, 426, 432
Child abuse 457
Child care 408, 417, 432
Communal living 304
Crime 408, 432
Criminology 425
Cross-cultural studies 419
Deaths 484
Demography 406
Deviant behavior 484
Discrimination 417
Divorce 212, 413, 414, 419, 432
Drug abuse 408, 412, 499
Elderly 341, 426
Ethnic groups 408, 410, 417
Ethnicity 406
Ethnology 406
Families 238, 404, 408, 410, 413-415, 417, 419, 423, 426
Family planning 403, 413, 414, 432
Family violence 457
Fertility 403, 415, 423
Hispanics 406, 410
Homosexuality 404, 408, 419, 425, 426
Immigrants 432
Incest 457
Lesbianism 412
Marital status 417

Marriage 404, 408, 410, 413, 414, 419, 423, 432
Mental health 412
Mexican-Americans 382, 383
Migration 403
Minority groups 406
Occupations 417
Population 256
Pornography 457
Poverty 412, 417, 432
Prostitution 419, 425, 432
Racial groups 410
Rape 408, 425, 432, 457
Role models 411
Sex discrimination 412
Sex roles 404, 408, 410-414, 417, 423, 425, 426, 432, 457, 470
Sexual stereotypes 423
Sexuality 404, 413, 414, 426, 474
Social casework 585
Social change 127, 412
Social characteristics 406
Social classes 404, 413, 414
Social conflict 412
Social groups 417
Social life 413, 414, 432, 484
Social policy 412
Social status 404, 413, 414, 417, 432
Socialization 403, 404, 413, 414, 417, 419, 426, 457
Sociology 404, 406, 408, 410, 413, 414, 425, 426
Southern whites 516
Spouse abuse 412, 457
Suicide 412, 484
Urban affairs 541
Urbanization 415

Work release
Institutionalization 547

Work roles
Families 238

Working women
Families 402

Youth 494, 495
Alcoholism 477, 483
Black-Americans 281, 282, 284
Child abuse 218
Community development 448
Day care 218
Death 231
Death and dying 201, 205
Divorce 211-213, 215, 231
Drug abuse 448, 494, 495, 499, 501
Families 211, 218
Handicapped 448
Homosexuality 460, 461
Incest 451
Juvenile delinquency 448
Leisure 448
Marihuana 503
Mental health 218
One-parent families 231
Polish-Americans 374
Poverty 514
Race relations 393
Sexual abuse 442
Sexuality 474
Social casework 585
Social change 533
Social indicators 538
Social issues 231
Social relations 231
Social services 448
Social welfare 582
Socialization 218
Stepfamilies 211
Suicide 210
Television 518
Urban affairs 315

BICULTURALISM

See Acculturation

BIGOTRY

  See Discrimination

BIOGRAPHIES

  RT Directories
   Anthropologists 51, 54
   Demography
     Dictionaries 241
   Dictionaries
     Demography 241
   Social sciences
     Directories 45
   Social scientists 54
   Sociologists 51, 54
   Sociology
     Directories 45

BIRTH CONTROL

  See Family planning

BIRTHRATE

  See Natality

BIRTHS

  BT Life events
  RT Fertility
  RT Illegitimacy
   Almanacs
     Statistics (Great Britain) 155
     Statistics (U.S.) 43, 168, 169
   Bibliographies
     Family planning 226
   Cities
     Statistics (U.S.) 158
   Counties
     Statistics (U.S.) 158
   Family planning
     Bibliographies 226
   History
     Statistics (U.S.) 163
   Indexes
     Statistics (International) 159
     Statistics (U.S.) 159
   Statistics (Great Britain)
     Almanacs 155
   Statistics (International)
     Indexes 159
     Women 405
     Yearbooks 32, 160, 170
   Statistics (U.S.) 173
     Almanacs 43, 168, 169
     Cities 158
     Counties 158
     History 163
     Indexes 159
   Women
     Statistics (International) 405
   Yearbooks
     Statistics (International) 32, 160, 170

BLACK-AMERICANS

  UF Afro-Americans
  BT Minority groups
   Abortion
     Bibliographies 290
   Abstracts
     Families 297
     Fertility 297
     Mortality 297
     Population 297
     Statistics (U.S.) 297
   Adoption
     Bibliographies 217, 234, 282
   Alcoholism
     Bibliographies 477
   Almanacs
     Families 293
     Intermarriage 293
     Population 293
     Poverty 293
     Statistics 293
   Anthropology
     Encyclopedias 292
   Atlases
     Urban affairs 9
   Audio-visual sources
     Guides 349
   Bibliographies 151, 345
     Abortion 290
     Adoption 217, 234, 282
     Alcoholism 477
     Crime 295, 298
     Demography 290
     Desegregation 287
     Divorce 213
     Drug abuse 501
     Elderly 325, 329

Ethnic groups 288
Ethnicity 285, 329
Families 238, 282-284, 290, 296
Family planning 282, 290
Folklore 294
Homosexuality 286
Immigration 285
Juvenile delinquency 281, 295
Lesbianism 286
Marriage 294
Mental health 282, 296
Migration 294
Minority groups 307
Population 256, 290, 294
Poverty 284, 325, 505
Prejudice 288
Race relations 288, 295, 298, 393
Racism 286, 288
Riots 295
Segregation 287
Sex roles 284, 466
Social change 127
Social classes 294
Social conditions 294-296, 298
Social identity 287
Social institutions 294
Social life 282, 296
Social relations 294
Social welfare 582
Socialization 281
Sociology 283
Sociology of education 183
Television 517
Urban affairs 299, 300, 308, 541, 546
Urban communities 314
Urbanization 290
Women 283, 289, 296, 404, 406, 410, 423, 426, 432
Youth 281, 282, 284

Crime
Bibliographies 295, 298
Handbooks 291

Demography
Bibliographies 290

Desegregation
Bibliographies 287

Directories
Organizations 42
Statistics (U.S.) 161

Discrimination
Encyclopedias 280

Divorce
Bibliographies 213

Drug abuse
Bibliographies 501

Elderly
Bibliographies 325, 329
Guides 334, 342

Encyclopedias
Anthropology 292
Discrimination 280
Families 280
Popular culture 280
Population 280
Poverty 280
Prejudice 280
Racism 280
Social conditions 292
Sociology 292
Women 280
Youth 280

Ethnic groups
Bibliographies 288

Ethnicity
Bibliographies 285, 329

Families
Abstracts 297
Almanacs 293
Bibliographies 238, 282-284, 290, 296
Encyclopedias 280
Guides 222

Family planning
Bibliographies 282, 290

Fertility
Abstracts 297

Folklore
Bibliographies 294

Guides
Audio-visual sources 349
Elderly 334, 342
Families 222
Popular culture 522

Handbooks
Crime 291
Popular culture 519

Population 291
Statistics 291
Women 291
Homosexuality
Bibliographies 286
Immigration
Bibliographies 285
Indexes
Public opinion 523
Intermarriage
Almanacs 293
Juvenile delinquency
Bibliographies 281, 295
Lesbianism
Bibliographies 286
Marriage
Bibliographies 294
Mental health
Bibliographies 282, 296
Migration
Bibliographies 294
Minority groups
Bibliographies 307
Mortality
Abstracts 297
Organizations
Directories 42
Popular culture
Encyclopedias 280
Guides 522
Handbooks 519
Population
Abstracts 297
Almanacs 293
Bibliographies 256, 290, 294
Encyclopedias 280
Handbooks 291
Poverty
Almanacs 293
Bibliographies 284, 325, 505
Encyclopedias 280
Prejudice
Bibliographies 288
Encyclopedias 280
Public opinion 524, 527
Indexes 523
Race relations
Bibliographies 288, 295, 298, 393
Racism
Bibliographies 286, 288
Encyclopedias 280
Riots
Bibliographies 295
Segregation
Bibliographies 287
Sex roles
Bibliographies 284, 466
Social change
Bibliographies 127
Social classes
Bibliographies 294
Social conditions
Bibliographies 294-296, 298
Encyclopedias 292
Social identity
Bibliographies 287
Social institutions
Bibliographies 294
Social life
Bibliographies 282, 296
Social relations
Bibliographies 294
Social welfare
Bibliographies 582
Socialization
Bibliographies 281
Sociology
Bibliographies 283
Encyclopedias 292
Sociology of education
Bibliographies 183
Statistics
Almanacs 293
Handbooks 291
Statistics (U.S.)
Abstracts 297
Directories 161
Urban affairs 9
Women 409
Television
Bibliographies 517
Urban affairs
Atlases 9
Bibliographies 299, 300, 308, 541, 546
Statistics (U.S.) 9
Urban communities
Bibliographies 314
Urbanization
Bibliographies 290
Women
Bibliographies 283, 289, 296, 404, 406,

410, 423, 426, 432
Encyclopedias 280
Handbooks 291
Statistics (U.S.) 409
Youth
Bibliographies 281, 282, 284
Encyclopedias 280

BLACKS (AFRICAN)

RT African cultures
RT Tribal groups
Bibliographies
Ethnography 77
Tribal groups 77
Guides
Anthropology 98
Cultures 98
Physical anthropology 98
Social conflict 98
Social control 98
Social life 98
Social organization 98

BLINDNESS

BT Handicapped
Directories
Information sources 31
Organizations 13, 42
Social programs 33

BOOK REVIEWS

Social sciences
Indexes 25

BRAIN DRAIN

SN Emigration of scientists, scholars, etc. to countries where rewards and opportunities are greater
BT Social trends
Abstracts
Immigration 247

BURIAL PRACTICES

BT Customs
RT Death and dying
Archaeology
Atlases 1

CANADA

BT Countries of the world
Homosexuality
Bibliographies 464

CANADIAN-AMERICANS

BT Ethnic groups
Almanacs 348

CANADIAN ORGANIZATIONS

BT Organizations
RT International organizations
Directories
Alcoholism 11
Criminology 11
Family planning 11
Mental health 11
Social work 11
Youth 11

CARIBBEAN

Bibliographies
Ethnic relations 398
Race relations 398
Dictionaries
Ethnic relations 398
Race relations 398

CARIBBEAN WOMEN

BT Women
RT African women
RT Arab women
RT Asian women
RT Chinese women
RT Indian women
RT Latin American women
Bibliographies
Ethnicity 436
Social norms 436
Social status 436
Social values 436

CASE STUDIES

SN Intensive analysis

focusing on an individual or group
BT Social research
Bibliographies
Child abuse 441
Incest 450

CATEGORIZATIONS

See Classifications

CENSUSES

RT Demography
RT Population
RT Statistics
Population
Bibliographies 250
Handbooks 245
Statistics (U.S.) 260, 261

CENTRAL AMERICA

BT Latin America
Criminal justice
Bibliographies 553

CHICANOS

See Mexican-Americans

CHANGE, SOCIAL

See Social change

CHILD ABUSE

UF Abused children
BT Family violence
RT Physical abuse
RT Sexual abuse
RT Spouse abuse
Abstracts
Social research 577
Alcoholism
Bibliographies 475
Almanacs 220
Appalachia
Women 428
Bibliographies
Alcoholism 475
Case studies 441
Child welfare 444
Demographic factors 442
Families 235, 574
Family dysfunction 442
Social factors 237, 441, 442
Social research 441
Social work 578
Treatment 237, 442
Women 457
Youth 218
Case studies
Bibliographies 441
Child welfare
Bibliographies 444
Crisis intervention
Directories 36
Demographic factors
Bibliographies 442
Directories
Crisis intervention 36
Organizations 447, 581
Families
Bibliographies 235, 574
Guides 222
Family dysfunction
Bibliographies 442
Guides
Families 222
Organizations 35, 443
Social services 443
Statistics (U.S.) 443
Organizations
Directories 447, 581
Guides 35, 443
Social factors
Bibliographies 237, 441, 442
Social research
Abstracts 577
Bibliographies 441
Social services
Guides 443
Social work
Bibliographies 578
Statistics (U.S.)
Guides 443
Treatment
Bibliographies 237, 442
Women
Appalachia 428
Bibliographies 457
Youth

Bibliographies 218

CHILD CARE

UF Child rearing
BT Social services
NT Day care
Bibliographies
African women 427
Women 408, 417, 432

CHILD MOLESTING

BT Sexual abuse
Bibliographies 456
Guides 456

CHILD REARING

See Child care

CHILD WELFARE

BT Social welfare
Bibliographies
Adoption 444
American Indians 444
Child abuse 444
Foster care 444
Mexican-Americans 444
Minority groups 444
Organizations
Directories 447

CHILDREN

See Youth

CHINESE-AMERICANS

BT Ethnic groups
Adoption
Bibliographies 217, 234
Audio-visual sources
Guides 349
Bibliographies 371
Adoption 217, 234
Mental health 563
Race relations 378
Social life 378
Directories
Statistics (U.S.) 161
Guides
Audio-visual sources 349
Mental health
Bibliographies 563
Race relations
Bibliographies 378
Social life
Bibliographies 378
Statistics (U.S.)
Directories 161

CHINESE WOMEN

BT Women
RT African women
RT Arab women
RT Asian women
RT Caribbean women
RT Indian women
RT Latin American women
Bibliographies
Customs 433
Families 433
Family planning 433
Fertility 433
Marriage 433
Sex roles 433
Social status 433

CITATION RESEARCH

SN Analyses of patterns and frequencies of quoting references
Bibliographies 185

CITATIONS

RT Bibliographies
RT Indexes
Indexes
Anthropology 27
Social sciences 27
Sociology 27

CITIES

UF Towns
BT Counties
RT Municipalities
RT Rural areas
RT Suburbs
RT Townships
RT Urban communities
Bibliographies 308
Statistics (U.S.)
Births 158
Crime 158

Deaths 158
Divorce 158
Marriage 158
Population 158

CLASSIFICATIONS

SN Ordering data into groups according to attributes
UF Categorizations
UF Labeling
Folklore
Bibliographies 118

CLINICAL SOCIOLOGY

See Applied sociology

COCAINE

BT Stimulants
RT Tobacco
Bibliographies 499

COGNITIVE ANTHROPOLOGY

UF Anthropology, cognitive
BT Anthropology
Handbooks 120

COLLECTIVE BEHAVIOR

BT Social behavior
RT Antisocial behavior
RT Group behavior
RT Urban behavior
Bibliographies 529

COLLEGE STUDENTS

BT Social groups
RT Adults
RT Youth
Bibliographies
Alcoholism 477
Drug abuse 499

COMMUNAL LIVING

SN Collective settlements having shared ownership and cooperative life styles
UF Kibbutz
RT Rural areas
Bibliographies
Families 304
Mental health 304
Sex roles 304
Social change 304
Socialization 304
Women 304

COMMUNITY-BASED CORRECTIONS

BT Corrections
RT Halfway houses
RT Work release
Bibliographies 547

COMMUNITY DEVELOPMENT

SN Planning and implementation of community improvements
BT Societal development
RT Development planning
RT World development
Bibliographies
Great Britain 544
Information sources 316
Youth 448
Countries of the world
Guides 319
Directories 316
Great Britain
Bibliographies 544
Guides
Countries of the world 319
Rural social welfare 579
Urban affairs 306
Handbooks 576
Information sources
Bibliographies 316
Rural social welfare
Guides 579
Urban affairs
Guides 306
Youth
Bibliographies 448

COMMUNITY LIFE

See Social life

COMMUNITY ORGANIZATION

SN Interrelationships among community groups that provide for needs of members
BT Social organization
RT Social participation
Elderly
Guides 322

COMPARATIVE CRIMINOLOGY

BT Criminology
Guides 189
Handbooks 197

COMPUTER CRIME

BT White collar crime
Bibliographies 486

CONFIDENTIALITY

SN Protection of sensitive information
RT Ethics
RT Privacy
Social research
Guides 67

CONFLICT RESOLUTION

BT Social conflict
Bibliographies 530

CONGRESSIONAL DISTRICTS

SN Districts in each U.S. state served by a Congressional representative
RT Counties
RT Minor Civil Divisions
RT Townships
Statistics (U.S.)
Demography 156
Population 156, 157
Racial composition 156
Social characteristics 157

CONTRACEPTION

See Family planning

CONVICTS

See Prisoners

CORRECTIONAL INSTITUTIONS

See Prisons

CORRECTIONS

BT Criminal justice
NT Community-based corrections
NT Halfway houses
NT Institutionalization
NT Parole
NT Probation
NT Rehabilitation
NT Work release
Bibliographies
Criminal justice 550
Social casework 585
Social group work 575
Directories
Information sources 557

COUNSELING

See Treatment

COUNTIES

NT Cities
RT Congressional districts
RT Minor civil divisions
RT Townships
Atlases 172
Demography 3
Population density 3
Statistics (U.S.)
Age composition 3
Births 158
Crime 158
Deaths 158
Divorce 158
Families 158
Marriage 158
Population 158
Population density 3
Racial composition 3

COUNTRIES OF THE WORLD

SN See also entries for specific countries, i.e. Canada, Great Britain, Soviet Union, etc.
RT Third World
Bibliographies
Families 223
Kinship 223
Social research 535
Social work education 583
Community development
Guides 319
Criminology
Guides 189, 192
Handbooks 197
Demography
Guides 319
Families
Bibliographies 223
Family planning
Guides 319
Guides
Community development 319
Criminology 189, 192
Demography 319
Family planning 319
Migration 319
Social structures 319
Village studies 319
Handbooks
Criminology 197
Kinship
Bibliographies 223
Migration
Guides 319
Social research
Bibliographies 535
Social structures
Guides 319
Social work education
Bibliographies 583
Village studies
Guides 319

COURTS

BT Criminal justice
RT Law enforcement
Criminal justice
Bibliographies 550

CRIME

BT Social issues
NT Arson
NT Organized crime
NT Police corruption
NT Sex crimes
NT White collar crime
RT Juvenile delinquency
Abbreviations
Dictionaries 487
Abstracts
Urban affairs 309, 312
Alcoholism
Bibliographies 475, 477, 483
Almanacs
Statistics (Great Britain) 155
Statistics (U.S.) 43, 168
Asian women
Bibliographies 434
Bibliographies 151, 188
Alcoholism 475, 477, 483
Asian women 434
Drug abuse 499
Elderly 341
Ethnic groups 352
Great Britain 144
Homosexuality 461
Italian-Americans 369
Juvenile delinquency 446
Latin America 56
Mental health 565
Mental retardation 568
Poverty 515
Social change 127
Social indicators 538
Urban affairs 308, 541, 546
Urban communities 314
Women 408, 432
Black-Americans
Bibliographies 298
Handbooks 291
Cities
Statistics (U.S.) 158
Counties
Statistics (U.S.) 158
Death and dying
Guides 208
Dictionaries 487
Abbreviations 487

Slang 487
Directories
Organizations 42
Organizations (Elderly) 339
Statistics (U.S.) 161
Urban affairs 301
Drug abuse
Bibliographies 499
Guides 500
Elderly
Bibliographies 341
Guides 320, 330
Encyclopedias 196, 488
Social work 573
Ethnic groups
Bibliographies 352
Great Britain
Bibliographies 144
Guides
Death and dying 208
Drug abuse 500
Elderly 320, 330
Radical sociology 60
Statistics (Great Britain) 167
Urban affairs 306
Handbooks 197
Black-Americans 291
Homosexuality
Bibliographies 461
Indexes 26, 126, 551
Public opinion 523, 528
Statistics (International) 159
Statistics (U.S.) 159
Italian-Americans
Bibliographies 369
Juvenile delinquency
Bibliographies 446
Latin America
Bibliographies 56
Mental health
Bibliographies 565
Mental retardation
Bibliographies 568
Organizations
Directories 42
Organizations (Elderly)
Directories 339
Poverty
Bibliographies 515
Public opinion 527
Indexes 523, 528
Radical sociology
Guides 60
Slang
Dictionaries 487
Social change
Bibliographies 127
Social indicators
Bibliographies 538
Social work
Encyclopedias 573
Statistics (Canada) 165
Statistics (Great Britain)
Almanacs 155
Guides 167
Statistics (International)
Indexes 159
Yearbooks 40
Statistics (U.S.)
Almanacs 43, 168
Cities 158
Counties 158
Directories 161
History 163
Indexes 159
Women 409
Urban affairs
Abstracts 309, 312
Bibliographies 299, 300, 308, 541, 546
Directories 301
Guides 306
Urban communities
Bibliographies 314
Women
Bibliographies 408, 432
Statistics (U.S.) 409
Yearbooks
Statistics (International) 40

CRIME CONTROL POLICIES

BT Social policy
Bibliographies 187

CRIME PREVENTION

RT Community organization
Bibliographies 187
Organizations
Directories 30
Guides 35

CRIMINAL DETERRENCE

RT Rehabilitation
Bibliographies 187

CRIMINAL JUSTICE

BT Social welfare
NT Corrections
NT Juvenile justice
Abstracts 548
Alcoholism
Encyclopedias 558
Almanacs
Women 422
Bibliographies 191
Central America 553
Corrections 550
Courts 550
Cuba 553
Dominican Republic 553
Haiti 553
Latin America 553
Law enforcement 550
Puerto Rico 553
Rape 454
South America 553
Central America
Bibliographies 553
Corrections
Bibliographies 550
Courts
Bibliographies 550
Cuba
Bibliographies 553
Dictionaries 549, 554, 556
Directories 559
Information sources 557
Dominican Republic
Bibliographies 553
Drug abuse
Encyclopedias 558
Guides 562
Encyclopedias
Alcoholism 558
Drug abuse 558
Family violence 558
Juvenile delinquency 558
Mental health 558
Prostitution 558
Rape 558
Statistics (U.S.) 558
Family violence
Encyclopedias 558
Guides
Drug abuse 562
Juvenile delinquency 562
Prisoners 562
Statistics (U.S.) 562
Haiti
Bibliographies 553
Indexes 551
Information sources 559
Directories 557
Juvenile delinquency
Encyclopedias 558
Guides 562
Latin America
Bibliographies 553
Law enforcement
Bibliographies 550
Mental health
Encyclopedias 558
Prisoners
Guides 562
Prostitution
Encyclopedias 558
Puerto Rico
Bibliographies 553
Rape
Bibliographies 454
Encyclopedias 558
Research guides 552
South America
Bibliographies 553
Statistics (U.S.)
Encyclopedias 558
Guides 562
Women
Almanacs 422

CRIMINAL ORGANIZATIONS

BT Organizations
NT Mafia
RT Secret organizations
Bibliographies 493

CRIMINOLOGY

SN Study of criminal behavior
NT Comparative criminology
Abstracts 190
Bibliographies 186, 188, 191

Theses 150
Women 425
Canadian organizations
Directories 11
Countries of the world
Guides 189, 192
Handbooks 197
Dictionaries 194, 549, 554-556
Polyglots 195
Slang 490
Directories 559
Canadian organizations 11
Grants 15
Information sources 557
International organizations 24, 192
Publications 37, 41
Drug abuse
Encyclopedias 558
Guides 562
Encyclopedias 51, 54, 196, 558
Grants
Directories 15
Guides 555
Countries of the world 189, 192
Slang 490
Social research 192
Handbooks
Countries of the world 197
Indexes 28, 551
Information sources 559
Directories 557
International organizations
Directories 24, 192
Juvenile delinquency
Guides 562
Polyglots
Dictionaries 195
Publications
Directories 37, 41
Research guides 63, 552
Social research 198
Statistics 198
Slang
Dictionaries 490
Guides 490
Social research
Guides 192
Research guides 198
Statistics
Research guides 198
Statistics (U.S.)
Encyclopedias 558
Guides 562
Theses
Bibliographies 150
Women
Bibliographies 425

CRIMINOLOGY (U.S.)

Indexes 193

CRIMINOLOGY, COMPARATIVE

See Comparative criminology

CRISIS INTERVENTION

RT Assistance programs
RT Suicide prevention
Directories
Child abuse 36
Drug abuse 36
Rape 36
Suicide 36

CROSS-CULTURAL STUDIES

SN Studies comparing behavior of individuals or groups in two or more cultures
RT Cultural pluralism
RT Subcultures
Acculturation
Bibliographies 84
Anthropology
Bibliographies 84
Applied anthropology 84
Atlases
Ethnography 8
Bibliographies
Acculturation 84
Anthropology 84
Applied anthropology 84
Economic anthropology 84
Social anthropology 84
Urban anthropology 84
Women 419
Cultural characteristics

85
Cultures 85
Death education
  Guides 203
Economic anthropology
  Bibliographies 84
Ethnography 85
  Atlases 8
Guides
  Death education 203
Handbooks 120
Social anthropology
  Bibliographies 84
Urban anthropology
  Bibliographies 84
Women
  Bibliographies 419

CUBA

BT Latin America
Criminal justice
  Bibliographies 553

CUBAN-AMERICANS

BT Hispanics
Audio-visual sources
  Guides 349
Bibliographies 346, 384
  Immigrants 375
Guides
  Audio-visual sources 349
  Sociology 392
Immigrants
  Bibliographies 375
Organizations (Voluntary) 385
Sociology
  Guides 392

CULTS

Handbooks 134

CULTURAL ADAPTION

See Acculturation

CULTURAL ANTHROPOLOGISTS

BT Anthropologists
Directories 90

CULTURAL ANTHROPOLOGY

UF Anthropology, cultural
BT Anthropology
NT Ethnography
NT Ethnology
RT Social anthropology
Abstracts 76, 190
Bibliographies 122
  History 89
  New Guinea 81
  South Asia 78, 79
  Theses 92
Dictionaries 86
Directories
  Publications 97
Encyclopedias 54, 121
Field research
  Handbooks 119
Guides 59, 61
  Publications 64
Handbooks 120
  Field research 119
  Research methods 119
History
  Bibliographies 89
Indexes 28, 80
New Guinea
  Bibliographies 81
Publications
  Directories 97
  Guides 64
Research methods
  Handbooks 119
South Asia
  Bibliographies 78, 79
Theses
  Bibliographies 92

CULTURAL AREAS

SN Geographic area inhabited by a homogeneous culture
BT Social systems
Anthropology
  Handbooks 99

CULTURAL ASSIMILATION

See Acculturation

CULTURAL CHANGE

RT Alienation
RT Social change
Hispanics

Bibliographies 566

CULTURAL CHARACTERISTICS

RT Social characteristics
Cross-cultural studies 85

CULTURAL CONTINUITY

American Indians
Bibliographies 564

CULTURAL GROUPS

BT Cultures
RT Ethnic groups
RT Minority groups
RT Nationalities
RT Racial groups
RT Religious groups
RT Social groups
Encyclopedias 121
Guides 124

CULTURAL LIFE

RT Family life
RT Social life
Bibliographies
Polish-Americans 374
Urbanization 317

CULTURAL PLURALISM

SN Coexistence of different ethnic and minority groups within a society
UF Multiculturalism
RT Ethnic relations
RT Race relations
Bibliographies
Ethnic groups (Canadian) 344
Hispanics 566

CULTURAL VALUES

SN Standards of cultural interaction regarded as important by group members
RT Belief systems
RT Social values
Mexican-Americans
Bibliographies 387

CULTURALLY DISADVANTAGED

SN Those with low societal status for reasons of ethnicity or language
RT Social status
RT Socially disadvantaged
Bibliographies 508

CULTURES

SN Socially transmitted behaviors, beliefs, customs, norms, languages, etc.
NT African cultures
NT Cultural groups
NT Popular culture
NT Subcultures
American Indians
Bibliographies 274, 275
Encyclopedias 277
Handbooks 271
Indexes 272
Anthropology
Bibliographies 87
Bibliographies 140
American Indians 274, 275
Anthropology 87
Ethnic groups 352
German-Americans 364, 365
Homosexuality 461
Latin America 55, 56
Mexican-Americans 382
Romanian-Americans 376
Southern whites 516
Ukrainian-Americans 379
Urban communities 314
Blacks (African)
Guides 98
Cross-cultural studies 85
Encyclopedias 121
American Indians 277
Ethnic groups 353
Ethnic groups

Bibliographies 352
Encyclopedias 353
German-Americans
Bibliographies 364, 365
Guides 124
Blacks (African) 98
Publications 64
Handbooks
American Indians 271
Homosexuality
Bibliographies 461
Indexes
American Indians 272
Latin America
Bibliographies 55, 56
Mexican-Americans
Bibliographies 382
Publications
Guides 64
Romanian-Americans
Bibliographies 376
Southern whites
Bibliographies 516
Ukrainian-Americans
Bibliographies 379
Urban communities
Bibliographies 314

CUSTOMS

SN Traditional social behavior
NT Marriage customs
RT Social norms
Almanacs
American Indians 267
American Indians
Almanacs 267
Dictionaries 269
Encyclopedias 277
Archaeology
Atlases 1
Atlases
Archaeology 1
Bibliographies
Chinese women 433
Dutch-Americans 362
German-Americans 364, 365
Jewish-Americans 372
Chinese women
Bibliographies 433
Death and dying
Guides 208
Dictionaries
American Indians 269
Dutch-Americans
Bibliographies 362
Encyclopedias
American Indians 277
German-Americans
Bibliographies 364, 365
Guides
Death and dying 208
Jewish-Americans
Bibliographies 372

DANISH-AMERICANS

BT Ethnic groups
Mental health
Bibliographies 563

DATING

BT Interpersonal relations
RT Social life
Bibliographies 224, 225, 227

DAY CARE

BT Child care
Almanacs 220
Bibliographies
Youth 218

DEAFNESS

BT Handicapped
Directories
Information sources 31
Organizations 13
Publications 41

DEATH AND DYING

BT Life events
RT Bereavement
RT Burial practices
RT Euthanasia
RT Hospices
RT Mortality
RT Sociology of death
RT Suicide
RT Widowhood
Bereavement
Bibliographies 201,

    204
  Guides 208
  Handbooks 202
 Bibliographies 202,
  205
  Bereavement 201, 204
  Elderly 201, 321,
   323, 326
  Families 201, 204
  Gerontology 332
  Jews 228
  Social attitudes 201
  Social behavior 204
  Social problems 204
  Social sciences 201
  Social welfare 204
  Youth 201, 205
 Crime
  Guides 208
 Customs
  Guides 208
 Directories
  Organizations 202
 Elderly
  Bibliographies 201,
   321, 323, 326
  Handbooks 202, 335
 Families
  Bibliographies 201,
   204
 Gerontology
  Bibliographies 332
 Glossaries 202
 Guides
  Bereavement 208
  Crime 208
  Customs 208
  Statistics 208
 Handbooks
  Bereavement 202
  Elderly 202, 335
  Popular culture 519
  Social anthropology
   94
  Youth 202
 Hospices
  Guides 208
 Indexes 126
 Jews
  Bibliographies 228
 Organizations
  Directories 202
 Popular culture
  Handbooks 519
 Social anthropology
  Handbooks 94
 Social attitudes
  Bibliographies 201
 Social behavior
  Bibliographies 204
 Social problems
  Bibliographies 204
 Social sciences
  Bibliographies 201
 Social welfare
  Bibliographies 204
 Statistics
  Guides 298
 Youth
  Bibliographies 201,
   205
  Handbooks 202

DEATH EDUCATION

 BT Education
 Guides
  Cross-cultural studies
   203
  Elderly 203
  Suicide 203
  Widowhood 203
  Youth 203

DEATHS

 RT Mortality
 Almanacs
  Statistics (Great
   Britain) 155
  Statistics (U.S.)
   168, 169
 Bibliographies
  Elderly 341
  Women 484
  Youth 231
 Cities
  Statistics (U.S.) 158
 Counties
  Statistics (U.S.) 158
 Elderly
  Bibliographies 341
 History
  Statistics (U.S.) 163
 Indexes
  Statistics (Interna-
   tional) 159
  Statistics (U.S.) 159
 Statistics (Great
  Britain)
  Almanacs 155
 Statistics (Interna-

tional)
Indexes 159
Women 495
Yearbooks 32, 170
Statistics (U.S.) 173
Almanacs 43, 168, 169
Cities 158
Counties 158
History 163
Indexes 159
Women
Bibliographies 484
Statistics (International) 405
Yearbooks
Statistics (International) 170
Youth
Bibliographies 231

DELINQUENCY

See Juvenile delinquency

DEMOGRAPHIC FACTORS

RT Social factors
Bibliographies
Baby boom 239
Child abuse 442
Warfare 100

DEMOGRAPHY

SN Study of human population size, composition, distribution and development
BT Social sciences
NT Age composition
NT Fertility
NT Migration
NT Mortality
NT Population density
NT Population distribution
NT Racial composition
RT Population studies
Abstracts
Immigration 247
Urban affairs 312
Africa
Bibliographies 318
American Indians
Bibliographies 268, 279
Asian-Americans
Guides 360
Atlases
Counties 3
Australia
Guides 545
Bibliographies 252
Africa 318
American Indians 268, 279
Black-Americans 290
Elderly 323, 341
Ethnic groups (Canadian) 344
Ethnicity 110
Families 238
Family planning 226
Fertility 263
Gerontology 332
Filipino-Americans 363
Italian-Americans 369
Japanese-Americans 371
Latin America 55, 56
Minority groups 307, 346
Social research 535
Theses 150
Urbanization 303
Women 406
Biographies
Dictionaries 241
Black-Americans
Bibliographies 290
Congressional districts
Statistics (U.S.) 156
Counties
Atlases 3
Countries of the world
Guides 319
Dictionaries 240, 254
Biographies 241
Glossaries 243
Organizations 243
Polyglots 242, 244
Directories
International organizations 24, 248
Organizations 255
Drug abuse
Guides 500
Elderly
Bibliographies 323,

341
Guides 330, 342
Handbooks 338
Encyclopedias 54, 249
Organizations 14
Ethnic groups (Canadian)
Bibliographies 344
Ethnic groups (Soviet Union)
Guides 366
Ethnicity
Bibliographies 110
Families
Bibliographies 238
Family planning
Bibliographies 226
Fertility
Bibliographies 263
Filipino-Americans
Bibliographies 363
Gerontology
Bibliographies 332
Glossaries 244
Dictionaries 243
Guides 59, 253
Asian-Americans 360
Australia 545
Countries of the world 319
Drug abuse 500
Elderly 330, 342
Ethnic groups (Soviet Union) 366
Poverty 506
Publications 64
Urban affairs 306
Handbooks
Elderly 338
Research methods 75
Soviet Union 114
Statistics (Soviet Union) 536
Immigration
Abstracts 247
Indexes 148, 259
International organizations
Directories 24, 248
Italian-Americans
Bibliographies 369
Japanese-Americans
Bibliographies 371
Latin America
Bibliographies 55, 56
Minority groups
Bibliographies 307, 346
Organizations
Dictionaries 243
Directories 255
Encyclopedias 14
Polyglots
Dictionaries 242, 244
Poverty
Guides 506
Statistics (U.S.) 506
Publications
Guides 64
Research methods
Handbooks 75
Social research
Bibliographies 535
Soviet Union
Handbooks 114
Statistics (International)
Yearbooks 160
Statistics (Soviet Union)
Handbooks 536
Statistics (U.S.)
Congressional districts 156
Poverty 506
Theses
Bibliographies 150
Urban affairs
Abstracts 312
Guides 306
Urbanization
Bibliographies 303
Women
Bibliographies 406
Yearbooks
Statistics (International) 160

DEPRESSANTS

BT Drugs
NT Alcohol
RT Hallucinogens
RT Narcotics
RT Sedatives
RT Stimulants
Encyclopedias 502

DESEGREGATION

SN Process of dismantling barriers to social separation

UF Integration
RT Segregation
Bibliographies
Black-Americans 287
Ethnic groups 343, 351
Sociology of education 183
Urban affairs 308

DEVELOPING NATIONS

See Third World

DEVELOPMENT PLANNING

BT Societal development
RT Community development
RT Social planning
RT World development
Bibliographies
Migration 258
Population 258

DEVIANCE

See Deviant behavior

DEVIANT BEHAVIOR

SN Departure from social norms
UF Deviance
UF Social deviance
NT Sexual deviance
RT Antisocial behavior
RT Sociopathy
American Indians
Bibliographies 564
Bibliographies 153, 191, 485
American Indians 564
Latin American women 435
Mental health 565
Social mobility 147
Women 484
Handbooks
Small groups 70
Indexes 126, 139
Latin American women
Bibliographies 435
Mental health
Bibliographies 565
Small groups
Handbooks 70
Social mobility
Bibliographies 147
Women
Bibliographies 484

DIALECTICS

SN Study of change through conflict in society
BT Marxism
RT Social conflict
Bibliographies 143
Dictionaries 142

DICTIONARIES

RT Encyclopedias
RT Glossaries
RT Polyglots
RT Thesauri
Abbreviations
Crime 487
Alcohol 481
Alcoholism 481
Slang 480
American Indians
Customs 269
Marriage 269
Social life 269
Tribal groups 269
Anthropology 48, 86, 142
Archaeologists 105
Archaeology 86, 103-106
Biographies
Demography 241
Caribbean
Ethnic relations 398
Race relations 398
Crime 487
Abbreviations 487
Slang 487
Criminal justice 549, 554, 556
Criminology 194, 549, 554-556
Polyglots 195
Slang 490
Cultural anthropology 86
Customs
American Indians 269
Demography 240, 254
Biographies 241

Glossaries 243
Organizations 243
Polyglots 242, 244
Dialectics 142
Drug abuse 504
Slang 498
Ethnic groups
Soviet Union 116
Ethnic relations 394
Caribbean 398
Latin America 398
Ethnography
Soviet Union 116
Ethnology
Europe 123
Europe
Ethnology 123
Folklore 123
Families
Polyglots 244
Folklore
Europe 123
Fraternal organizations 10
Glossaries
Demography 243
Graduate departments
Sociology 135
Hallucinogens 498
Latin America
Ethnic relations 398
Race relations 398
Linguistics 86
Marihuana 498, 504
Marriage
American Indians 269
Marxism 142
Sociological theory 133
Migration
Polyglots 244
Nationalities
Soviet Union 116
Organizations
Demography 243
Physical anthropology 86
Polyglots
Criminology 195
Demography 242, 244
Families 244
Migration 244
Population 244
Population
Polyglots 244
Soviet Union 116
Population studies 254
Quotations
Sociology 129
Race relations 305, 394
Caribbean 398
Latin America 398
Secret organizations 10
Slang
Alcoholism 480
Crime 487
Criminology 490
Drug abuse 498
Subcultures 490
Social administration 49
Social change 532
Social life
American Indians 269
Social psychology 142
Social sciences 47-49, 58
Research methods 66
Social welfare 305
Social work 49
Sociological theory 142
Marxism 133
Sociology 47, 48, 58, 128, 141, 142, 145, 146
Graduate departments 135
Quotations 129
Soviet Union
Ethnic groups 116
Ethnography 116
Nationalities 116
Population 116
Subcultures
Slang 490
Tribal groups
American Indians 269
Urban affairs 305

DIGESTS

See Abstracts

DIRECTORIES

RT Biographies
RT Indexes
RT Information sources
Abortion
Organizations 255, 424
Adoption
Organizations 13, 581

Alcoholism 316
Canadian organizations 11
Grants 15
Organizations 30
Publications 37, 41
American Indians
Statistics (U.S.) 161
Anthropologists 90
Anthropology
Grants 15
International organizations 24
Organizations 12
Publications 37, 41, 97
Research centers 21
Archaeologists 90
Archaeology
Grants 15
International organizations 24
Organizations 101
Proceedings 50
Publications 37, 41, 97
Biographies
Social sciences 45
Sociology 45
Black-Americans
Organizations 42
Statistics (U.S.) 161
Blindness
Information sources 31
Organizations 13, 42
Social programs 33
Canadian organizations
Alcoholism 11
Criminology 11
Family planning 11
Mental health 11
Social work 11
Youth 11
Child abuse
Crisis intervention 36
Organizations 447, 581
Child welfare
Organizations 447
Chinese-Americans
Statistics (U.S.) 161
Community development 316
Corrections
Information sources 557
Crime
Organizations 42
Organizations (Elderly) 339
Statistics (U.S.) 161
Urban affairs 301
Crime prevention
Organizations 30
Criminal justice 559
Information sources 557
Criminology
Canadian organizations 11
Grants 15
Information sources 557
International organizations 24, 192
Publications 37, 41
Crisis intervention
Child abuse 36
Drug abuse 36
Rape 36
Suicide 36
Cultural anthropologists 90
Cultural anthropology
Publications 97
Deafness
Information sources 31
Organizations 13
Publications 41
Death and dying
Organizations 202
Demography
International organizations 24, 248
Organizations 255
Divorce
Organizations 424
Drug abuse 316
Crisis intervention 36
Organizations 30, 581
Publications 37, 41
Urban affairs 301
Elderly
International organizations 337
Organizations 13, 30, 42, 331, 337, 581
Social programs 33

Ethnic groups
  Organizations 347, 350, 424
  Publications 37, 41, 357
  Research centers 21, 350
  Statistics (U.S.) 161
Ethnology
  International organizations 24
  Publications 97
  Research centers 21
Families
  Organizations 30, 235
  Publications 149
  Statistics (U.S.) 161
Family planning 316
  Canadian organizations 11
  International organizations 248
  Organizations 42, 255, 424, 581
  Publications 37, 41
  Social services 418
Family studies
  Research centers 21
Filipino-Americans
  Statistics (U.S.) 161
Folklore
  Publications 37
  Research centers 21
Gerontology
  International organizations 24
  Publications 37, 41
  Research centers 21
Grants
  Alcoholism 15
  Anthropology 15
  Archaeology 15
  Criminology 15
  Handicapped 15
  Population 15
  Social sciences 15
  Sociology 15
Handicapped
  Grants 34
  Information sources 31
  Organizations 13, 30
  Organizations (Elderly) 339
Homosexuality
  Publications 37, 41
Hospices 202
Information sources
  Blindness 31
  Corrections 557
  Criminal justice 557
  Criminology 557
  Deafness 31
  Handicapped 31
  Mental retardation 31
International grants
  Social welfare 20
International organizations
  Anthropology 24
  Archaeology 24
  Criminology 24, 192
  Demography 24, 248
  Elderly 337
  Ethnology 24
  Family planning 248
  Gerontology 24
  Population 248
  Sociology 24
Japanese-Americans
  Statistics (U.S.) 161
Juvenile delinquency
  Organizations 447, 581
  Urban affairs 301
Juvenile justice
  Organizations 560
Linguistics
  Publications 97
Local areas
  Statistics (U.S.) 161
Medical sociology
  Research centers 21
Mental health
  Canadian organizations 11
  Organizations 13, 30, 42, 447
  Organizations (Youth) 447
  Research centers 21
  Social programs 33
  Treatment 567
Mental health facilities 567
Mental retardation
  Information sources 31
  Social programs 33
Migration
  Publications 149
  Organizations 255

Minority groups
Organizations 42, 447
Organizations (Elderly) 339
Organizations (Youth) 447
Urban affairs 301
Organizations
Abortion 255, 424
Adoption 13, 581
Alcoholism 30, 581
Anthropology 12
Archaeology 101
Black-Americans 42
Blindness 13, 42
Child abuse 447, 581
Child welfare 447
Crime 42
Crime prevention 30
Deafness 13
Death and dying 202
Demography 255
Divorce 424
Drug abuse 30, 581
Elderly 13, 30, 42, 331, 337, 581
Ethnic groups 347, 350, 424
Families 30, 235
Family planning 42, 255, 424, 581
Handicapped 13, 30
Juvenile delinquency 447, 581
Juvenile justice 560
Mental health 13, 30, 42, 447
Migration 255
Minority groups 42, 447
Population 255
Prison reform 560
Rehabilitation 560
Sex roles 424
Sexuality 424
Social research 13, 572
Social sciences 12, 13, 23
Social services 42, 424, 581
Social status 424
Social welfare 572
Social work 424
Sociology 12, 424
Spouse abuse 581
Women 255, 424
Youth 13, 30, 42
Organizations (Elderly)
Crime 339
Handicapped 339
Minority groups 339
Retirement 339
Sexuality 339
Women 339
Organizations (Voluntary)
Social services 571
Social work 571
Organizations (Youth)
Mental health 447
Minority groups 447
Physical anthropologists 90
Population
Grants 15
International organizations 248
Organizations 255
Publications 37, 41, 149
Research centers 21
Statistics (U.S.) 161
Urban affairs 301
Poverty
Urban affairs 301
Prevention
Rape 452
Prison reform
Organizations 560
Proceedings
Archaeology 50
Social sciences 50
Social work 50
Sociology 50
Publications
Alcoholism 37, 41
Anthropology 37, 41, 97
Archaeology 37, 41, 97
Criminology 37, 41
Cultural anthropology 97
Deafness 41
Drug abuse 37, 41
Ethnic groups 37, 41, 357
Ethnology 97
Families 149
Family planning 37,

41
Folklore 37
Gerontology 37, 41
Homosexuality 37, 41
Linguistics 97
Migration 149
Population 37, 41, 149
Social change 149
Social conditions 149
Social sciences 37, 41, 149
Social welfare 37, 41
Sociology 37, 41, 149
Urban communities 149
Puerto Ricans
Statistics (U.S.) 161
Race relations
Urban affairs 301
Rape
Crisis intervention 36
Prevention 452
Social services 418
Treatment 452
Rehabilitation
Organizations 560
Research centers
Anthropology 21
Ethnic groups 21, 350
Ethnology 21
Family studies 21
Folklore 21
Gerontology 21
Medical sociology 21
Mental health 21
Population 21
Race relations 21
Rural sociology 21
Social sciences 21
Social services 21
Sociology 21
Sociology of education 21
Sociology of religion 21
Sociology of sciences 21
Urban affairs 301, 311
Urban sociology 21
Retirement
Organizations (Elderly) 339
Sex roles
Organizations 424
Sexuality
Organizations 424
Organizations (Elderly) 339
Social change
Publications 149
Social conditions
Publications 149
Social programs
Blindness 33
Elderly 33
Mental health 33
Mental retardation 33
Veterans 33
Youth 33
Social research
Organizations 13, 572
Social welfare 572
Urban affairs 311
Social sciences
Biographies 45
Grants 15
Organizations 12, 13, 23
Proceedings 50
Publications 37, 41, 149
Social services 316
Family planning 418
Organizations 42, 424, 581
Organizations (Voluntary) 571
Rape 418
Spouse abuse 418
Women 418
Social status
Organizations 424
Social welfare
International grants 20
Organizations 572
Publications 37, 41
Social research 572
Urban affairs 301
Social work
Canadian organizations 11
Organizations 424
Organizations (Voluntary) 571
Proceedings 50
Social work education 586
Social work programs 586

Sociologists (American) 130
Sociology
Biographies 45
Grants 15
International organizations 24
Organizations 12, 424
Proceedings 50
Publications 37, 41, 149
Spouse abuse
Organizations 581
Social services 418
Statistics (U.S.)
American Indians 161
Black-Americans 161
Chinese-Americans 161
Crime 161
Ethnic groups 161
Families 161
Filipino-Americans 161
Japanese-Americans 161
Local areas 161
Population 161
Puerto Ricans 161
Suicide
Crisis intervention 36
Treatment
Mental health 567
Rape 452
Urban affairs
Crime 301
Drug abuse 301
Juvenile delinquency 301
Minority groups 301
Population 301
Poverty 301
Race relations 301
Research centers 301, 311
Social research 311
Social welfare 301
Urban communities
Publications 149
Veterans
Social programs 33
Women
Organizations 255, 424
Organizations (Elderly) 339
Social services 418
Youth
Canadian organizations 11
Organizations 13, 30, 42
Social programs 33

DISABLED

See Handicapped

DISADVANTAGED

See Socially disadvantaged

DISCRIMINATION

SN Differential treatment of individuals on the basis of some attribute
UF Bigotry
BT Social issues
NT Sex discrimination
NT Social discrimination
RT Prejudice
Almanacs
Ethnic groups 348
American Indians
Bibliographies 564
Arabs
Bibliographies 377
Asian-Americans
Guides 360
Bibliographies 531
American Indians 564
Arabs 377
Hispanics 566
Immigration 355
Mexican-Americans 387
Minority groups 307
Poverty 505
Urban affairs 308
Women 417
Black-Americans
Encyclopedias 280
Encyclopedias
Black-Americans 280
Ethnic groups
Almanacs 348
Guides
Asian-Americans 360
Hispanics
Bibliographies 566

Immigration
Bibliographies 355
Mexican-Americans
Bibliographies 387
Minority groups
Bibliographies 307
Poverty
Bibliographies 505
Urban affairs
Bibliographies 308
Women
Bibliographies 417

DISCRIMINATION, SEXUAL

See Sex discrimination

DISCRIMINATION, SOCIAL

See Social discrimination

DISSERTATIONS

See Theses

DIVORCE

BT Social issues
NT Parent-child separation
RT Marital separation
RT One-parent families
African women
Bibliographies 427
Almanacs
Statistics (Great Britain) 155
Statistics (U.S.) 43, 168, 169
Women 422
Arab women
Bibliographies 431
Asian women
Bibliographies 429, 434
Bibliographies 224, 225, 227
African women 427
Arab women 431
Asian women 429, 434
Black-Americans 213
Families 235
Homosexuality 460
Jews 228
One-parent families 212, 213, 216
Religion 181
Sociology 212
Statistics (U.S.) 212, 213
Women 212, 413, 414, 419, 432
Youth 212, 213, 215, 231
Black-Americans
Bibliographies 213
Cities
Statistics (U.S.) 158
Counties
Statistics (U.S.) 158
Directories
Organizations 424
Families
Bibliographies 235
Father absence
Guides 214
Guides
Father absence 214
Marital separation 214
Organizations 214
Remarriage 214
Statistics 214
Youth 214
History
Statistics (U.S.) 163
Homosexuality
Bibliographies 460
Jews
Bibliographies 228
Marital separation
Guides 214
One-parent families
Bibliographies 212, 213, 216
Organizations
Directories 424
Guides 214
Religion
Bibliographies 181
Remarriage
Guides 214
Sociology
Bibliographies 212
Statistics
Guides 214
Statistics (Great Britain)
Almanacs 155
Statistics (International)
Yearbooks 160

Statistics (U.S.) 173, 540
Almanacs 43, 168, 169
Bibliographies 212, 213
Cities 158
Counties 158
History 163
Women
Almanacs 422
Bibliographies 212, 413, 414, 419, 432
Yearbooks
Statistics (International) 160
Youth
Bibliographies 212, 213, 215, 231
Guides 214

DOMINICAN REPUBLIC

BT Latin America
Criminal justice
Bibliographies 553

DRINKING PATTERNS

RT Alcoholism
Alcoholism
Encyclopedias 482

DRIVING

Alcoholism
Bibliographies 477

DRUG ABUSE

BT Social issues
NT Alcoholism
Almanacs
Statistics (U.S.) 43
American Indians
Bibliographies 501, 564
Asian-Americans
Bibliographies 501
Bibliographies 188, 494, 495, 531
American Indians 501, 564
Asian-Americans 501
Black-Americans 501
College students 499
Crime 499
Elderly 476, 499
Families 235, 499, 574
Hispanics 501
Information sources 316
Mexican-Americans 501
Minority groups 501
Puerto Ricans 501
Social casework 585
Social change 127
Social policy 543
Social research 499
Social work 578
Sociology 496, 499
Suicide 200, 210
Treatment 494, 495, 496, 501
Women 408, 412, 499
Youth 448, 494, 495, 499, 501
Black-Americans
Bibliographies 501
College students
Bibliographies 499
Crime
Bibliographies 499
Guides 500
Criminal justice
Encyclopedias 558
Guides 562
Crisis intervention
Directories 36
Demography
Guides 500
Dictionaries 504
Slang 498
Directories 316
Crisis intervention 36
Organizations 30, 581
Publications 37, 41
Urban affairs 301
Elderly
Bibliographies 476, 499
Encyclopedias
Criminal justice 558
Organizations 14
Social work 573
Treatment 502
Ethnic groups
Guides 500
Families
Bibliographies 235, 499, 574

Guides 222
Grants
Guides 22
Guides
Crime 500
Criminal justice 562
Demography 500
Ethnic groups 500
Families 222
Grants 22
Institutionalization 324
Organizations 35
Social characteristics 500
Social research 500
Women 500
Youth 500
Handbooks
Social services 576
Hispanics
Bibliographies 501
Indexes 193, 551
Public opinion 523, 528
Information sources
Bibliographies 316
Institutionalization
Guides 324
Mexican-Americans
Bibliographies 501
Minority groups
Bibliographies 501
Organizations
Directories 30, 581
Encyclopedias 14
Guides 35
Public opinion
Indexes 523, 528
Publications
Directories 37, 41
Puerto Ricans
Bibliographies 501
Research guides 198
Slang
Dictionaries 498
Social case work
Bibliographies 585
Social change
Bibliographies 127
Social characteristics
Guides 500
Social policy
Bibliographies 543
Social research
Bibliographies 499
Guides 500
Social services
Handbooks 576
Social work
Bibliographies 578
Encyclopedias 573
Sociology
Bibliographies 496, 499
Statistics (U.S.)
Almanacs 43
Suicide
Bibliographies 200, 210
Treatment
Bibliographies 494, 495, 496, 501
Encyclopedias 502
Urban affairs
Directories 301
Women
Bibliographies 408, 412, 499
Guides 500
Youth
Bibliographies 448, 494, 495, 499, 501
Guides 500

DRUGS

NT Depressants
NT Hallucinogens
NT Narcotics
NT Sedatives
NT Stimulants
Encyclopedias 482

DUAL-CAREER FAMILIES

See Two-career families

DURKHEIMIAN SCHOOL

BT Sociological theory
RT Structural functionalism
Sociological theory
Bibliographies 131

DUTCH-AMERICANS

BT Ethnic groups
Bibliographies
Assimilation 362
Customs 362

Immigration 362
Population 362
Social conditions 362
Social life 362

EASTERN EUROPE

BT Europe
RT Northern Europe
RT Southern Europe
RT Western Europe
Handbooks
Ethnic groups 109
Minority groups 109
Sociological research 136

ECOLOGICAL ANTHROPOLOGY

UF Anthropology, ecological
BT Anthropology
Handbooks 120

ECONOMIC ANTHROPOLOGY

UF Anthropology, economic
BT Anthropology
Cross-cultural studies
Bibliographies 84
Encyclopedias 54
Handbooks 119, 120

ECONOMIC SOCIOLOGY

BT Sociology
Encyclopedias 54
Guides 62

EDUCATION

NT Death education
NT Social work education
Bibliographies
Anthropology 87
Urban affairs 313
Guides
Alcoholism 478

EDUCATIONAL SOCIOLOGY

See Sociology of education

ELDERLY

UF Aging
UF Older adults
BT Social groups
RT Gerontology
RT Hospices
RT Retirement
RT Sociology of aging
Abstracts 510
Social research 584
Urban affairs 312
Alcoholism
Bibliographies 327, 341, 476
American Indians
Bibliographies 329
Guides 334
Anomie
Bibliographies 327
Anthropology
Handbooks 335
Asian-Americans
Bibliographies 329
Guides 334, 360
Atlases
Urban affairs 9
Bibliographies
Alcoholism 327, 341, 476
American Indians 329
Anomie 327
Asian-Americans 329
Black-Americans 325, 329
Crime 341
Death and dying 201, 321, 323, 326
Deaths 341
Demography 323, 341
Drug abuse 476, 499
Ethnic groups 323, 329
Families 323, 326, 341, 473
Family relations 328
Family violence 328
Fertility 473
Hispanics 329
Homelessness 327
Homosexuality 473
Marriage 473
Mental health 321, 326, 341
Minority groups 341
Mortality 476
Physical abuse 328
Polish-Americans 374

Population 256
Poverty 325, 505
Religion 340
Retirement 321, 323, 326, 340
Rural areas 341
Sex roles 470, 473
Sexuality 323, 326, 473
Social casework 585
Social change 127, 341
Social isolation 326, 327
Social life 326
Social participation 341
Social policy 543
Social role loss 326
Social sciences 321
Social welfare 340, 582
Social work 512, 513
Sociology 321
Suicide 210
Urban communities 314
Widowhood 326, 341
Women 341, 426
Black-Americans
Bibliographies 325, 329
Guides 334, 342
Community organization
Guides 322
Crime
Bibliographies 341
Guides 320, 330
Death and dying
Bibliographies 201, 321, 323, 326
Handbooks 202, 335
Death education
Guides 203
Deaths
Bibliographies 341
Demography
Bibliographies 323, 341
Guides 330, 342
Handbooks 338
Directories
International organizations 337
Organizations 13, 30, 42, 331, 337, 581
Social programs 33
Drug abuse
Bibliographies 476, 499
Encyclopedias
Organizations 14
Social work 573
Ethnic groups
Handbooks 336
Ethnicity
Bibliographies 323, 329
Handbooks 335
Ethnogerontology
Handbooks 335
Families
Bibliographies 323, 326, 341, 473
Family life
Handbooks 335
Family relations
Bibliographies 328
Family violence
Bibliographies 328
Fertility
Bibliographies 473
Gerontology
Handbooks 338
Grants
Guides 22, 331
Guides
American Indians 334
Asian-Americans 334, 360
Black-Americans 334, 342
Community organization 322
Crime 320, 330
Death education 203
Demography 330, 342
Grants 22, 331
Hispanics 334
Institutionalization 324
Mental health 322
Minority groups 322, 334
Mortality 342
Organizations 35
Physical abuse 320
Population 330, 342
Rural social welfare 579
Statistics (U.S.) 330, 342
Victimization 320

Handbooks
  Anthropology 335
  Death and dying 202, 335
  Demography 338
  Ethnic groups 336
  Ethnicity 335
  Ethnogerontology 335
  Family life 335
  Gerontology 338
  Handicapped 336
  Mental health 335
  Population 335
  Religious groups 336
  Retirement 335
  Social behavior 335
  Social research 335, 338
  Social roles 335
  Social sciences 335
  Social services 576
  Social statuses 335
  Social stratification 335
  Social support 335
  Societal development 335
  Statistics (International) 338
Handicapped
  Handbooks 336
Hispanics
  Bibliographies 329
  Guides 334
Homelessness
  Bibliographies 327
Homosexuality
  Bibliographies 473
Indexes
  Public opinion 528
Institutionalization
  Guides 324
International organizations
  Directories 337
Marriage
  Bibliographies 473
Men
  Sexuality 473
Mental health
  Bibliographies 321, 326, 341
  Guides 322
  Handbooks 335
Mexican-Americans
  Research guides 386
Minority groups
  Bibliographies 341
  Guides 322, 334
Mortality
  Bibliographies 476
  Guides 342
Municipalities
  Statistics (U.S.) 38
Organizations
  Directories 13, 30, 42, 331, 337, 581
  Encyclopedias 14
  Guides 35
Physical abuse
  Bibliographies 328
  Guides 320
Polish-Americans
  Bibliographies 374
Population
  Bibliographies 256
  Guides 330, 342
  Handbooks 335
Poverty
  Bibliographies 325, 505
Public opinion
  Indexes 528
Religion
  Bibliographies 340
Religious groups
  Handbooks 336
Research guides
  Mexican-Americans 386
Retirement
  Bibliographies 321, 323, 326, 340
  Handbooks 335
Rural areas
  Bibliographies 341
Rural social welfare
  Guides 579
Sex roles
  Bibliographies 470, 473
Sexuality
  Bibliographies 323, 326, 473
  Men 473
  Women 473
Social behavior
  Handbooks 335
Social case work
  Bibliographies 585
Social change
  Bibliographies 127, 341

Social isolation
Bibliographies 326, 327
Social life
Bibliographies 326
Social participation
Bibliographies 341
Social policy
Bibliographies 543
Social programs
Directories 33
Social research
Abstracts 584
Handbooks 335, 338
Social role loss
Bibliographies 326
Social roles
Handbooks 335
Social sciences
Bibliographies 321
Handbooks 335
Social services
Handbooks 576
Social statistics
Handbooks 335
Social stratification
Handbooks 335
Social support
Handbooks 335
Social welfare
Bibliographies 340, 582
Social work
Bibliographies 512, 513
Encyclopedias 573
Societal development
Handbooks 335
Sociology
Bibliographies 321
Statistics (Canada) 165
Statistics (International)
Handbooks 338
Statistics (U.S.)
Guides 330, 342
Municipalities 38
Urban affairs 9
Stereotypes
Television 520
Suicide
Bibliographies 210
Television
Stereotypes 520
Urban affairs
Abstracts 312
Atlases 9
Statistics (U.S.) 9
Urban communities
Bibliographies 314
Victimization
Guides 320
Widowhood
Bibliographies 326, 341
Women
Bibliographies 341, 426
Sexuality 473

EMIGRATION

SN Departure of persons from their home country for residence in another
BT Migration
RT Immigration
Bibliographies
German-Americans 365
Italian-Americans 369

EMOTIONAL HEALTH

See Mental health

ENCYCLOPEDIAS

RT Almanacs
RT Dictionaries
RT Handbooks
Abortion 249
Women 407
Adoption
Organizations 14
Alcohol 482, 502
Alcoholism 482
Criminal justice 558
Drinking patterns 482
Organizations 14
Treatment 482, 502
American Indians
Archaeology 277
Cultures 277
Customs 277
Ethnology 277
Social life 277
Amphetamines 502
Anthropologists 88
Anthropology 51, 54, 88
Black-Americans 292
Organizations 14

Women 407
Applied anthropology 54
Archaeology 54, 103
American Indians 277
Research methods 103
Assimilation
Ethnic groups 353
Barbiturates 502
Beer 482
Black-Americans
Anthropology 292
Discrimination 280
Families 280
Popular culture 280
Population 280
Poverty 280
Prejudice 280
Racism 280
Social conditions 292
Sociology 292
Women 280
Youth 280
Crime 196, 488
Social work 573
Criminal justice
Alcoholism 558
Drug abuse 558
Family violence 558
Juvenile delinquency 558
Mental health 558
Prostitution 558
Rape 558
Statistics (U.S.) 558
Criminology 51, 54, 196, 558
Cultural anthropology 54, 121
Cultural groups 121
Cultures 121
American Indians 277
Ethnic groups 353
Customs
American Indians 277
Demography 54, 249
Organizations 14
Discrimination
Black-Americans 280
Drinking patterns
Alcoholism 482
Drug abuse
Criminal justice 558
Organizations 14
Social work 573
Treatment 502
Drugs 482
Economic anthropology 54
Economic sociology 54
Elderly
Organizations 14
Social work 573
Ethnic groups
Assimilation 353
Cultures 353
Immigration 353
Migration 353
Organizations 18, 347
Social life 353
Social organization 353
Social relations 353
Social structures 353
Ethnography 54, 121
Kinship 115
Marriage 115
Muslims 115
Social structures 115
Women 115
Ethnology 54, 121
American Indians 277
Women 407
Families
Black-Americans 280
Social work 573
Women 407
Family planning 249
Organizations 14
Women 407
Family violence
Criminal justice 558
Fertility 249
Fraternal organizations 18
Hallucinogens 502
Homosexuality
Organizations 14
Human ecology 54
Immigration
Ethnic groups 353
Juvenile Delinquency 196
Criminal justice 558
Social work 573
Kinship
Ethnography 115
Linguistics 54, 121
Marihuana 502
Marriage 249
Ethnography 115
Women 407
Medical sociology 54

Mental health
  Criminal justice 558
  Social work 573
Migration 249
  Ethnic groups 353
Minority groups
  Social work 573
Mortality 249
Motherhood 407
Muslims
  Ethnography 115
Narcotics 502
Organizations
  Adoption 14
  Alcoholism 14
  Anthropology 14
  Demography 14
  Drug abuse 14
  Elderly 14
  Ethnic groups 18, 347
  Family planning 14
  Homosexuality 14
  Population 14
  Social groups 18
  Social services 580
  Social welfare 580
  Sociology 14
Physical anthropology 54
Political sociology 54
Popular culture
  Black-Americans 280
Population 249
  Black-Americans 280
  Organizations 14
  Urban affairs 302
Poverty
  Black-Americans 280
  Social work 573
Prejudice
  Black-Americans 280
Prisons 488
Prostitution 488
  Criminal justice 558
Racism
  Black-Americans 280
Rape
  Criminal justice 558
  Women 407
Research methods
  Archaeology 103
Riots 488
Rural sociology 54
Sedatives 502
Sex roles
  Women 407
Sexuality
  Women 407
Social anthropology 54, 121
Social conditions
  Black-Americans 292
Social groups
  Organizations 18
Social life
  American Indians 277
  Ethnic groups 353
Social organization 121
  Ethnic groups 353
Social relations
  Ethnic groups 353
Social sciences 51, 54
Social services
  Organizations 580
Social structures
  Ethnic groups 353
  Ethnography 115
Social welfare
  Organizations 580
Social work
  Crime 573
  Drug abuse 573
  Elderly 573
  Families 573
  Juvenile delinquency 573
  Mental health 573
  Minority groups 573
  Poverty 573
  Statistics (U.S.) 573
  Youth 573
Sociology 51, 54, 132, 141
  Black-Americans 292
  Organizations 14
Sociology of knowledge 54
Sociology of law 54
Sociology of organizations 54
Sociology of religion 54
Sociometry 54
Statistics (U.S.)
  Criminal justice 558
  Social work 573
Survey methods 54
Treatment
  Alcoholism 482, 502
  Drug abuse 502
Urban affairs
  Population 302

Urban behavior 121
Urban sociology 54
Urbanization 302
Wine 482
Women
Abortion 407
Anthropology 407
Black-Americans 280
Ethnography 115
Ethnology 407
Families 407
Family planning 407
Marriage 407
Rape 407
Sex roles 407
Sexuality 407
Youth
Black-Americans 280
Social work 573

ESKIMOS

BT Ethnic groups
Linguistics
Bibliographies 266

ETHICS

UF Morals
RT Confidentiality
RT Privacy
RT Social values
Social group work
Bibliographies 575
Social research
Guides 67

ETHNIC GROUPS

SN See also entries for specific ethnic groups, i.e., American Indians, German-Americans, Hispanics, etc.
RT Ethnicity
RT Nationalities
Abstracts 510
Almanacs
Discrimination 348
Assimilation
Encyclopedias 353
Audio-visual sources
Guides 349
Bibliographies 151
Black-Americans 288
Crime 352
Cultures 352
Desegregation 343, 351
Europe 113
Families 351, 352
Immigration 343
Latin America 55, 56
Population 351
Poverty 505
Race relations 343
Social conditions 352
Social organization 351, 352
Social policy 351
Social relations 343
Social roles 351
Social status 352
Social theory 351
Social welfare 351
Social work 578
Urban affairs 300, 308, 546
Women 408, 410, 417
Black-Americans
Bibliographies 288
Crime
Bibliographies 352
Cultures
Bibliographies 352
Encyclopedias 353
Desegregation
Bibliographies 343, 351
Dictionaries
Soviet Union 116
Directories
Organizations 347, 350, 424
Publications 37, 41, 357
Research centers 21, 350
Statistics (U.S.) 161
Discrimination
Almanacs 348
Drug abuse
Guides 500
Eastern Europe
Handbooks 109
Elderly
Handbooks 336
Encyclopedias
Assimilation 353
Cultures 353
Immigration 353

Migration 353
Organizations 18, 347
Social life 353
Social organization 353
Social relations 353
Social structures 353
Europe
Bibliographies 113
Families
Bibliographies 351, 352
Guides 124
Audio-visual sources 349
Drug abuse 500
Migration 246
Handbooks
Eastern Europe 109
Elderly 336
Soviet Union 116
Immigration
Bibliographies 343
Encyclopedias 353
Latin America
Bibliographies 55, 56
Mexican-Americans
Research guides 386
Migration
Encyclopedias 353
Guides 246
Organizations
Directories 347, 350, 424
Encyclopedias 18, 347
Population
Bibliographies 351
Poverty
Bibliographies 505
Publications
Directories 37, 41, 357
Race relations
Bibliographies 343
Research centers
Directories 21, 350
Research guides
Mexican-Americans 386
Social conditions
Bibliographies 352
Social life
Encyclopedias 353
Social organization
Bibliographies 351, 352
Encyclopedias 353
Social policy
Bibliographies 351
Social relations
Bibliographies 343
Encyclopedias 353
Social roles 351
Social status
Bibliographies 352
Social structures
Encyclopedias 353
Social theory
Bibliographies 351
Social welfare
Bibliographies 351
Social work
Bibliographies 578
Soviet Union
Dictionaries 116
Handbooks 116
Statistics (International)
Yearbooks 32
Statistics (U.S.)
Directories 161
Urban affairs
Bibliographies 300, 308, 546
Women
Bibliographies 408, 410, 417
Yearbooks
Statistics (International) 32

ETHNIC GROUPS (CANADIAN)

Bibliographies
Cultural pluralism 344
Demography 344
Ethnicity 344
Immigration 344
Social structures 344

ETHNIC GROUPS (SOVIET UNION)

Guides
Anthropology 366
Demography 366
Folklore 366
Sociology 366

ETHNIC RELATIONS

BT Social relations

RT Race relations
Bibliographies
Caribbean 398
Latin America 398
Research methods 397
Social theory 397
Dictionaries 394
Caribbean 398
Latin America 398

ETHNICITY

SN Awareness of an ethnic character
RT Ethnic groups
RT Socialization
RT Subcultures
Acculturation
Bibliographies 355
American Indians
Bibliographies 329, 564
Anthropology
Bibliographies 110
Asian-Americans
Bibliographies 329
Assimilation
Bibliographies 355
Basque-Americans
Bibliographies 380
Bibliographies
Acculturation 355
American Indians 329, 564
Anthropology 110
Asian-Americans 329
Assimilation 355
Basque-Americans 380
Black-Americans 285, 329
Caribbean women 436
Demography 110
Elderly 323, 329
Ethnic groups (Canadian) 344
Families 110
German-Americans 365
Hispanics 329
Italian-Americans 369
Jewish-Americans 372
Migration 110
Romanian-Americans 376
Social identity 110
Social stratification 110
Social work 512, 513
Sociology 110
Ukrainian-Americans 379
Urban affairs 313
Urban communities 314
Women 406
Black-Americans
Bibliographies 285, 329
Caribbean women
Bibliographies 436
Demography
Bibliographies 110
Elderly
Bibliographies 323, 329
Handbooks 335
Ethnic groups (Canadian)
Bibliographies 344
Families
Bibliographies 110
German-Americans
Bibliographies 365
Guides
Mental health 570
Handbooks
Elderly 335
Youth 440
Hispanics
Bibliographies 329
Indexes 126
Italian-Americans
Bibliographies 369
Theses 370
Jewish-Americans
Bibliographies 372
Mental health
Guides 570
Migration
Bibliographies 110
Research guides
Youth 440
Romanian-Americans
Bibliographies 376
Social identity
Bibliographies 110
Social stratification
Bibliographies 110
Social work
Bibliographies 512, 513
Sociology
Bibliographies 110
South Africa
Indexes 83

Theses
  Italian-Americans 370
Ukrainian-Americans
  Bibliographies 379
Urban affairs
  Bibliographies 313
Urban communities
  Bibliographies 314
Women
  Bibliographies 406
Youth
  Handbooks 440
  Research guides 440

ETHNOGERONTOLOGY

BT Gerontology
Elderly
  Handbooks 335

ETHNOGRAPHY

SN Descriptive study of human culture
BT Cultural anthropology
American Indians
  Bibliographies 108, 111
Atlases 5
  Cross-cultural studies 8
  Kinship 5
  Marriage customs 5
  Social organization 5
Bibliographies 113
  American Indians 108, 111
  Filipino-Americans 117
  Latin American women 435
  South America 112
  Tribal groups 111, 112
Blacks (African)
  Bibliographies 77
Cross-cultural studies 85
  Atlases 8
Dictionaries
  Soviet Union 116
Encyclopedias 54, 121
  Kinship 115
  Marriage 115
  Muslims 115
  Social structures 115
  Women 115
Filipino-Americans
  Bibliographies 117
Guides 59, 124
Handbooks 120
  Soviet Union 116
Indexes 28
Kinship
  Atlases 5
  Encyclopedias 115
Latin American women
  Bibliographies 435
Marriage
  Encyclopedias 115
Marriage customs
  Atlases 5
Muslims
  Encyclopedias 115
Social organization
  Atlases 5
Social structures
  Encyclopedias 115
South America
  Bibliographies 112
Soviet Union
  Dictionaries 116
  Handbooks 116
Theses
  Bibliographies 92
Tribal groups
  Bibliographies 111, 112
Women
  Encyclopedias 115

ETHNOHISTORY

American Indians
  Bibliographies 108

ETHNOLOGY

SN Historical or comparative study of human culture
BT Cultural anthropology
RT Cross-cultural studies
American Indians
  Encyclopedias 277
  Handbooks 271
Arab women
  Bibliographies 437
Bibliographies
  Arab women 437
  Europe 96

Theses 92
Women 406
Dictionaries
Europe 123
Directories
International organizations 24
Publications 97
Research centers 21
Encyclopedias 54, 121
American Indians 277
Women 407
Europe
Bibliographies 96
Dictionaries 123
Guides 91
Publications 64
Handbooks
American Indians 271
Indexes 28
International organizations
Directories 24
Publications
Directories 97
Guides 64
Research centers
Directories 21
Theses
Bibliographies 92
Women
Bibliographies 406
Encyclopedias 407

EUROPE

NT Eastern Europe
NT Northern Europe
NT Southern Europe
NT Western Europe
RT Africa
RT Asia
RT Australia
Bibliographies
Anthropology 96
Archaeology 96
Ethnic groups 113
Ethnology 96
Dictionaries
Ethnology 123
Folklore 123

EUTHANASIA

UF Mercy killing
RT Death and dying
Bibliographies 205, 206
Statistics (International) 206

EXCERPTS

See Abstracts

FACULTY

Graduate departments
Sociology 135

FAMILIES

BT Social organization
NT Foster families
NT One-parent families
NT Step families
NT Two-career families
RT Family structures
RT Kinship
Abstracts
Black-Americans 297
Social research 577, 584
Women 421
African women
Bibliographies 427
Alcoholism
Bibliographies 477, 574
Guides 222, 478
Almanacs
Black-Americans 293
Statistics (Great Britain) 155
Statistics (U.S.) 220
Women 422
Ambition
Bibliographies 411
American Indians
Guides 222
Arab women
Bibliographies 430, 431, 437
Arabs
Bibliographies 377
Asian women
Bibliographies 429
Assistance programs 219
Bibliographies 140, 151, 224, 225, 227
African women 427
Alcoholism 477, 574
Ambition 411

Arab women 430, 431, 437
Arabs 377
Asian women 429
Black-Americans 238, 282-284, 290, 296
Child abuse 235, 574
Chinese women 433
Communal living 304
Countries of the world 223
Death and dying 201, 204
Demography 238
Divorce 235
Drug abuse 235, 499, 574
Elderly 323, 326, 341, 473
Ethnic groups 351, 352
Ethnicity 110
History 223
Homosexuality 460, 461
Incest 451
Jews 228
Juvenile delinquency 446, 574
Latin America 56
Latin American women 435
Marriage 235, 574
Maternal employment 402
Mental health 235, 563
Mental retardation 568
Mexican-Americans 382, 383
Minority groups 346
Parents 574
Polish-Americans 374
Poverty 505, 509, 514, 515
Publications 149
Religion 181
Research methods 221
Sex roles 232
Single parents 235
Social change 127, 574
Social indicators 538
Social life 235
Social mobility 147
Social policy 238
Social problems 235
Social research 535
Social roles 232, 238
Social trends 232
Social welfare 582
Social work 512, 513, 578
Socialization 235
Suicide 200
Television 518
Treatment 574
Urban affairs 315, 534
Violence 574
Women 238, 404, 408, 410, 413-415, 417, 419, 423, 426
Work roles 238
Working women 402
Youth 211, 218

Black-Americans
Abstracts 297
Almanacs 293
Bibliographies 238, 282-284, 290, 296
Encyclopedias 280
Guides 222

Child abuse
Bibliographies 235, 574
Guides 222

Chinese women
Bibliographies 433

Cities
Statistics (U.S.) 158

Communal living
Bibliographies 304

Counties
Statistics (U.S.) 158

Countries of the world
Bibliographies 223

Death and dying
Bibliographies 201, 204

Demography
Bibliographies 238

Dictionaries
Polyglots 244

Directories
Organizations 30, 235
Publications 149
Statistics (U.S.) 161

Divorce
Bibliographies 235

Drug abuse
Bibliographies 235,

499, 574
Guides 222
Elderly
Bibliographies 323, 326, 341, 473
Encyclopedias
Black-Americans 280
Social work 573
Women 407
Ethnic groups
Bibliographies 351, 352
Ethnicity
Bibliographies 110
Glossaries 244
Guides
Alcoholism 222, 478
American Indians 222
Black-Americans 222
Child abuse 222
Drug abuse 222
Mental health 222, 570
Migration 246
Organizations 229
Popular culture 522
Poverty 222
Puerto Ricans 390
Social problems 229
Social research 222
Social services 229
Socialization 222
Statistics (International) 229
Handbooks 138
Social anthropology 94
Social services 576
History
Bibliographies 223
Homosexuality
Bibliographies 460, 461
Incest
Bibliographies 451
Indexes 126, 259
Public opinion 523, 528
Jews
Bibliographies 228
Juvenile delinquency
Bibliographies 446, 574
Latin America
Bibliographies 56
Latin American women
Bibliographies 435
Marriage
Bibliographies 235, 574
Maternal employment
Bibliographies 402
Mental health
Bibliographies 235, 563
Guides 222, 570
Mental retardation
Bibliographies 568
Mexican-Americans
Bibliographies 382, 383
Migration 219
Guides 246
Military (U.S.) 219
Minority groups
Bibliographies 346
Organizations
Directories 30, 235
Guides 229
Parents
Bibliographies 574
Polish-Americans
Bibliographies 374
Polyglots
Dictionaries 244
Popular culture
Guides 522
Poverty
Bibliographies 505, 509, 514, 515
Guides 222
Research guides 509
Social characteristics 507
Public opinion 524-526,
Indexes 523, 528
Publications
Bibliographies 149
Directories 149
Puerto Ricans
Guides 390
Religion
Bibliographies 181
Research guides
Poverty 509
Research methods
Bibliographies 221
Sex roles
Bibliographies 232
Single parents
Bibliographies 235
Social anthropology

Handbooks 94
Social change
Bibliographies 127, 574
Social characteristics
Poverty 507
Social indicators
Bibliographies 538
Social life
Bibliographies 235
Social mobility
Bibliographies 147
Social policy
Bibliographies 238
Social problems
Bibliographies 235
Guides 229
Social research
Abstracts 577, 584
Bibliographies 535
Guides 222
Social roles 219
Bibliographies 232, 238
Women 238
Social services
Guides 229
Handbooks 576
Social trends
Bibliographies 232
Social welfare
Bibliographies 582
Social work
Bibliographies 512, 513, 578
Encyclopedias 573
Socialization
Bibliographies 235
Guides 222
Statistics (Canada) 165
Statistics (Great Britain)
Almanacs 155
Statistics (International)
Guides 229
Statistics (U.S.) 164, 540
Almanacs 43, 220
Counties 158
Directories 161
Suicide
Bibliographies 200
Television
Bibliographies 518
Treatment
Bibliographies 574
Urban affairs
Bibliographies 315, 534
Violence
Bibliographies 574
Women
Abstracts 421
Almanacs 422
Bibliographies 238, 404, 408, 410, 413-415, 417, 419, 423, 426
Encyclopedias 407
Social roles 238
Work roles
Bibliographies 238
Working women
Bibliographies 402
Youth
Bibliographies 211, 218

FAMILY DYSFUNCTION

SN Aspect of a family that causes disturbance to the stability of the unit
BT Group behavior
Child abuse
Bibliographies 442

FAMILY LIFE

RT Cultural life
RT Social life
Elderly
Handbooks 335
Public opinion
Indexes 523

FAMILY PLANNING

SN Voluntary regulation of births
UF Birth control
UF Contraception
Abstracts
Women 421
Almanacs
Women 422
Arab women
Bibliographies 431
Asia
Handbooks 233

Asian women
  Bibliographies 434
Bibliographies 140, 224, 225, 227, 256, 401
  Arab women 431
  Asian women 434
  Births 226
  Black-Americans 282, 290
  Chinese women 433
  Demography 226
  Information sources 316
  Latin American women 435
  Population policy 226
  Poverty 514
  Sex discrimination 472
  Social casework 585
  Social programs 226
  Women 403, 413, 414, 432
Births
  Bibliographies 226
Black-Americans
  Bibliographies 282, 290
Canadian organizations
  Directories 11
Chinese women
  Bibliographies 433
Countries of the world
  Guides 319
Demography
  Bibliographies 226
Directories 316
  Canadian organizations 11
  International organizations 248
  Organizations 42, 255, 424, 581
  Publications 37, 41
  Social services 418
Encyclopedias 249
  Organizations 14
  Women 407
Guides
  Countries of the world 319
  Organizations 35
Handbooks
  Asia 233
Indexes
  Public opinion 523
Information sources
  Bibliographies 316
International organizations
  Directories 248
Latin American women
  Bibliographies 435
Organizations
  Directories 42, 255, 424, 581
  Encyclopedias 14
  Guides 35
Population policy
  Bibliographies 226
Poverty
  Bibliographies 514
Public opinion
  Indexes 523
Publications
  Directories 37, 41
Sex discrimination
  Bibliographies 472
Social casework
  Bibliographies 585
Social programs
  Bibliographies 226
Social services
  Directories 418
Union lists 264
Women
  Abstracts 421
  Almanacs 422
  Bibliographies 403, 413, 414, 432
  Encyclopedias 407
  World development 416
World development
  Women 416

FAMILY RELATIONS

  BT Social relations
  RT Ethnic relations
  RT Race relations
  Bibliographies
    Elderly 328
    Sex discrimination 472

FAMILY ROLES

  BT Social roles
  RT Fatherhood
  RT Motherhood
  RT Parenting

RT Sex roles
Hispanics
Bibliographies 566

FAMILY STRUCTURES

SN Organizational frameworks of families
BT Social structures
RT Families
American Indians
Bibliographies 564
Asian-Americans
Guides 360
Hispanics
Bibliographies 566

FAMILY STUDIES

RT Sociology of the family
Research centers
Directories 21

FAMILY VIOLENCE

BT Violence
NT Child abuse
NT Spouse abuse
Bibliographies 235, 237, 574
Elderly 328
Women 457
Encyclopedias
Criminal justice 558

FATHER ABSENCE

BT Parental absence
Divorce
Guides 214

FATHERHOOD

BT Sex roles
RT Men
RT Parenting
Sex roles
Bibliographies 466

FEMALES

See Women

FERTILITY

SN Rate of reproduction
BT Demography
RT Baby boom
RT Births
Abstracts
Black-Americans 297
African women
Bibliographies 427
Arab women
Bibliographies 437
Asian women
Bibliographies 429, 434
Bibliographies 252
African women 427
Arab women 437
Asian women 429, 434
Chinese women 433
Demography 263
Elderly 473
Research methods 263
Social mobility 147
Social norms 263
Social stratification 263
Social structures 263
Urbanization 317
Women 403, 415, 423
Black-Americans
Abstracts 297
Chinese women
Bibliographies 433
Demography
Bibliographies 263
Elderly
Bibliographies 473
Encyclopedias 249
Indexes 259
Latin America
Bibliographies 55
Research methods
Bibliographies 263
Social mobility
Bibliographies 147
Social norms
Bibliographies 263
Social stratification
Bibliographies 263
Social structures
Bibliographies 263
Statistics (International)
Women 405
Yearbooks 160
Statistics (U.S.) 164, 173, 540

Women 409
Urbanization
Bibliographies 317
Women
Bibliographies 403, 415, 423
Statistics (International) 405
Statistics (U.S.) 409
World development 416
World development
Women 416
Yearbooks
Statistics (International) 160

FIELD INSTRUCTION

Social work education
Bibliographies 583

FIELD RESEARCH

UF Field work
BT Social research
RT Sociological research
Bibliographies
Archaeology 102
Handbooks
Anthropology 99
Cultural anthropology 119

FIELD WORK

See Field research

FILIPINO-AMERICANS

BT Ethnic groups
Adoptions
Bibliographies 234
Anthropology
Bibliographies 117
Bibliographies 371
Adoptions 234
Anthropology 117
Demography 363
Ethnography 117
Immigration 373
Mental health 563
Migration 363
Race relations 378
Racism 373
Social conditions 363, 373
Social life 378
Sociology 117
Demography
Bibliographies 363
Directories
Statistics (U.S.) 161
Ethnography
Bibliographies 117
Immigration
Bibliographies 373
Mental health
Bibliographies 563
Migration
Bibliographies 363
Race relations
Bibliographies 378
Racism
Bibliographies 373
Social conditions
Bibliographies 363, 373
Social life
Bibliographies 378
Sociology
Bibliographies 117
Statistics (U.S.)
Directories 161

FOLKLORE

SN Unwritten, traditional literature, including stories, legends, proverbs, etc.
BT Anthropology
RT Customs
Anthropology
Bibliographies 118
Appalachia
Women 428
Archaeology
Bibliographies 118
Bibliographies
Anthropology 118
Archaeology 118
Black-Americans 294
Classifications 118
Puerto Ricans 391
Southern whites 516
Black-Americans
Bibliographies 294
Classifications
Bibliographies 118
Dictionaries
Europe 123

Directories
Research centers 21
Ethnic groups (Soviet Union)
Guides 366
Europe
Dictionaries 123
Guides
Ethnic groups (Soviet Union) 366
History
Bibliographies 89
Publications
Directories 37
Puerto Ricans
Bibliographies 391
Research centers
Directories 21
Southern whites
Bibliographies 516
Women
Appalachia 428

FOSTER CARE

RT Adoption
RT Child welfare
Child welfare
Bibliographies 444

FOSTER FAMILIES

BT Families
RT One-parent families
RT Step families
RT Two-career families
Social research
Abstracts 577

FRATERNAL ORGANIZATIONS

BT Organizations
RT International organizations
RT Secret organizations
Dictionaries 10
Encyclopedias 18
Handbooks 19

FRENCH-AMERICANS

BT Ethnic groups
Bibliographies 345
Mental health 563

GAZETTEERS

UF Place-names
Archaeology 2

GERMAN-AMERICANS

BT Ethnic groups
Almanacs 348
Bibliographies 345
Acculturation 365
Cultures 364, 365
Customs 364, 365
Emigration 365
Ethnicity 365
Immigration 364, 365
Mental health 563
Social conditions 364
Social life 364

GERONTOLOGY

SN Study of the elderly and the aging process
UF Social gerontology
BT Social sciences
NT Ethnogerontology
RT Elderly
RT Retirement
RT Sociology of aging
Bibliographies 333
Death and dying 332
Demography 332
Hospices 332
Retirement 332
Social research 535
Social services 332
Theses 150
Death and dying
Bibliographies 332
Demography
Bibliographies 332
Directories
International organizations 24
Publications 37, 41
Research centers 21
Elderly
Handbooks 338
Handbooks
Elderly 338
Hospices
Bibliographies 332
International organizations
Directories 24
Publications
Directories 37, 41

Research centers
  Directories 21
Retirement
  Bibliographies 332
Social research
  Bibliographies 535
Social services
  Bibliographies 332
Theses
  Bibliographies 150

GLOSSARIES

RT Dictionaries
RT Polyglots
RT Thesauri
Archaeology 2, 106
Death and dying 202
Demography 244
  Dictionaries 243
Dictionaries
  Demography 243
Families 244
Migration 244
Population 244

GRADUATE DEPARTMENTS

RT Theses
Sociology
  Dictionaries 135
  Special programs 135

GRANT RECIPIENTS

RT Grants
Indexes
  Anthropology 16
  Social sciences 16
  Sociology 16

GRANTS

SN Funds given by an organization
NT International grants
RT Grant recipients
Alcoholism
  Directories 15
  Guides 22
Anthropology
  Directories 15
  Guides 17
Archaeology
  Directories 15
Criminology
  Directories 15
Directories
  Alcoholism 15
  Anthropology 15
  Archaeology 15
  Criminology 15
  Handicapped 34
  Population 15
  Social sciences 15
  Sociology 15
Drug abuse
  Guides 22
Elderly
  Guides 22, 331
Guides
  Alcoholism 22
  Anthropology 17
  Drug abuse 22
  Elderly 22, 331
  Handicapped 22
  Mental health 22
  Social sciences 17
  Sociology 17
  Women 22
  Youth 22
Handicapped
  Directories 34
  Guides 22
Mental health
  Guides 22
Population
  Directories 15
Social sciences
  Directories 15
  Guides 17
Sociology
  Directories 15
  Guides 17
Women
  Guides 22
Youth
  Guides 22

GREAT BRITAIN

BT Countries of the world
Bibliographies
  Community development 544
  Crime 144
  Leisure 144
  Migration 144
  Minority groups 144
  Population 144
  Poverty 544

Sex roles 144
Social classes 144
Social policy 144, 544
Social work 544
Urbanization 144

GREEK-AMERICANS

BT Ethnic groups
Bibliographies 345
Mental health 563

GROUP BEHAVIOR

BT Social behavior
RT Antisocial behavior
RT Collective behavior
RT Group dynamics
RT Urban behavior
Handbooks 138

GROUP DYNAMICS

BT Social interaction
RT Group behavior
RT Sociometry
Social group work
Bibliographies 575

GROUPS, SOCIAL

See Social groups

GUIDES

NT Research guides
RT Handbooks
Aborigines
Social organization 107
Tribal groups 107
Women 107
Abortion
Asian women 439
Australia 545
Acculturation
Asian-Americans 360
Puerto Ricans 390
Adoption
Organizations 35
Alcoholism
Education 478
Families 222, 478
Grants 22
Institutionalization 324
Organizations 35
Treatment 478
Youth 478
American Indians
Archaeology 270
Audio-visual sources 349
Elderly 334
Families 222
Population 270
Social life 270
Social organization 270
Anthropology 52, 59, 62, 91
Blacks (African) 98
Ethnic groups (Soviet Union) 366
Grants 17
Mexican-Americans 392
Puerto Ricans 392
Social research 74
Applied anthropology 62, 82
Archaeology 52
American Indians 270
Publications 64
Asian-Americans
Acculturation 360
Demography 360
Discrimination 360
Elderly 334, 360
Family structures 360
Immigrants 360
Immigration 360
Mental health 360
Population 360
Poverty 360
Social organization 360
Social services 360
Social structures 360
Social welfare 360
Asian women
Abortion 439
Kinship 439
Marriage 439
Population 439
Sexuality 439
Social change 439
Assimilation
Migration 246
Audio-visual sources
American Indians 349

Black-Americans 349
Chinese-Americans 349
Cuban-Americans 349
Ethnic groups 349
Japanese-Americans 349
Jewish-Americans 349
Mexican-Americans 349
Puerto Ricans 349

Australia
Abortion 545
Demography 545
Social policy 545
Social services 545
Social welfare 545
Urban affairs 545

Bereavement
Death and dying 208

Black-Americans
Audio-visual sources 349
Elderly 334, 342
Families 222
Popular culture 522

Blacks (African)
Anthropology 98
Cultures 98
Physical anthropology 98
Social conflict 98
Social control 98
Social life 98
Social organization 98

Child abuse
Families 222
Organizations 35, 443
Social services 443
Statistics (U.S.) 443

Child molesting 456

Chinese-Americans
Audio-visual sources 349

Community development
Countries of the world 319
Rural social welfare 579
Urban affairs 306

Community organization
Elderly 322

Comparative criminology 189

Confidentiality
Social research 67

Countries of the world
Community development 319
Criminology 189, 192
Death and dying 208
Demography 319
Family planning 319
Migration 319
Radical sociology 60
Social structures 319
Statistics (Great Britain) 167
Village studies 319

Crime
Drug abuse 500
Elderly 320, 330
Urban affairs 306

Crime prevention
Organizations 35

Criminal justice
Drug abuse 562
Juvenile delinquency 562
Prisoners 562
Statistics (U.S.) 562

Criminology 555
Countries of the world 189, 192
Slang 490
Social research 192

Cross-cultural studies
Death education 203

Cuban-Americans
Audio-visual sources 349
Sociology 392

Cultural anthropology 59, 61
Publications 64

Cultural groups 124

Cultures 124
Blacks (African) 98
Publications 64

Customs
Death and dying 208

Death and dying
Bereavement 208
Crime 208
Customs 208
Hospices 208
Statistics 208

Death education
Cross-cultural studies 203
Elderly 203
Suicide 203
Widowhood 203

Youth 203
Demography 59, 253
Asian-Americans 360
Australia 545
Countries of the world 319
Drug abuse 500
Elderly 330, 342
Ethnic groups (Soviet Union) 366
Poverty 506
Publications 64
Urban affairs 306
Discrimination
Asian-Americans 360
Divorce
Father absence 214
Marital separation 214
Organizations 214
Remarriage 214
Statistics 214
Youth 214
Drug abuse
Crime 500
Criminal justice 562
Demography 500
Ethnic groups 500
Families 222
Grants 22
Institutionalization 324
Organizations 35
Social characteristics 500
Social research 500
Women 500
Youth 500
Economic sociology 62
Education
Alcoholism 478
Elderly
American Indians 334
Asian-Americans 334, 360
Black-Americans 334, 342
Community organizations 322
Crime 320, 330
Death education 203
Demography 330, 342
Grants 22, 331
Hispanics 334
Institutionalization 324
Mental health 322
Minority groups 322, 334
Mortality 342
Organizations 35
Physical abuse 320
Population 330, 342
Rural social welfare 579
Statistics (U.S.) 330, 342
Victimization 320
Ethics
Social research 64
Ethnic groups 124
Audio-visual sources 349
Drug abuse 500
Migration 246
Ethnic groups (Soviet Union)
Anthropology 366
Demography 366
Folklore 366
Sociology 366
Ethnicity
Mental health 570
Ethnography 59, 124
Ethnology 91
Publications 64
Families
Alcoholism 222, 478
American Indians 222
Black-Americans 222
Child abuse 222
Drug abuse 222
Mental health 222, 570
Migration 246
Organizations 229
Popular culture 522
Poverty 222
Puerto Ricans 390
Social problems 229
Social research 222
Social services 229
Socialization 222
Statistics (International) 229
Family planning
Countries of the world 319
Organizations 35
Family structures
Asian-Americans 360
Father absence

Divorce 214
Folklore
Ethnic groups (Soviet Union) 366
Grants
Alcoholism 22
Anthropology 17
Drug abuse 22
Elderly 22, 331
Handicapped 22
Mental health 22
Social sciences 17
Sociology 17
Women 22
Youth 22
Handicapped
Grants 22
Leisure 39
Organizations 39
Sexuality 39
Hispanics
Elderly 334
Sociolinguistics 392
Homosexuality
Prisons 555
Human evolution
Physical anthropology 4
Immigrants
Asian-Americans 360
Immigration
Asian-Americans 360
Incest 456
Informed consent
Social research 67
Institutionalization
Alcoholism 324
Drug abuse 324
Elderly 324
Juvenile delinquency 324
Mental health 324
Internal migration
Social research 262
Japanese-Americans
Audio-visual sources 349
Jewish-Americans
Audio-visual sources 349
Juvenile delinquency
Criminal justice 562
Institutionalization 324
Organizations 35
Urban affairs 306
Kinship
Asian women 439
Latin America
Urban affairs 306
Leisure
Handicapped 39
Linguistics 62
Social change 91
Social roles 91
Socialization 91
Marihuana 497
Youth 497
Marital separation
Divorce 214
Marriage
Asian women 439
Mental health 570
Migration 246
Mental health
Asian-Americans 360
Elderly 322
Ethnicity 570
Families 570
Grants 22
Institutionalization 324
Marriage 570
Migration 570
Organizations 35
Rural social welfare 579
Social classes 570
Social groups 570
Social roles 570
Social status 570
Youth 570
Mental health
Families 222
Mexican-Americans
Anthropology 392
Audio-visual sources 349
Sociology 392
Middle classes
Popular culture 522
Migrants
Social research 262
Migration 253
Assimilation 246
Countries of the world 319
Ethnic groups 246
Families 246
Marriage 246
Mental health 570
Puerto Ricans 390

Social life 246
Social mobility 246
Social problems 246
Social research 262
Social structures 246
Urban affairs 306
Urbanization 246
Youth 246
Minority groups
Elderly 322, 334
Mortality 253
Elderly 342
Natality 253
Organizations
Adoption 35
Alcoholism 35
Child abuse 35, 443
Crime prevention 35
Divorce 214
Drug abuse 35
Elderly 35
Families 229
Family planning 35
Handicapped 39
Juvenile delinquency 35
Mental health 35
Parenting 35
Rape 35
Sexual assault 35
Spouse abuse 35, 449
Suicide prevention 35
Treatment 35
Volunteerism 35
Youth 35
Organized crime 491
Parenting
Organizations 35
Physical abuse
Elderly 320
Physical anthropology 62
Blacks (African) 98
Human evolution 4
Police
Social roles 491
Subcultures 491
Police corruption 491
Political sociology 62
Popular culture
Black-Americans 522
Families 522
Middle classes 522
Sexuality 522
Women 522
Population 253
Asian-Americans 360
Asian women 439
Elderly 330, 342
Social research 74
Statistics (Great Britain) 167
Third World 257
World development 257
Poverty
Asian-Americans 360
Demography 506
Families 222
Social factors 506
Social issues 506
Social programs 506
Social trends 506
Prison riots 555
Prison systems 555
Prisoners
Criminal justice 562
Statistics (U.S.) 555
Prisons
Homosexuality 555
Privacy
Social research 67
Publications
Archaeology 64
Cultural anthropology 64
Cultures 64
Demography 64
Ethnology 64
Social anthropology 64
Social problems 64
Social sciences 64
Sociology 64, 125
Publishing
Social sciences 53
Puerto Ricans
Acculturation 390
Anthropology 392
Audio-visual sources 349
Families 390
Migration 390
Social conflict 390
Sociology 392
Statistics (U.S.) 390
Racism
Radical sociology 60
Radical sociology
Crime 60
Racism 60
Social classes 60
Urban affairs 60

Women 60
Rape
Organizations 35
Rehabilitation 555
Remarriage
Divorce 214
Research methods 59
Sociology 71
Sociology of aging 182
Rural social welfare
Community development 579
Elderly 579
Mental health 579
Social policy 579
Social research 579
Social services 579
Youth 579
Rural sociology 62
Sexual abuse 456
Organizations 35
Sexuality
Asian women 439
Handicapped 39
Popular culture 522
Slang
Criminology 490
Subcultures 490
Social anthropology 59
Publications 64
Social behavior
Youth 445
Social change
Asian women 439
Linguistics 91
Social research 262
Urban affairs 306
Social characteristics
Drug abuse 500
Social classes
Mental health 570
Radical sociology 60
Social conditions
Urban affairs 306
Social conflict
Blacks (African) 98
Puerto Ricans 390
Social control
Blacks (African) 98
Social control 67
Social factors
Poverty 506
Social groups
Mental health 570
Social inequality
Sociology of aging 182
Social institutions
Sociology of aging 182
Social issues
Poverty 506
Urban affairs 306
Social life
American Indians 270
Blacks (African) 98
Migration 246
Social mobility
Migration 246
Social organization 59
Aborigines 107
American Indians 270
Asian-Americans 360
Blacks (African) 98
Social policy
Australia 545
Rural social welfare 579
Social problems 62
Families 229
Migration 246
Publications 64
Sociology of aging 182
Social programs
Poverty 506
Social psychology 59
Social research
Anthropology 74
Confidentiality 67
Criminology 192
Drug abuse 500
Ethics 67
Families 222
Informed consent 67
Internal migration 262
Migrants 262
Migration 262
Population 74
Privacy 67
Rural social welfare 579
Social change 262
Social control 67
Social sciences 74
Sociology 74
Spouse abuse 449
Volunteerism 67
Social roles
Linguistics 91

Mental health 570
Police 491
Social sciences 52, 59, 61
Grants 17
Publications 64
Publishing 53
Social research 74
Writing 53
Social services
Asian-Americans 360
Australia 545
Child abuse 443
Families 229
Organizations 449
Rural social welfare 579
Social research 449
Statistics (Great Britain) 167
Social status
Mental health 570
Social structures
Asian-Americans 360
Countries of the world 319
Migration 246
Social theory 59
Sociology of aging 182
Social trends
Poverty 506
Social welfare 52
Asian-Americans 360
Australia 545
Statistics (Great Britain) 167
Urban affairs 306
Socialization
Families 222
Linguistics 91
Sociolinguistics
Hispanics 392
Sociology 52, 59, 61, 62
Cuban-Americans 392
Ethnic groups (Soviet Union) 366
Grants 17
Mexican-Americans 392
Publications 64, 125
Puerto Ricans 392
Research methods 71
Social research 74
Sociology of aging
Research methods 182
Social inequality 182
Social institutions 182
Social problems 182
Social theory 182
Sociology of education 62, 180
Sociology of religion 62
Sociology of sciences 62
Sociology of the family 62
Spouse abuse
Organizations 35
Statistics
Death and dying 208
Divorce 214
Statistics (Great Britain)
Crime 167
Population 167
Social services 167
Social welfare 167
Statistics (International)
Families 229
Statistics (U.S.)
Child abuse 443
Criminal justice 562
Elderly 330, 342
Prisoners 555
Puerto Ricans 390
Subcultures
Police 491
Slang 490
Suicide
Death education 203
Suicide prevention
Organizations 35
Third World
Population 257
Treatment
Alcoholism 478
Organizations 35
Tribal groups
Aborigines 107
Urban affairs 62
Australia 545
Community development 306
Crime 306
Demography 306
Juvenile delinquency 306
Latin America 306

Migration 306
Radical sociology 60
Social change 306
Social conditions 306
Social issues 306
Social welfare 306
Urbanization 306
Migration 246
Victimization
Elderly 320
Village studies
Countries of the world
319
Volunteerism
Organizations 35
Social research 67
Widowhood
Death education 203
Women
Aborigines 107
Drug abuse 500
Grants 22
Popular culture 522
Radical sociology 60
World development
Population 257
Writing
Social sciences 53
Youth
Alcoholism 478
Death education 203
Divorce 214
Drug abuse 500
Grants 22
Marihuana 497
Mental health 570
Migration 246
Organizations 35
Rural social welfare
579
Social behavior 445

HAITI

BT Latin America
Criminal justice
Bibliographies 553

HALFWAY HOUSES

UF Rehabilitation
centers
BT Corrections
RT Community-based
corrections
Bibliographies 547

HALLUCINOGENS

BT Drugs
NT LSD
NT Marihuana
RT Depressants
RT Narcotics
RT Sedatives
RT Stimulants
Bibliographies 494,
495
Dictionaries 498
Encyclopedias 502

HANDBOOKS

RT Almanacs
RT Encyclopedias
RT Guides
Abortion 202
Acculturation
Social research 68
Adults
Socialization 137
Africa
Sociological research
136
Alcoholism
Social services 576
American Indians
Archaeology 271
Cultures 271
Ethnology 271
Linguistics 271
Physical anthropology
271
Social anthropology
271
Youth 440
Anthropology 197
Cultural areas 99
Elderly 335
Field research 99
Library research 99
Regional studies 99
Research methods 75
Anthropology of war 120
Applied sociology 174
Archaeology 101
American Indians 271
Asia
Family planning 233
Population 233
Sociological research
136
Belief systems 120

Bereavement
  Death and dying 202
Black-Americans
  Crime 291
  Popular culture 519
  Population 291
  Statistics 291
  Women 291
Censuses
  Population 245
Cognitive anthropology 120
Community development 576
Comparative criminology 197
Countries of the world
  Criminology 197
Crime 197
  Black-Americans 291
Criminology
  Countries of the world 197
Cross-cultural studies 120
Cults 134
Cultural anthropology 120
  Field research 119
  Research methods 119
Cultural areas
  Anthropology 99
Cultures
  American Indians 271
Death and dying
  Bereavement 202
  Elderly 202, 335
  Popular culture 519
  Social anthropology 94
  Youth 202
Demography
  Elderly 338
  Research methods 75
  Soviet Union 114
  Statistics (Soviet Union) 536
Deviant behavior
  Small groups 70
Drug abuse
  Social services 576
Eastern Europe
  Ethnic groups 109
  Minority groups 109
  Sociological research 136
Economic anthropology 119, 120
Elderly
  Anthropology 335
  Death and dying 202, 335
  Demography 338
  Ethnic groups 336
  Ethnicity 335
  Ethnogerontology 335
  Family life 335
  Gerontology 338
  Handicapped 336
  Mental health 335
  Population 335
  Religious groups 336
  Retirement 335
  Social behavior 335
  Social research 335, 338
  Social roles 335
  Social sciences 335
  Social services 576
  Social statistics 335
  Social stratification 335
  Social support 335
  Societal development 335
  Statistics (International) 338
Ethnic groups
  Eastern Europe 109
  Elderly 336
  Soviet Union 116
Ethnicity
  Elderly 335
  Youth 440
Ethnogerontology
  Elderly 335
Ethnography 120
  Soviet Union 116
Ethnology
  American Indians 271
Families 138
  Social anthropology 94
  Social services 576
Family life
  Elderly 335
Family planning
  Asia 233
Field research
  Anthropology 99
  Cultural anthropology 119

Fraternal organizations 19
Gerontology
  Elderly 338
Group behavior 138
Handicapped
  Elderly 336
Historic archaeology 101
History
  Youth 440
Hospices 202
Immigrants 358
Immigration
  Soviet Union 114
Juvenile delinquency 197
Kinship 120
  Social anthropology 94
Library research
  Anthropology 99
Linguistics
  American Indians 271
Marriage
  Social anthropology 94
Mathematical anthropology 120
Medical anthropology 120
Medical sociology 175
Mental health 175
  Elderly 335
  Social services 576
Migration
  Social research 68
  Soviet Union 114
Minority groups
  Eastern Europe 109
  Popular culture 519
Nationalities
  Soviet Union 114, 116
Northern Europe
  Sociological research 136
Occupations
  Statistics (Soviet Union) 162
  Statistics (Eastern Europe) 162
Offenders
  Rape 455
Physical anthropology 94
  American Indians 271
Political anthropology 119, 120
Popular culture 519
  Black-Americans 519
  Death and dying 519
  Minority groups 519
  Pornography 519
Population 138
  Asia 233
  Black-Americans 291
  Censuses 245
  Elderly 335
  Soviet Union 114, 116
  Statistics (Eastern Europe) 162
  Statistics (Soviet Union) 162
Pornography
  Popular culture 519
Prevention
  Rape 455
Psychological anthropology 120
Public archaeology 101
Rape 455
  Offenders 455
  Prevention 455
  Victims 455
Recidivism 197
Refugees 358
Regional studies
  Anthropology 99
Religious groups
  Elderly 336
Research methods
  Anthropology 75
  Cultural anthropology 119
  Demography 75
  Social sciences 69, 72, 75
  Sociology 69, 75, 154
  Sociometry 69
Retirement
  Elderly 335
Secret organizations 19
Sex roles
  Socialization 137
Sexual abuse 455
Small groups
  Deviant behavior 70
  Social control 70
  Social interaction 70
  Social norms 70
  Social research 70
  Social roles 70

Social anthropology 120
American Indians 271
Death and dying 94
Families 94
Kinship 94
Marriage 94
Social life 94
Social stratification 94
Social structures 94
Social behavior
Elderly 335
Social biology 175
Social casework 576
Social change 138
Social classes
Statistics (Eastern Europe) 162
Statistics (Soviet Union) 162
Social control 138, 197
Small groups 70
Social disorganization 138
Social research 68
Social group work 576
Social indicators
Social patterns 542
Statistics (Eastern Europe) 162
Statistics (International) 542
Statistics (Soviet Union) 162, 536
Social interaction
Small groups 70
Social life
Social anthropology 94
Social network analysis 120
Social norms
Small groups 70
Social organization 138
Social research 68
Social patterns
Social indicators 542
Social planning 576
Social research
Acculturation 68
Elderly 335, 338
Migration 68
Small groups 70
Social disorganization 68
Social organization 68
Socialization 137
Urban affairs 68
Social roles
Elderly 335
Small groups 70
Social sciences
Elderly 335
Research methods 69, 72, 75
Statistics (Soviet Union) 536
Social services
Alcoholism 576
Drug abuse 576
Elderly 576
Families 576
Mental health 576
Youth 576
Social statistics
Elderly 335
Social stratification 138
Elderly 335
Social anthropology 94
Social structures
Social anthropology 94
Social support
Elderly 335
Social theory
Socialization 137
Social welfare 576
Social work 576
Socialization 138
Adults 137
Sex roles 137
Social research 137
Social theory 137
Youth 137
Societal development
Elderly 335
Sociolinguistics 120
Sociological research
Africa 136
Asia 136
Eastern Europe 136
Northern Europe 136
Southern Europe 136
Western Europe 136
Sociology 138, 197
Research methods 69, 75, 154
Sociology of education 176

Sociometry
Research methods 69
Southern Europe
Sociological Research 136
Soviet Union
Demography 114
Ethnic groups 116
Ethnography 116
Immigration 114
Migration 114
Nationalities 114, 116
Population 114, 116
Statistics 114
Urbanization 114
Statistics
Black-Americans 291
Soviet Union 114
Statistics (Eastern Europe)
Occupations 162
Population 162
Social classes 162
Social indicators 162
Statistics (International)
Elderly 338
Social indicators 542
Statistics (Soviet Union)
Demography 536
Occupations 162
Population 162
Social classes 162
Social indicators 162, 536
Social sciences 536
Structural anthropology 120
Suicide 202
Urban affairs
Social research 68
Urban anthropology 120
Urbanization
Soviet Union 114
Victims
Rape 455
Western Europe
Sociological research 136
Youth
American Indians 440
Death and dying 202
Ethnicity 440
History 440
Social services 576
Socialization 137
Women
Black-Americans 291

HANDICAPPED

SN Sensory, physical and/or mental deficiencies that make normal functioning more difficult
UF Disabled
NT Blindness
NT Deafness
Abstracts
Urban affairs 312
Bibliographies
Social work 578
Youth 448
Directories
Grants 34
Information sources 31
Organizations 13, 30
Organizations (Elderly) 339
Elderly
Handbooks 336
Grants
Directories 34
Guides 22
Guides
Grants 22
Leisure 39
Organizations 39
Sexuality 39
Handbooks
Elderly 336
Information sources
Directories 31
Leisure
Guides 39
Municipalities
Statistics (U.S.) 38
Organizations
Directories 13, 30
Guides 39
Organizations (Elderly)
Directories 339
Sexuality
Guides 39
Social work
Bibliographies 578
Statistics (U.S.)

Municipalities 38
Stereotypes
Television 520
Television
Stereotypes 520
Urban affairs
Abstracts 312
Youth
Bibliographies 448

HEROIN

BT Narcotics
RT Methadone
Bibliographies 501

HISPANICS

BT Ethnic groups
NT Cuban-Americans
NT Mexican-Americans
NT Puerto Ricans
Abstracts
Immigration 247
Acculturation
Bibliographies 566
Alcoholism
Bibliographies 566
Bibliographies 345
Acculturation 566
Alcoholism 566
Cultural change 566
Cultural pluralism 566
Discrimination 566
Drug abuse 501
Elderly 329
Ethnicity 329
Family roles 566
Family structures 566
Interpersonal relations 566
Mental health 566
Poverty 566
Prejudice 566
Race relations 393
Sex roles 466, 566
Women 406, 410
Cultural change
Bibliographies 566
Cultural pluralism
Bibliographies 566
Discrimination
Bibliographies 566
Drug abuse
Bibliographies 501
Elderly
Bibliographies 329
Guides 334
Ethnicity
Bibliographies 329
Family roles
Bibliographies 566
Family structures
Bibliographies 566
Guides
Elderly 334
Sociolinguistics 392
Immigration
Abstracts 247
Indexes
Public opinion 523
Interpersonal relations
Bibliographies 566
Mental health
Bibliographies 566
Organizations (Voluntary) 385
Poverty
Bibliographies 566
Prejudice
Bibliographies 566
Public opinion
Indexes 523
Race relations
Bibliographies 393
Sex roles
Bibliographies 466, 566
Sociolinguistics
Guides 392
Statistics (U.S.)
Women 409
Women
Bibliographies 406, 410
Statistics (U.S.) 409

HISTORIC ARCHAEOLOGY

BT Archaeology
RT Ancient archaeology
Abstracts 76
Handbooks 101

HISTORY

BT Social sciences
Anthropology
Bibliographies 89
Archaeology
Bibliographies 89

Atlases
  Population 6
Bibliographies
  Anthropology 89
  Archaeology 89
  Cultural anthropology 89
  Families 223
  Folklore 89
  Kinship 223
  Linguistics 89
  Physical anthropology 89
  Social anthropology 89
  Social welfare 582
Births
  Statistics (U.S.) 163
Crime
  Statistics (U.S.) 163
Cultural anthropology
  Bibliographies 89
Deaths
  Statistics (U.S.) 163
Divorce
  Statistics (U.S.) 163
Families
  Bibliographies 223
Folklore
  Bibliographies 89
Handbooks
  Youth 440
Kinship
  Bibliographies 223
Linguistics
  Bibliographies 89
Marriage
  Statistics (U.S.) 163
Migration
  Statistics (U.S.) 163
Physical anthropology
  Bibliographies 89
Population
  Atlases 6
  Statistics (U.S.) 163
Research guides
  Youth 440
Social anthropology
  Bibliographies 89
Social welfare
  Bibliographies 582
Statistics (U.S.)
  Births 163
  Crime 163
  Deaths 163
  Divorce 163
  Marriage 163
  Migration 163
  Population 163
Youth
  Handbooks 440
  Research guides 440

HOMELESSNESS

BT Social issues
RT Refugees
Elderly
  Bibliographies 327

HOMOSEXUALITY

BT Sexuality
NT Lesbianism
RT Sex roles
RT Transsexualism
Alcoholism
  Bibliographies 460, 461, 475
Anthropology
  Bibliographies 458, 460, 461
Bibliographies 462, 463, 469
  Alcoholism 460, 461, 475
  Anthropology 458, 460, 461
  Black-Americans 286
  Canada 464
  Crime 461
  Cultures 461
  Divorce 460
  Elderly 473
  Families 460, 461
  Juvenile delinquency 461
  Marriage 460, 461
  Prisons 561
  Sex roles 461
  Sexuality 465
  Social life 460, 461
  Sociology 458, 460
  Women 404, 408, 419, 425, 426
  Youth 460, 461
Black-Americans
  Bibliographies 286
Canada
  Bibliographies 464
Crime
  Bibliographies 461

Cultures
Bibliographies 461
Directories
Publications 37, 41
Divorce
Bibliographies 460
Elderly
Bibliographies 473
Encyclopedias
Organizations 14
Families
Bibliographies 460, 461
Guides
Prisons 555
Indexes
Public opinion 523
Juvenile delinquency
Bibliographies 461
Marriage
Bibliographies 460, 461
Organizations
Encyclopedias 14
Prisons
Bibliographies 561
Guides 555
Public opinion
Indexes 523
Publications
Directories 37, 41
Sex roles
Bibliographies 461
Sexuality
Bibliographies 465
Social life
Bibliographies 460, 461
Sociology
Bibliographies 458, 460
Women
Bibliographies 404, 408, 419, 425, 426
Youth
Bibliographies 460, 461

HOMOSEXUALS

NT Lesbians
Almanacs
Women 422

HOSPICES

RT Death and dying
RT Elderly
Bibliographies
Gerontology 332
Directories 202
Guides
Death and dying 208
Handbooks 202

HUMAN ECOLOGY

SN Study of the effects of spatial distributions and interrelations of people on the development and composition of communities
UF Social ecology
BT Urban sociology
Encyclopedias 54

HUMAN EVOLUTION

RT Physical anthropology
RT Socialization
Physical anthropology
Atlases 4
Guides 4

HUMAN SERVICES

See Social services

HUNGARIAN-AMERICANS

BT Ethnic groups
Bibliographies 367
Mental health 563

ILLEGAL ALIENS

SN Illegal residents in a country
BT Immigrants
Immigration
Abstracts 247

ILLEGITIMACY

RT Adoption
RT One-parent families
Bibliographies 224, 225, 227

IMMIGRANTS

UF-Used For, BT-Broader Term, NT-Narrower Term, RT-Related Term

NT Illegal aliens
RT Migrants
RT Refugees
Asian-Americans
Bibliographies 375
Guides 360
Bibliographies 354
Asian-Americans 375
Cuban-Americans 375
Russian-Americans 375
Women 432
Cuban-Americans
Bibliographies 375
Guides
Asian-Americans 360
Handbooks 358
Russian-Americans
Bibliographies 375
Women
Bibliographies 432

IMMIGRATION

SN Entrance into a new country to establish permanent residence
BT Migration
RT Emigration
Abstracts 399
Asians 247
Brain drain 247
Demography 247
Hispanics 247
Illegal aliens 247
Social policy 247
Social research 247
Acculturation
Bibliographies 355
Asian-Americans
Guides 360
Asians
Abstracts 247
Assimilation
Bibliographies 355
Bibliographies
Acculturation 355
Assimilation 355
Black-Americans 285
Discrimination 355
Dutch-Americans 362
Ethnic groups 343
Ethnic groups (Canadian) 344
Filipino-Americans 373
German-Americans 364, 365
Italian-Americans 369
Jewish-Americans 372
Mexican-Americans 388
Minority groups 346
Romanian-Americans 376
Social life 355
Ukrainian-Americans 379
Black-Americans
Bibliographies 285
Brain drain
Abstracts 247
Demography
Abstracts 247
Discrimination
Bibliographies 355
Dutch-Americans
Bibliographies 362
Encyclopedias
Ethnic groups 353
Ethnic groups
Bibliographies 343
Encyclopedias 353
Ethnic groups (Canadian)
Bibliographies 344
Filipino-Americans
Bibliographies 373
German-Americans
Bibliographies 364, 365
Guides
Asian-Americans 360
Handbooks
Soviet Union 114
Hispanics
Abstracts 247
Illegal aliens
Abstracts 247
Italian-Americans
Bibliographies 369
Theses 370
Jewish-Americans
Bibliographies 372
Mexican-Americans
Bibliographies 388
Research guides 386
Minority groups
Bibliographies 346
Research guides
Mexican-Americans 386
Romanian-Americans
Bibliographies 376
Social life

Bibliographies 355
Social policy
Abstracts 247
Social research
Abstracts 247
Soviet Union
Handbooks 114
Statistics (U.S.)
Almanacs 43
Theses
Italian-Americans 370
Ukrainian-Americans
Bibliographies 379

INCEST

SN Sexual relations with closely related persons (parents, siblings, children)
BT Sexual abuse
Almanacs
Women 422
Anthropology
Bibliographies 451
Bibliographies 224, 225, 227, 456
Anthropology 451
Case studies 450
Families 451
Sociology 451
Treatment 450
Women 457
Youth 451
Case studies
Bibliographies 450
Families
Bibliographies 451
Guides 456
Sociology
Bibliographies 451
Treatment
Bibliographies 450
Women
Almanacs 422
Bibliographies 457
Youth
Bibliographies 451

INDEXES

RT Abstracts
RT Directories
RT Information sources
Abortion
Public opinion 523, 528
Statistics (International) 159
Statistics (U.S.) 159
Acculturation
American Indians 272
Adoption 551
Alcoholism
American Indians 272
Alienation 139
American Indians
Acculturation 272
Alcoholism 272
Anthropology 272
Archaeology 272
Cultures 272
Linguistics 272
Sociology 272
Urban affairs 272
Women 272
Anthropology 28, 80, 126
American Indians 272
Citations 27
Grant recipients 16
South Africa 83
Women 420
Applied anthropology 28, 126
Applied sociology 148
Archaeology 28, 80
American Indians 272
Women 420
Births
Statistics (International) 159
Statistics (U.S.) 159
Black-Americans
Public opinion 523
Book reviews
Social sciences 25
Citations
Anthropology 27
Social sciences 27
Sociology 27
Crime 26, 126, 551
Public opinion 523, 528
Statistics (International) 159
Statistics (U.S.) 159
Criminal justice 551
Criminology 28, 551
Criminology (U.S.) 193
Cultural anthropology

28, 80
Cultures
American Indians 272
Death and dying 126
Deaths
Statistics (International) 159
Statistics (U.S.) 159
Demography 148, 259
Deviant behavior 126, 139
Drug abuse 193, 551
Public opinion 523, 528
Elderly
Public opinion 528
Ethnicity 126
South Africa 83
Ethnography 28
Ethnology 28
Families 126, 259
Public opinion 523, 528
Family life
Public opinion 523
Family planning
Public opinion 523
Fertility 259
Grant recipients
Anthropology 16
Social sciences 16
Sociology 16
Hispanics
Public opinion 523
Homosexuality
Public opinion 523
Juvenile delinquency 193, 551
Linguistics
American Indians 272
Marriage
Public opinion 523, 528
Mental health 26
Migration 259
Mortality 259
Physical anthropology 80
Political sociology 28, 139
Population 259
Public opinion 528
Statistics (International) 159
Statistics (U.S.) 159
Poverty 26, 126, 148
Theses 152
Public opinion
Abortion 523, 528
Black-Americans 523
Crime 523, 528
Drug abuse 523, 528
Elderly 528
Families 523, 528
Family life 523
Family planning 523
Hispanics 523
Homosexuality 523
Marriage 523, 528
Population 528
Social issues 528
Social life 523
Social programs 523
Social status 528
Social values 523, 528
Statistics 523, 528
Race relations 126
Rural sociology 148
Sex roles 126
Women 420
Social anthropology 28, 80
Social change 126, 139, 148
Social classes 551
Social conditions 26
Social control 148, 193, 551
Social differentiation 148
Social disorganization 126
Social ecology 126
Social issues
Public opinion 528
Social life
Public opinion 523
Social norms 139
Social policy 26
Social problems 148
Social programs
Public opinion 523
Social psychology 148, 551
Social research 139
Social roles
Women 420
Social sciences 28
Book reviews 25
Citations 27
Grant recipients 16

Statistics (International) 159
Statistics (U.S.) 159
Women 420
Social services
Statistics (International) 159
Statistics (U.S.) 159
Social status
Public opinion 528
Social stratification 126
Social structures 148, 193
Social theory 139
Social values
Public opinion 523, 528
Social welfare 26
Women 420
Social work 551
Women 420
Socialization 148, 193
Theses 152
Sociology 28, 126, 139, 148
American Indians 272
Citations 27
Grant recipients 16
Theses 152
Sociology of education 148
Sociology of religion 148
Sociology of sciences 148
Sociology of the family 148
Sociopathy 193
South Africa
Anthropology 83
Ethnicity 83
Statistics
Public opinion 523, 528
Statistics (International)
Abortion 159
Births 159
Crime 159
Deaths 159
Population 159
Social sciences 159
Social services 159
Suicide 159
Statistics (U.S.)
Abortion 159
Births 159
Crime 159
Deaths 159
Population 159
Social sciences 159
Social services 159
Suicide 159
Structural functionalism 139
Suicide
Statistics (International) 159
Statistics (U.S.) 159
Theses
Poverty 152
Socialization 152
Sociology 152
Urban affairs 26
Urban sociology 139
American Indians 272
Women
American Indians 272
Anthropology 420
Archaeology 420
Sex roles 420
Social roles 420
Social sciences 420
Social welfare 420
Social work 420

INDIAN-AMERICANS

BT Ethnic groups
Bibliographies
Race relations 378
Social life 378

INDIAN WOMEN

BT Women
RT African women
RT Arab women
RT Asian women
RT Caribbean women
RT Chinese women
RT Latin American women
Bibliographies 438

INDIANS (NORTH AMERICAN)

See American Indians

INDUSTRIALIZATION

BT Social change

RT Modernization
RT Urbanization
Urban affairs
Bibliographies 534

INFORMATION SOURCES

RT Bibliographies
RT Directories
RT Indexes
Bibliographies
Alcoholism 316
Community development 316
Drug abuse 316
Family planning 316
Social services 316
Directories
Blindness 31
Corrections 557
Criminal justice 557
Criminology 557
Deafness 31
Handicapped 31
Mental retardation 31

INFORMED CONSENT

SN Consent to participation in research conditional on the subject's understanding of what is involved
RT Confidentiality
RT Ethics
RT Privacy
Social research
Guides 67

INITIALISMS

See Abbreviations

INMATES

See Prisoners

INSTITUTIONALIZATION

BT Corrections
NT Prisons
RT Community-based corrections
RT Halfway houses
RT Mental health facilities
Bibliographies
Juvenile delinquency 547
Parole 547
Probation 547
Rehabilitation 547
Work release 547
Guides
Alcoholism 324
Drug abuse 324
Elderly 324
Juvenile delinquency 324
Mental health 324

INTEGRATION

See Desegregation

INTERGROUP RELATIONS

See Interpersonal relations

INTERMARRIAGE

SN Marriage between persons from different racial, ethnic or religious backgrounds
BT Marriage
RT Remarriage
Almanacs
Black-Americans 293
Bibliographies 224, 225, 227
Jews 228

INTERNAL MIGRATION

SN Movement of persons within a country
BT Migration
Social research
Guides 262

INTERNATIONAL GRANTS

BT Grants
Social welfare
Directories 20

INTERNATIONAL ORGANIZATIONS

UF Organizations (International)
BT Organizations
RT Canadian organizations
RT Fraternal organizations
RT Secret organizations
Directories
Anthropology 24
Archaeology 24
Criminology 24, 192
Demography 24, 248
Elderly 337
Ethnology 24
Family planning 248
Gerontology 24
Population 248
Sociology 24

INTERPERSONAL RELATIONS

UF Intergroup relations
NT Dating
NT Social relations
RT Social networks
RT Sociometry
Bibliographies
Hispanics 566
Social research 535
Suicide 210
Urban affairs 299

INVISIBLE COLLEGES

SN Communication between members of a profession that serves to facilitate the exchange of ideas
BT Social networks
Bibliographies 185

IRISH-AMERICANS

BT Ethnic groups
Almanacs 348
Bibliographies 345
Mental health 563
Migration 368
Social mobility 368
Social status 368

ISOLATION, SOCIAL

See Social isolation

ITALIAN-AMERICANS

BT Ethnic groups
Almanacs 348
Bibliographies 345
Acculturation 369
Anthropology 369
Crime 369
Demography 369
Emigration 369
Ethnicity 369
Immigration 369
Mental health 563
Social life 369
Social structures 369
Theses
Acculturation 370
Assimilation 370
Ethnicity 370
Immigration 370

JAPANESE-AMERICANS

BT Ethnic groups
Adoption
Bibliographies 217, 234
Assimilation
Bibliographies 371
Audio-visual sources
Guides 349
Bibliographies
Adoption 217, 234
Assimilation 371
Demography 371
Mental health 371, 563
Race relations 371, 378
Social life 378
Demography
Bibliographies 371
Directories
Statistics (U.S.) 161
Guides
Audio-visual sources 349
Mental health
Bibliographies 371, 563
Race relations
Bibliographies 371, 378
Social life
Bibliographies 378
Statistics (U.S.)

Directories 161

JARGON

See Slang

JEWISH-AMERICANS

BT Ethnic groups
Bibliographies 345, 346
Acculturation 372
Assimilation 372
Customs 372
Ethnicity 372
Immigration 372
Mental health 563
Race relations 372
Social change 372
Social conditions 372
Social mobility 372
Social organization 372
Guides
Audio-visual sources 349
Yearbooks
Population 359
Social conditions 359
Social life 359
Social relations 359
Statistics 359

JEWS

BT Religious groups
Bibliographies
Death and dying 228
Divorce 228
Families 228
Intermarriage 228
Marriage 228
Sexuality 228
Social life 228
Social welfare 228

JUVENILE DELINQUENCY

UF Delinquency
BT Antisocial behavior
RT Crime
RT Youth
Abstracts 548
Social research 577
Alcoholism
Bibliographies 477
Bibliographies 140, 151, 188, 531
Alcoholism 477
Black-Americans 281, 295
Crime 446
Families 446, 574
Homosexuality 461
Institutionalization 547
Leisure 446
Mental health 565, 568
Parent-child separation 230
Poverty 515
Social behavior 446
Social change 127
Social institutions 446
Social issues 446
Social welfare 582
Theses 150
Youth 448
Black-Americans
Bibliographies 281, 295
Crime
Bibliographies 446
Criminal justice
Encyclopedias 558
Guides 562
Directories
Organizations 447, 581
Urban affairs 301
Encyclopedias 196
Criminal justice 558
Social work 573
Families
Bibliographies 446, 574
Guides
Criminal justice 562
Institutionalization 324
Organizations 35
Urban affairs 306
Handbooks 197
Homosexuality
Bibliographies 461
Indexes 193, 551
Institutionalization
Bibliographies 547
Guides 324
Leisure
Bibliographies 446
Mental health

Bibliographies 565
Mental retardation
Bibliographies 568
Organizations
Directories 447, 581
Guides 35
Parent-child separation
Bibliographies 230
Poverty
Bibliographies 515
Social behavior
Bibliographies 446
Social change
Bibliographies 127
Social institutions
Bibliographies 446
Social issues
Bibliographies 446
Social research
Abstracts 577
Social welfare
Bibliographies 582
Social work
Encyclopedias 573
Theses
Bibliographies 150
Urban affairs
Directories 301
Guides 306
Youth
Bibliographies 448

JUVENILE JUSTICE

BT Criminal justice
Organizations
Directories 560

KIBBUTZ

See Communal living

KINSHIP

SN Relations based on genetic descent or marriage
RT Families
RT Marriage
American Indians
Bibliographies 279
Asian women
Bibliographies 429
Guides 439
Atlases
Ethnography 5
Bibliographies
American Indians 279
Asian women 429
Countries of the world 223
History 223
Countries of the world
Bibliographies 223
Encyclopedias
Ethnography 115
Ethnography
Atlases 5
Encyclopedias 115
Guides
Asian women 439
Handbooks 120
Social anthropology 94
History
Bibliographies 223
Social anthropology
Handbooks 94

KOREAN-AMERICANS

BT Ethnic groups
Bibliographies
Adoption 217, 234
Mental health 563

KU KLUX KLAN

BT Secret organizations
RT Racism
Bibliographies 395, 396

LSD

UF Lysergic acid diethylamide
BT Hallucinogens
RT Marihuana
Bibliographies 495

LABELING

See Classifications

LATIN AMERICA

NT Central America
NT Cuba
NT Dominican Republic
NT Haiti
NT Puerto Rico
RT South America

Anthropology
Bibliographies 55, 56
Archaeology
Bibliographies 55, 56
Bibliographies
Anthropology 55, 56
Archaeology 55, 56
Crime 56
Criminal justice 553
Cultures 55, 56
Demography 55, 56
Ethnic groups 55, 56
Ethnic relations 398
Families 56
Fertility 55
Migration 55, 56
Population 55, 56
Poverty 56
Race relations 55, 398
Social change 55, 56
Social classes 55, 56
Social conflict 55
Social organization 55, 56
Social structures 56
Crime
Bibliographies 56
Criminal justice
Bibliographies 553
Cultures
Bibliographies 55, 56
Demography
Bibliographies 55, 56
Dictionaries
Ethnic relations 398
Race relations 398
Ethnic groups
Bibliographies 55, 56
Ethnic relations
Bibliographies 398
Dictionaries 398
Families
Bibliographies 56
Fertility
Bibliographies 55
Guides
Urban affairs 306
Migration
Bibliographies 55, 56
Population
Bibliographies 55, 56
Poverty
Bibliographies 56
Race relations
Bibliographies 55, 398
Dictionaries 398
Social change
Bibliographies 55, 56
Social classes
Bibliographies 55, 56
Social conflict
Bibliographies 55
Social organization
Bibliographies 55, 56
Social structures
Bibliographies 56
Urban affairs
Guides 306

LATIN AMERICAN WOMEN

BT Women
RT African women
RT Arab women
RT Asian women
RT Caribbean women
RT Chinese women
RT Indian women
Bibliographies
Abortion 435
Deviant behavior 435
Ethnography 435
Families 435
Family planning 435
Marriage 435
Prostitution 435
Sex roles 435
Sexuality 435
Socialization 435
Statistics 435

LAW ENFORCEMENT

BT Criminal justice
NT Recidivism
RT Police
RT Social control
Criminal justice
Bibliographies 550

LEISURE

RT Retirement
RT Social life
Bibliographies
Great Britain 144
Juvenile delinquency 446
Mental retardation 568

Social indicators 538
Social mobility 147
Television 518
Youth 448
Great Britain
Bibliographies 144
Guides
Handicapped 39
Handicapped
Guides 39
Juvenile delinquency
Bibliographies 446
Mental retardation
Bibliographies 568
Social indicators
Bibliographies 538
Social mobility
Bibliographies 147
Statistics 521
Statistics (Canada) 165
Statistics (U.S.) 540
Television 521
Bibliographies 518
Youth
Bibliographies 448

LESBIANISM

BT Homosexuality
Bibliographies
Black-Americans 286
Women 412

LESBIANS

BT Homosexuals
RT Women
Sexuality
Bibliographies 474

LIBRARY RESEARCH

RT Social research
Anthropology
Handbooks 99

LIFE EVENTS

NT Births
NT Death and dying
NT Marriage
NT Retirement
Bibliographies 533

LINGUISTICS

SN Study of language
BT Anthropology
American Indians
Handbooks 271
Indexes 272
Bibliographies
Eskimos 266
History 89
Micronesia 93
New Guinea 81
Dictionaries 86
Directories
Publications 97
Encyclopedias 54, 121
Eskimos
Bibliographies 266
Guides 62
Social change 91
Social roles 91
Socialization 91
Handbooks
American Indians 271
History
Bibliographies 89
Indexes
American Indians 272
Micronesia
Bibliographies 93
New Guinea
Bibliographies 81
Publications
Directories 97
Social change
Guides 91
Social roles
Guides 91
Socialization
Guides 91

LOCAL AREAS

RT Minor Civil Divisions
RT Municipalities
RT Townships
Statistics (U.S.)
Directories 161

LYSERGIC ACID DIETHYLAMIDE

See LSD

MAFIA

BT Criminal organizations
RT Organized crime

Bibliographies 492

MALES

See Men

MARIHUANA

BT Hallucinogens
RT LSD
Alcoholism
Bibliographies 477
Bibliographies 494, 495, 499, 501
Alcoholism 477
Social behavior 503
Sociology 503
Youth 503
Dictionaries 498, 504
Encyclopedias 502
Guides 497
Youth 497
Social behavior
Bibliographies 503
Social interaction
Bibliographies 503
Sociology
Bibliographies 503
Youth
Bibliographies 503
Guides 497

MARITAL SEPARATION

UF Separation
RT Divorce
Bibliographies 224, 225, 227
Guides
Divorce 214

MARITAL STATUS

BT Social status
Women
Bibliographies 417
Statistics (U.S.) 409

MARRIAGE

BT Life events
NT Intermarriage
NT Polygamy
NT Remarriage
RT Kinship
African women
Bibliographies 427
Almanacs 220
American Indians 267
Statistics (Great Britain) 155
Statistics (U.S.) 43, 168, 169
Women 422
American Indians
Almanacs 267
Dictionaries 269
Arab women
Bibliographies 430, 431, 437
Asian women
Bibliographies 429, 434
Guides 439
Bibliographies 151, 224, 225, 227
African women 427
Arab women 430, 431, 437
Asian women 429, 434
Black-Americans 294
Chinese women 433
Elderly 473
Families 235, 574
Homosexuality 460, 461
Jews 228
Latin American women 435
Mexican-Americans 382, 383
Religion 181
Research methods 221
Sex roles 466
Women 404, 408, 410, 413, 414, 419, 423, 432
Black-Americans
Bibliographies 294
Chinese women
Bibliographies 433
Cities
Statistics (U.S.) 158
Counties
Statistics (U.S.) 158
Dictionaries
American Indians 269
Elderly
Bibliographies 473
Encyclopedias 249
Ethnography 115
Women 407

Ethnography
  Encyclopedias 115
Families
  Bibliographies 235, 574
Guides
  Asian women 439
  Mental health 570
  Migration 246
Handbooks
  Social anthropology 94
History
  Statistics (U.S.) 163
Homosexuality
  Bibliographies 460, 461
Indexes
  Public opinion 523, 528
Jews
  Bibliographies 228
Latin American women
  Bibliographies 435
Mental health
  Guides 570
Mexican-Americans
  Bibliographies 382, 383
Migration
  Guides 246
Public opinion 526
  Indexes 523, 528
Religion
  Bibliographies 181
Research methods
  Bibliographies 221
Sex roles
  Bibliographies 466
Social anthropology
  Handbooks 94
Statistics
  Yearbooks 32
Statistics (Great Britain)
  Almanacs 155
Statistics (International)
  Women 405
  Yearbooks 32, 160
Statistics (U.S.) 173, 540
  Almanacs 43, 168, 169
  Cities 158
  Counties 158
  History 163
Women
  Almanacs 422
  Bibliographies 404, 408, 410, 413, 414, 419, 423, 432
  Encyclopedias 407
  Statistics (International) 405
Yearbooks
  Statistics (International) 32, 160

MARRIAGE CUSTOMS

BT Customs
Ethnography
  Atlases 5

MARXISM

BT Sociological theory
NT Dialectics
Bibliographies 143
Dictionaries 142
  Sociological theory 133

MASS CULTURE

See Popular culture

MATHEMATICAL ANTHROPOLOGY

UF Anthropology, mathematical
BT Anthropology
Handbooks 120

MATHEMATICAL SOCIOLOGY

UF Sociology, mathematical
BT Sociology
Bibliographies 178

MEDICAL ANTHROPOLOGY

UF Anthropology, medical
BT Anthropology
Handbooks 120

MEDICAL SOCIOLOGY

UF Sociology of medicine
BT Sociology
Bibliographies 179

Directories
  Canadian organizations 11
  Organizations 13, 30, 42, 447
  Organizations (Youth) 447
  Research centers 21
  Social programs 33
  Treatment 567
Elderly
  Bibliographies 321, 326, 341
  Guides 322
  Handbooks 335
Encyclopedias
  Criminal justice 558
  Social work 573
Ethnicity
  Guides 570
Families
  Bibliographies 235, 563
  Guides 222, 570
Filipino-Americans
  Bibliographies 563
French-Americans
  Bibliographies 563
German-Americans
  Bibliographies 563
Greek-Americans
  Bibliographies 563
Grants
  Guides 22
Guides
  Asian-Americans 360
  Elderly 322
  Ethnicity 570
  Families 222, 570
  Grants 22
  Institutionalization 324
  Marriage 570
  Migration 570
  Organizations 35
  Rural social welfare 579
  Social classes 570
  Social groups 570
  Social roles 570
  Social status 570
  Youth 570
Handbooks 175
  Elderly 335
  Social services 576
Hispanics
  Bibliographies 566
Hungarian-Americans
  Bibliographies 563
Indexes 26
Institutionalization
  Guides 324
Irish-Americans
  Bibliographies 563
Italian-Americans
  Bibliographies 563
Japanese-Americans
  Bibliographies 371, 563
Jewish-Americans
  Bibliographies 563
Juvenile delinquency
  Bibliographies 565
Korean-Americans
  Bibliographies 563
Marriage
  Guides 570
Mexican-Americans
  Bibliographies 383, 387, 563
Migration
  Guides 570
Norwegian-Americans
  Bibliographies 563
Organizations
  Directories 13, 30, 42, 447
  Guides 35
Organizations (Youth)
  Directories 447
Polish-Americans
  Bibliographies 563
Portuguese-Americans
  Bibliographies 563
Poverty
  Bibliographies 514, 515
Puerto Ricans
  Bibliographies 563
Refugees
  Bibliographies 375
Research centers
  Directories 21
Rural social welfare
  Guides 579
Russian-Americans
  Bibliographies 563
Scandinavian-Americans
  Bibliographies 563
Sex roles
  Bibliographies 466
Social casework

Bibliographies 585
Social classes
Bibliographies 563
Guides 570
Social groups
Guides 570
Social mobility
Bibliographies 147
Social networks
Bibliographies 569
Social programs
Directories 33
Social research
Abstracts 577
Bibliographies 563
Social roles
Guides 570
Social services
Handbooks 576
Social status
Guides 570
Social work
Bibliographies 578
Encyclopedias 573
Socialization
Bibliographies 563
Suicide
Bibliographies 209, 563
Support groups
Bibliographies 569
Swedish-Americans
Bibliographies 563
Swiss-Americans
Bibliographies 563
Treatment
Directories 567
Women
Abstracts 421
Bibliographies 412
Youth
Bibliographies 218
Guides 570

MENTAL HEALTH FACILITIES

BT Social institutions
RT Halfway houses
Directories 567

MENTAL ILLNESS

See Mental health

MENTAL RETARDATION

BT Mental health
Bibliographies
Crime 568
Families 568
Juvenile delinquency 568
Leisure 568
Social adjustment 568
Social life 568
Socialization 568
Directories
Information sources 31
Social programs 33

MERCY KILLING

See Euthanasia

METHADONE

BT Narcotics
RT Heroin
Bibliographies 501

MEXICAN-AMERICANS

UF Chicanos
BT Hispanics
Acculturation
Bibliographies 383, 387
Adoption
Bibliographies 234
Almanacs 348
Anthropology
Guides 392
Assimilation
Bibliographies 387
Audio-visual sources
Guides 349
Bibliographies 389
Acculturation 383, 387
Adoption 234
Assimilation 387
Child welfare 444
Cultural values 387
Cultures 382
Discrimination 387
Drug abuse 501
Families 382, 383
Immigration 388
Marriage 382, 383
Mental health 383, 387, 563

Migrants 383
Migration 388
Occupations 383
Poverty 387, 505
Race relations 388
Racism 383
Segregation 387
Sex roles 382
Social conditions 382, 388
Social life 388
Social status 387
Statistics 381, 383
Urbanization 387
Women 383, 387
Child welfare
Bibliographies 444
Cultural values
Bibliographies 382
Cultures
Bibliographies 382
Discrimination
Bibliographies 387
Drug abuse
Bibliographies 501
Elderly
Research guides 386
Ethnic groups
Research guides 386
Families
Bibliographies 382, 383
Guides
Anthropology 392
Audio-visual sources 349
Sociology 392
Immigration
Bibliographies 388
Research guides 386
Marriage
Bibliographies 382, 383
Mental health
Bibliographies 383, 387, 563
Migrants
Bibliographies 383
Migration
Bibliographies 388
Occupations
Bibliographies 383
Organizations (Voluntary) 385
Population
Research guides 386
Poverty
Bibliographies 387, 505
Race relations
Bibliographies 388
Racism
Bibliographies 383
Research guides
Elderly 386
Ethnic groups 386
Immigration 386
Population 386
Statistics 386
Women 386
Segregation
Bibliographies 387
Sex roles
Bibliographies 382
Social conditions
Bibliographies 382, 388
Social life
Bibliographies 388
Social status
Bibliographies 387
Sociology
Guides 392
Statistics
Bibliographies 381, 383
Research guides 386
Urbanization
Bibliographies 387
Women
Bibliographies 382, 383
Research guides 386

MICRONESIA

Bibliographies
Anthropology 93
Archaeology 93
Linguistics 93
Social organization 93

MIDDLE CLASSES

BT Social classes
Popular culture
Guides 522

MIGRANTS

SN Those having no

permanent residence
RT Immigrants
RT Refugees
Bibliographies
Mexican-Americans 383
Guides
Social research 262

MIGRATION

SN Movement of persons across political boundaries
UF Mobility
BT Demography
NT Emigration
NT Immigration
NT Internal migration
RT Population distribution
Abstracts 510
Almanacs
Statistics (Great Britain) 155
Statistics (U.S.) 169
Assimilation
Guides 246
Bibliographies 252, 256
Black-Americans 294
Development planning 258
Ethnicity 110
Filipino-Americans 363
Great Britain 144
Irish-Americans 368
Latin America 55, 56
Mexican-Americans 388
Poverty 505
Publications 149
Puerto Ricans 391
Social policy 543
Southern whites 516
Suburbs 310
Urban affairs 541
Urbanization 303, 317
Women 403
Black-Americans
Bibliographies 294
Countries of the world
Guides 319
Development planning
Bibliographies 258
Dictionaries
Polyglots 244
Directories
Organizations 255
Publications 149
Encyclopedias 249
Ethnic groups 353
Ethnic groups
Encyclopedias 353
Guides 246
Ethnicity
Bibliographies 110
Families 219
Guides 246
Filipino-Americans
Bibliographies 363
Glossaries 244
Great Britain
Bibliographies 144
Guides 253
Assimilation 246
Countries of the world 319
Ethnic groups 246
Families 246
Marriage 246
Mental health 570
Puerto Ricans 390
Social life 246
Social mobility 246
Social problems 246
Social research 262
Social structures 246
Urban affairs 306
Urbanization 246
Youth 246
Handbooks
Social research 68
Soviet Union 114
History
Statistics (U.S.) 163
Indexes 259
Irish-Americans
Bibliographies 368
Latin America
Bibliographies 55, 56
Marriage
Guides 246
Mental health
Guides 570
Mexican-Americans
Bibliographies 388
Organizations
Directories 255
Polyglots
Dictionaries 244
Poverty
Bibliographies 505
Publications

Bibliographies 149
Directories 149
Puerto Ricans
Bibliographies 391
Guides 390
Social life
Guides 246
Social mobility
Guides 246
Social policy
Bibliographies 543
Social problems
Guides 246
Social research
Guides 262
Handbooks 68
Social structures
Guides 246
Southern whites
Bibliographies 516
Soviet Union
Handbooks 114
Statistics (Great Britain)
Almanacs 155
Statistics (International)
Women 405
Statistics (U.S.) 164, 540
Almanacs 169
History 163
Suburbs
Bibliographies 310
Urban affairs
Bibliographies 541
Guides 306
Urbanization
Bibliographies 303, 317
Guides 246
Women
Bibliographies 403
Statistics (International) 405
Youth
Guides 246

MILITARY (U.S.)

RT Veterans
RT Warfare
Families 219

MINOR CIVIL DIVISIONS

RT Congressional districts
RT Counties
RT Local areas
RT Townships
Atlases 172

MINORITY GROUPS

SN See also entries for specific minority groups, i.e., Asian-Americans, Black-Americans, Jewish-Americans
BT Cultures
Abstracts 510
Adoption
Bibliographies 234
Ambition
Bibliographies 411
Bibliographies 356
Adoption 234
Ambition 411
Black-Americans 307
Child welfare 444
Demography 307, 346
Discrimination 307
Drug abuse 501
Elderly 341
Families 346
Great Britain 144
Immigration 346
Population 256, 346
Poverty 505, 515
Segregation 307
Sex discrimination 472
Slums 307
Social casework 585
Social stratification 147
Social work 512, 513
Social work education 583
Sociology of education 183
Urban affairs 308, 546
Urbanization 346
Women 406
Black-Americans
Bibliographies 307
Child welfare
Bibliographies 444
Demography

Bibliographies 307, 346
Directories
Organizations 42, 447
Organizations (Elderly) 339
Organizations (Youth) 447
Urban affairs 301
Discrimination
Bibliographies 307
Drug abuse
Bibliographies 501
Eastern Europe
Handbooks 109
Elderly
Bibliographies 341
Guides 322, 334
Encyclopedias
Social work 573
Families
Bibliographies 346
Great Britain
Bibliographies 144
Guides
Elderly 322, 334
Handbooks
Eastern Europe 109
Popular culture 519
Immigration
Bibliographies 346
Municipalities
Statistics (U.S.) 38
Organizations
Directories 42, 447
Organizations (Elderly)
Directories 339
Organizations (Youth)
Directories 447
Popular culture
Handbooks 519
Population
Bibliographies 256, 346
Poverty
Bibliographies 505, 515
Segregation
Bibliographies 307
Sex discrimination
Bibliographies 472
Slums
Bibliographies 307
Social casework
Bibliographies 585
Social stratification
Bibliographies 147
Social work
Bibliographies 512, 513
Encyclopedias 573
Social work education
Bibliographies 583
Sociology of education
Bibliographies 183
Statistics (U.S.)
Municipalities 38
Stereotypes
Television 520
Television
Stereotypes 520
Urban affairs
Bibliographies 308, 546
Directories 301
Urbanization
Bibliographies 346
Women
Bibliographies 406

MOBILITY

See Migration

MODERNIZATION

BT Social change
RT Industrialization
RT Urbanization
Urban affairs
Bibliographies 534

MORALS

See Ethics

MORTALITY

BT Demography
RT Death and dying
RT Deaths
RT Suicide
Abstracts
Black-Americans 297
Bibliographies 252
Elderly 476
Urbanization 317
Black-Americans
Abstracts 297
Elderly
Bibliographies 476
Guides 342

Encyclopedias 249
Guides 253
Elderly 342
Indexes 259
Statistics (International)
Yearbooks 160
Statistics (U.S.) 173
Women 409
Urbanization
Bibliographies 317
Women
Statistics (U.S.) 409
Yearbooks
Statistics (International) 160

MOTHERHOOD

BT Sex roles
RT Parenting
RT Women
Bibliographies 432
Encyclopedias 407

MULTICULTURALISM

See Cultural pluralism

MUNICIPALITIES

RT Cities
RT Local areas
RT Townships
Statistics (U.S.)
Elderly 38
Handicapped 38
Minority groups 38
Social services 38
Yearbooks 38

MUSLIMS

BT Religious groups
Ethnography
Encyclopedias 115

NARCOTICS

BT Drugs
NT Heroin
NT Methadone
RT Depressants
RT Hallucinogens
RT Sedatives
RT Stimulants
Encyclopedias 502

NATALITY

UF Birthrate
RT Births
Guides 253
Statistics (U.S.) 173

NATIONALITIES

SN Identification with a particular nation
RT Cultural groups
RT Ethnic groups
Dictionaries 116
Soviet Union
Dictionaries 116
Handbooks 114, 116

NATIVE AMERICANS

See American Indians

NEW GUINEA

Bibliographies
Cultural anthropology 81
Linguistics 81
Physical anthropology 81
Social anthropology 81

NORMS

See Social norms

NORTHERN EUROPE

BT Europe
RT Eastern Europe
RT Southern Europe
RT Western Europe
Sociological research
Handbooks 136

NORTHERN PLAINS

American Indians
Bibliographies 108

NORWEGIAN-AMERICANS

BT Ethnic groups

Mental health
Bibliographies 563

OCCUPATIONS

UF Vocations
RT Work roles
Bibliographies
Mexican-Americans 383
Women 417
Handbooks
Statistics (Eastern Europe) 162
Statistics (Soviet Union) 162

OCCUPATIONS, SEX-TYPED

See Sex-typed occupations

OFFENDERS

Rape
Handbooks 455

OLDER ADULTS

See Elderly

ONE-PARENT FAMILIES

BT Families
RT Stepfamilies
RT Two-career families
Bibliographies 215
Divorce 212, 213, 216
Remarriage 216
Widowhood 216
Youth 231

ORGANIZATIONAL SOCIOLOGY

See Sociology of organizations

ORGANIZATIONS

UF Associations
NT Canadian organizations
NT Criminal organizations
NT International organizations
NT Fraternal organizations
NT Secret organizations
RT Social institutions
RT Social structures
Abortion
Directories 255, 424
Adoption
Directories 13, 581
Encyclopedias 14
Guides 35
Alcoholism
Directories 30, 581
Encyclopedias 14
Guides 35
Anthropology
Directories 12
Encyclopedias 14
Yearbooks 44
Archaeology
Directories 101
Yearbooks 44
Black-Americans
Directories 42
Blindness
Directories 13, 42
Child abuse
Directories 447, 581
Guides 35, 443
Child welfare
Directories 447
Crime
Directories 42
Crime prevention
Directories 30
Guides 35
Deafness
Directories 13
Death and dying
Directories 202
Demography
Dictionaries 243
Directories 255
Encyclopedias 14
Dictionaries
Demography 243
Directories
Abortion 255, 424
Adoption 13, 581
Alcoholism 30, 581
Anthropology 12
Archaeology 101
Black-Americans 42
Blindness 13, 42
Child abuse 447, 581
Child welfare 447
Crime 42

Crime prevention 30
Deafness 13
Death and dying 202
Demography 255
Divorce 424
Drug abuse 30, 581
Elderly 13, 30, 42, 331, 337, 581
Ethnic groups 347, 350, 424
Families 30, 235
Family planning 42, 255, 424, 581
Handicapped 13, 30
Juvenile delinquency 447, 581
Juvenile justice 560
Mental health 13, 30, 42, 447
Migration 255
Minority groups 42, 447
Population 255
Prison reform 560
Rehabilitation 560
Sex roles 424
Sexuality 424
Social research 13, 572
Social sciences 12, 13
Social services 42, 424, 581
Social status 424
Social welfare 572
Social work 424
Sociology 12, 424
Spouse abuse 581
Women 255, 424
Youth 13, 30, 42

Divorce
Directories 424
Guides 214

Drug abuse
Directories 30, 581
Encyclopedias 14
Guides 35

Elderly
Directories 13, 30, 42, 331, 337, 581
Encyclopedias 14
Guides 35

Encyclopedias
Adoption 14
Alcoholism 14
Anthropology 14
Demography 14
Drug abuse 14
Elderly 14
Ethnic groups 18, 347
Family planning 14
Homosexuality 14
Population 14
Social groups 18
Social services 580
Social welfare 580
Sociology 14

Ethnic groups
Directories 347, 350, 424
Encyclopedias 18, 347

Families
Directories 30, 235
Guides 229

Family planning
Directories 42, 255, 424, 581
Encyclopedias 14
Guides 35

Guides
Adoption 35
Alcoholism 35
Child abuse 35, 443
Crime prevention 35
Divorce 214
Drug abuse 35
Elderly 35
Families 229
Family planning 35
Juvenile delinquency 35
Mental health 35
Parenting 35
Rape 35
Sexual assault 35
Spouse abuse 35, 449
Suicide prevention 35
Treatment 35
Volunteerism 35
Youth 35

Handicapped
Directories 13, 30
Guides 39

Homosexuality
Encyclopedias 14

Juvenile delinquency
Directories 447, 581
Guides 35

Juvenile justice
Directories 560

Mental health

Directories 13, 30, 42, 447
Guides 35
Migration
Directories 255
Minority groups
Directories 42, 447
Parenting
Guides 35
Population
Directories 255
Encyclopedias 14
Prison reform
Directories 560
Rape
Guides 35
Rehabilitation
Directories 560
Sex roles
Directories 424
Sexual assault
Guides 35
Sexuality
Directories 424
Social groups
Encyclopedias 18
Social research
Directories 13, 572
Social sciences
Directories 12, 13, 23
Social services
Directories 42, 424, 581
Encyclopedias 580
Social status
Directories 424
Social welfare
Directories 572
Encyclopedias 580
Social work
Directories 424
Sociology
Directories 12, 424
Encyclopedias 14
Yearbooks 44
Spouse abuse
Directories 581
Guides 35, 449
Statistics (International)
Yearbooks 44
Suicide prevention
Guides 35
Treatment
Guides 35
Volunteerism
Guides 35
Women
Directories 255, 424
Yearbooks
Anthropology 44
Archaeology 44
Sociology 44
Statistics (International) 44
Youth
Directories 13, 30, 42
Guides 35

ORGANIZATIONS (ELDERLY)

Directories
Crime 339
Handicapped 339
Minority groups 339
Retirement 339
Sexuality 339
Women 339

ORGANIZATIONS (INTERNATIONAL)

See International organizations

ORGANIZATIONS (VOLUNTARY)

Cuban-Americans 385
Directories
Social services 571
Social work 571
Hispanics 385
Mexican-Americans 385
Puerto Ricans 385

ORGANIZATIONS (YOUTH)

Directories
Mental health 447
Minority groups 447

ORGANIZED CRIME

BT Crime
RT Mafia
Bibliographies 493
Guides 491

PALEOANTHROPOLOGY

SN Study of extinct species of manlike creatures
BT Anthropology
Bibliographies 122

PARENT-CHILD SEPARATION

BT Divorce
Bibliographies
Juvenile delinquency 230
Suicide 230

PARENTAL ABSENCE

NT Father absence
Bibliographies 219

PARENTING

RT Family roles
RT Fatherhood
RT Motherhood
Organizations
Guides 35

PARENTS

BT Social groups
NT Single parents
Public opinion 526
Families
Bibliographies 574

PAROLE

BT Corrections
RT Probation
RT Rehabilitation
Bibliographies 191
Institutionalization 547

PHYSICAL ABUSE

RT Child abuse
RT Sexual abuse
RT Spouse abuse
RT Victimization
Elderly
Bibliographies 328
Guides 320

PHYSICAL ANTHROPOLOGISTS

BT Anthropologists
Directories 90

PHYSICAL ANTHROPOLOGY

UF Anthropology, physical
BT Anthropology
NT Anthropometry
Abstracts 76
American Indians
Handbooks 271
Basque-Americans
Bibliographies 380
Bibliographies 122
Basque-Americans 380
History 89
New Guinea 81
South Asia 78
Theses 92
Blacks (African)
Guides 98
Dictionaries 86
Encyclopedias 54
Guides 62
Blacks (African) 98
Human evolution 4
Handbooks 94
American Indians 271
History
Bibliographies 89
Human evolution
Atlases 4
Guides 4
Indexes 80
New Guinea
Bibliographies 81
South Asia
Bibliographies 78
Theses
Bibliographies 92

PLACE-NAMES

See Gazetteers

POLICE

RT Law enforcement
Guides
Social roles 491
Subcultures 491

POLICE CORRUPTION

BT Crime

Guides 491

POLISH-AMERICANS

BT Ethnic groups
Almanacs 348
Bibliographies
Assimilation 374
Cultural life 374
Elderly 374
Families 374
Mental health 563
Youth 374

POLITICAL ANTHROPOLOGY

UF Anthropology, political
BT Anthropology
Encyclopedias 54
Handbooks 119, 120

POLITICAL SOCIOLOGY

BT Sociology
Encyclopedias 54
Guides 62
Indexes 28, 139

POLYGAMY

SN Marriage involving more than one mate at a time
BT Marriage
Bibliographies
Arab women 430, 437

POLYGLOTS

SN Involving several languages
RT Dictionaries
RT Glossaries
RT Thesauri
Dictionaries
Criminology 195
Demography 242, 244
Families 244
Migration 244
Population 244

POPULAR CULTURE

UF Mass culture
RT Cultures
NT Pornography
NT Television
Bibliographies 151
Black-Americans
Encyclopedias 280
Guides 522
Handbooks 519
Death and dying
Handbooks 519
Encyclopedias
Black-Americans 280
Families
Guides 522
Guides
Black-Americans 522
Families 522
Middle classes 522
Sexuality 522
Women 522
Handbooks 519
Black-Americans 519
Death and dying 519
Minority groups 519
Pornography 519
Middle classes
Guides 522
Minority groups
Handbooks 519
Pornography
Handbooks 519
Sexuality
Guides 522
Women
Guides 522

POPULATION

RT Censuses
RT Demography
Abstracts
Black-Americans 297
Statistics (U.S.) 166
Almanacs
American Indians 267
Black-Americans 293
Statistics (Canada) 29
Statistics (Great Britain) 155
Statistics (International) 43
Statistics (U.S.) 43, 168, 169
American Indians
Almanacs 267
Guides 270

Arabs
  Bibliographies 377
Asia
  Handbooks 233
Asian-Americans
  Guides 360
Asian women
  Guides 439
Atlases
  History 6
  Urban affairs 9
Bibliographies 151
  Arabs 377
  Black-Americans 256, 290, 294
  Censuses 250
  Development planning 258
  Dutch-Americans 362
  Elderly 256
  Ethnic groups 351
  Great Britain 144
  Latin America 55, 56
  Minority groups 256, 346
  Puerto Ricans 391
  Social change 127
  Social indicators 538
  Social policy 543
  Urban affairs 256, 541, 546
  Urban communities 314
  Urbanization 303, 317
  Women 256
Black-Americans
  Abstracts 297
  Almanacs 293
  Bibliographies 256, 290, 294
  Encyclopedias 280
  Handbooks 291
Censuses
  Bibliographies 250
  Handbooks 245
  Statistics (U.S.) 260, 261
Cities
  Statistics (U.S.) 158
Congressional districts
  Statistics (U.S.) 156, 157
Counties
  Statistics (U.S.) 158
Development planning
  Bibliographies 258
Dictionaries
  Polyglots 244
  Soviet Union 116
Directories
  Grants 15
  International organizations 248
  Organizations 255
  Publications 37, 41, 149
  Research centers 21
  Statistics (U.S.) 161
  Urban affairs 301
Dutch-Americans
  Bibliographies 362
Elderly
  Bibliographies 256
  Guides 330, 342
  Handbooks 335
Encyclopedias 249
  Black-Americans 280
  Organizations 14
  Urban affairs 302
Ethnic groups
  Bibliographies 351
Glossaries 244
Grants
  Directories 15
Great Britain
  Bibliographies 144
Guides 253
  American Indians 270
  Asian-Americans 360
  Asian women 439
  Elderly 330, 342
  Social research 74
  Statistics (Great Britain) 167
  Third World 257
  World development 257
Handbooks 138
  Asia 233
  Black-Americans 291
  Censuses 245
  Elderly 335
  Soviet Union 114, 116
  Statistics (Eastern Europe) 162
  Statistics (Soviet Union) 162
History
  Atlases 6
  Statistics (U.S.) 163
Indexes 259
  Public opinion 528
  Statistics (International) 159

Statistics (U.S.) 159
International organizations
Directories 248
Jewish-Americans
Yearbooks 359
Latin America
Bibliographies 55, 56
Mexican-Americans
Research guides 386
Minority groups
Bibliographies 256, 346
Organizations
Directories 255
Encyclopedias 14
Polyglots
Dictionaries 244
Public opinion
Indexes 528
Publications
Directories 37, 41, 149
Puerto Ricans
Bibliographies 391
Research centers
Directories 21
Research guides
Mexican-Americans 386
Statistics (International) 171
Social change
Bibliographies 127
Social characteristics
Social trends 507
Statistics (U.S.) 507
Social indicators
Bibliographies 538
Social policy
Bibliographies 543
Social research
Guides 74
Social trends
Social characteristics 507
Statistics (Latin America) 251
Soviet Union
Dictionaries 116
Handbooks 114, 116
Statistics (Canada) 165
Almanacs 29
Statistics (Eastern Europe)
Handbooks 162
Statistics (Europe) 539
Statistics (Great Britain)
Almanacs 155
Guides 167
Statistics (International)
Almanacs 43
Indexes 159
Research guides 171
Yearbooks 32, 40, 160, 170
Statistics (Latin America)
Social trends 251
Statistics (Soviet Union)
Handbooks 162
Statistics (U.S.) 164, 540
Abstracts 166
Almanacs 43, 168, 169
Censuses 260, 261
Cities 158
Congressional districts 156, 157
Counties 158
Directories 161
History 163
Indexes 159
Social characteristics 507
Urban affairs 9
Third World
Guides 257
Urban affairs
Atlases 9
Bibliographies 256, 541, 546
Directories 301
Encyclopedias 302
Statistics (U.S.) 9
Urban communities
Bibliographies 314
Urbanization
Bibliographies 303, 317
Women
Bibliographies 256
World development
Guides 257
Yearbooks
Jewish-Americans 359
Statistics (International) 32, 40, 160, 170

POPULATION DENSITY

SN Size of population per unit area
BT Demography
RT Urbanization
Counties
Atlases 3
Statistics (U.S.) 3

POPULATION DISTRIBUTION

BT Demography
RT Migration
RT Segregation
Bibliographies 252

POPULATION PERIODICALS

BT Publications
Union lists 264

POPULATION POLICY

RT Social policy
Bibliographies 140, 265
Family planning 226

POPULATION STUDIES

SN Relationship of population to social and economic variables
UF Social demography
RT Demography
RT Human ecology
Bibliographies 252
Suburbs 310
Dictionaries 254

PORNOGRAPHY

RT Sexual stereotypes
Almanacs
Women 422
Bibliographies 412, 468, 531
Sex roles 470
Women 457
Handbooks
Popular culture 519

PORTUGUESE-AMERICANS

BT Ethnic groups
Bibliographies 345
Mental health 563

POVERTY

BT Social issues
NT Rural poverty
NT Urban poverty
RT Sociology of poverty
Abstracts 510
Almanacs
Black-Americans 293
Women 422
American Indians
Bibliographies 505
Appalachia
Bibliographies 505
Asian-Americans
Guides 360
Bibliographies
American Indians 505
Appalachia 505
Black-Americans 284, 325, 505
Crime 515
Discrimination 505
Elderly 325, 505
Ethnic groups 505
Families 505, 509, 514, 515
Family planning 514
Great Britain 544
Hispanics 566
Juvenile delinquency 515
Latin America 56
Mental health 514, 515
Mexican-Americans 387, 505
Migration 505
Minority groups 505, 515
Religious groups 515
Riots 505
Rural areas 505, 515
Social change 127
Social classes 514
Social indicators 509, 538
Social organization 515
Social research 509, 535
Social services 514
Social status 505

Social welfare 582
Social work 512, 513
Southern whites 516
Urban affairs 299, 300, 514, 515
Urban communities 314
Women 412, 417, 432
Youth 514
Black-Americans
Almanacs 293
Bibliographies 284, 325, 505
Encyclopedias 280
Crime
Bibliographies 515
Demography
Guides 506
Statistics (U.S.) 506
Directories
Urban affairs 301
Discrimination
Bibliographies 505
Elderly
Bibliographies 325, 505
Encyclopedias
Black-Americans 280
Social work 573
Ethnic groups
Bibliographies 505
Families
Bibliographies 505, 509, 514, 515
Guides 222
Research guides 509
Social characteristics 507
Family planning
Bibliographies 514
Great Britain
Bibliographies 544
Guides
Asian-Americans 360
Demography 506
Families 222
Social factors 506
Social issues 506
Social programs 506
Social trends 506
Hispanics
Bibliographies 566
Indexes 26, 126, 148
Theses 152
Juvenile delinquency
Bibliographies 515
Latin America
Bibliographies 56
Mental health
Bibliographies 514, 515
Mexican-Americans
Bibliographies 387, 505
Migration
Bibliographies 505
Minority groups
Bibliographies 505, 515
Religion
Bibliographies 515
Research guides
Families 509
Social indicators 509
Social research 509
Riots
Bibliographies 505
Rural areas
Bibliographies 505, 515
Social change
Bibliographies 127
Social characteristics
Families 507
Social classes
Bibliographies 514
Social factors
Guides 506
Social indicators
Bibliographies 509, 538
Research guides 509
Social issues
Guides 506
Social organization
Bibliographies 515
Social programs
Guides 506
Social research
Bibliographies 509, 535
Research guides 509
Social services
Bibliographies 514
Social status
Bibliographies 505
Social trends
Guides 506
Statistics (U.S.) 507
Social welfare
Bibliographies 582
Social work
Bibliographies 512,

513
Encyclopedias 573
Southern whites
Bibliographies 516
Statistics (U.S.) 164
Demography 506
Social trends 507
Women 409
Theses
Indexes 152
Urban affairs
Bibliographies 299, 300, 514, 515
Directories 301
Urban communities
Bibliographies 314
Women
Almanacs 422
Bibliographies 412, 417, 432
Statistics (U.S.) 409
Youth
Bibliographies 514

POWERLESSNESS

See Anomie

PREJUDICE

UF Bias
BT Social attitudes
NT Racism
RT Discrimination
Black-Americans
Bibliographies 288
Encyclopedias 280
Hispanics
Bibliographies 566

PREVENTION

Bibliographies
Alcoholism 477
Suicide 210
Directories
Rape 452
Handbooks
Rape 455

PRISON REFORM

BT Social change
Organizations
Directories 560

PRISON RIOTS

BT Riots
Guides 555

PRISON SYSTEMS

BT Social systems
Guides 555

PRISONERS

UF Convicts
UF Inmates
Guides
Criminal justice 562
Statistics (U.S.) 555

PRISONS

UF Correctional institutions
BT Institutionalization
Abstracts 548
Bibliographies
Homosexuality 561
Social life 561
Social research 561
Encyclopedias 488
Guides
Homosexuality 555

PRIVACY

RT Confidentiality
RT Ethics
Social research
Guides 67
Urban affairs
Bibliographies 315

PROBATION

SN Suspension of imprisonment for good behavior
BT Corrections
RT Parole
RT Rehabilitation
Institutionalization
Bibliographies 547

PROCEEDINGS

Directories
Archaeology 50

UF-Used For, BT-Broader Term, NT-Narrower Term, RT-Related Term

- Social sciences 50
- Social work 50
- Sociology 50

PROSTITUTION

- BT Social issues
- Almanacs
  - Women 422
- Bibliographies 412
  - Anthropology 459
  - Latin American women 435
  - Sociology 459
  - Women 419, 425, 432
- Encyclopedias 488
  - Criminal justice 558

PSYCHOLOGICAL ANTHROPOLOGY

- UF Anthropology, psychological
- BT Anthropology
- Handbooks 120

PUBLIC ARCHAEOLOGY

- BT Archaeology
- Handbooks 101

PUBLIC OPINION

- RT Social attitudes
- RT Social values
- Abortion 525-527
  - Indexes 523, 528
- Black-Americans 524, 527
  - Indexes 523
- Crime 527
  - Indexes 523, 528
- Drug abuse
  - Indexes 523, 528
- Elderly
  - Indexes 528
- Families 524-526
  - Indexes 523, 528
- Family life
  - Indexes 523
- Family planning
  - Indexes 523
- Hispanics
  - Indexes 523
- Homosexuality
  - Indexes 523
- Indexes
  - Abortion 523, 528
  - Black-Americans 523
  - Crime 523, 528
  - Drug abuse 523, 528
  - Elderly 528
  - Families 523, 528
  - Family life 523
  - Family planning 523
  - Hispanics 523
  - Homosexuality 523
  - Marriage 523, 528
  - Population 528
  - Social issues 528
  - Social life 523
  - Social programs 523
  - Social status 528
  - Social values 523, 528
  - Statistics 523, 528
- Marriage 526
  - Indexes 523, 528
- Parents 526
- Population
  - Indexes 528
- Race relations 525
- Social issues
  - Indexes 528
- Social life
  - Indexes 523
- Social programs
  - Indexes 523
- Social relations 526
- Social status
  - Indexes 528
- Social values
  - Indexes 523, 528
- Statistics 524-527
  - Indexes 523, 528
- Women 524

PUBLIC WELFARE

- See Social welfare

PUBLICATIONS

- NT Population periodicals
- Alcoholism
  - Directories 37, 41
- Anthropology
  - Directories 37, 41, 97
- Archaeology
  - Directories 37, 41, 97

Guides 64
Bibliographies
Families 149
Migration 149
Population 149
Social change 149
Social conditions 149
Social sciences 149
Sociology 149
Urban communities 149
Criminology
Directories 37, 41
Cultural anthropology
Directories 97
Guides 64
Cultures
Guides 64
Deafness
Directories 41
Demography
Guides 64
Directories
Alcoholism 37, 41
Anthropology 37, 41, 97
Archaeology 37, 41, 97
Criminology 37, 41
Cultural anthropology 97
Deafness 41
Drug abuse 37, 41
Ethnic groups 37, 41, 357
Ethnology 97
Families 149
Family planning 37, 41
Folklore 37
Gerontology 37, 41
Homosexuality 37, 41
Linguistics 97
Migration 149
Population 37, 41, 149
Social change 149
Social conditions 149
Social sciences 37, 41, 149
Social welfare 37, 41
Sociology 37, 41, 149
Urban communities 149
Drug abuse
Directories 37, 41
Ethnic groups
Directories 37, 41, 357
Ethnology
Directories 97
Guides 64
Families
Bibliographies 149
Directories 149
Family planning
Directories 37, 41
Folklore
Directories 37
Gerontology
Directories 37, 41
Guides
Archaeology 64
Cultural anthropology 64
Cultures 64
Demography 64
Ethnology 64
Social anthropology 64
Social problems 64
Social sciences 64
Sociology 64, 125
Homosexuality
Directories 37, 41
Linguistics
Directories 97
Migration
Bibliographies 149
Directories 149
Population
Bibliographies 149
Directories 37, 41, 149
Social anthropology
Guides 64
Social change
Bibliographies 149
Directories 149
Social conditions
Bibliographies 149
Directories 149
Social problems
Guides 64
Social sciences
Bibliographies 149
Directories 37, 41, 149
Guides 64
Social welfare
Directories 37, 41
Sociology
Bibliographies 149
Directories 37, 41,

149
Guides 64, 125
Urban communities
Bibliographies 149
Directories 149

PUBLISHING

Social sciences
Guides 53

PUERTO RICANS

BT Hispanics
Acculturation
Guides 390
Adoption
Bibliographies 217
Anthropology
Guides 392
Audio-visual sources
Guides 349
Bibliographies
Adoption 217
Drug abuse 501
Folklore 391
Mental health 563
Migration 391
Population 391
Social conditions 391
Social life 391
Directories
Statistics (U.S.) 161
Drug abuse
Bibliographies 501
Families
Guides 390
Folklore
Bibliographies 391
Guides
Acculturation 390
Anthropology 392
Audio-visual sources 349
Families 390
Migration 390
Social conflict 390
Sociology 392
Statistics (U.S.) 390
Mental health
Bibliographies 563
Migration
Bibliographies 391
Guides 390
Organizations (Voluntary) 385
Population
Bibliographies 391
Social conditions
Bibliographies 391
Social conflict
Guides 390
Social life
Bibliographies 391
Sociology
Guides 392
Statistics (U.S.)
Directories 161
Guides 390

PUERTO RICO

BT Latin America
Criminal justice
Bibliographies 553

QUALITY OF LIFE

BT Social indicators
Social indicators 511
Bibliographies 538

QUANTITATIVE METHODS

BT Research methods
RT Survey methods
Social research
Bibliographies 178

QUESTIONNAIRE DESIGN

RT Social research
RT Survey methods
Bibliographies 73

QUOTATIONS

Dictionaries
Sociology 129

RACE RELATIONS

BT Social relations
Abstracts 399
Bibliographies 531
American Indians 393
Black-Americans 288, 295, 298, 393
Caribbean 398
Chinese-Americans 378
Ethnic groups 343
Filipino-Americans

378
Hispanics 393
Indian-Americans 378
Japanese-Americans 371, 378
Jewish-Americans 372
Latin America 55, 398
Mexican-Americans 388
Research methods 397
Social groups 393
Social policy 543
Social theory 397
Socialization 393
Southern whites 516
Urban affairs 308
Urban communities 393
Youth 393
Black-Americans
Bibliographies 288, 295, 298, 393
Caribbean
Bibliographies 398
Dictionaries 398
Chinese-Americans
Bibliographies 378
Dictionaries 305, 394
Caribbean 398
Latin America 398
Directories
Research centers 21
Urban affairs 301
Ethnic groups
Bibliographies 343
Filipino-Americans
Bibliographies 378
Hispanics
Bibliographies 393
Indexes 126
Indian-Americans
Bibliographies 378
Japanese-Americans
Bibliographies 371, 378
Jewish-Americans
Bibliographies 372
Latin America
Bibliographies 55, 398
Dictionaries 398
Mexican-Americans
Bibliographies 388
Public opinion 525
Research centers
Directories 21
Research methods
Bibliographies 397
Social groups
Bibliographies 393
Social policy
Bibliographies 543
Social theory
Bibliographies 397
Socialization
Bibliographies 393
Southern whites
Bibliographies 516
Urban affairs
Bibliographies 308
Directories 301
Urban communities
Bibliographies 393
Youth
Bibliographies 393

RACIAL COMPOSITION

BT Demography
RT Population distribution
Statistics (U.S.)
Congressional districts 156
Counties 3

RACIAL GROUPS

BT Cultures
Women
Bibliographies 410

RACIAL SEGREGATION

BT Segregation
RT Social discrimination
Urban communities
Bibliographies 314

RACISM

BT Prejudice
RT Ku Klux Klan
Bibliographies 396
Black-Americans 286, 288
Filipino-Americans 373
Mexican-Americans 383
Urban affairs 299
Black-Americans
Bibliographies 286, 288
Encyclopedias 280

Encyclopedias
Black-Americans 280
Filipino-Americans
Bibliographies 373
Guides
Radical sociology 60
Mexican-Americans
Bibliographies 383
Radical sociology
Guides 60
Urban affairs
Bibliographies 299

RADICAL SOCIOLOGY

BT Sociology
Guides
Crime 60
Racism 60
Social classes 60
Urban affairs 60
Women 60

RAPE

BT Antisocial behavior
RT Sexual abuse
Almanacs
Women 422
Bibliographies 412
Criminal justice 454
Sex roles 454, 470
Social attitudes 453
Victims 453
Women 408, 425, 432, 457
Criminal justice
Bibliographies 454
Encyclopedias 558
Crisis intervention
Directories 36
Directories
Crisis intervention 36
Prevention 452
Social services 418
Treatment 452
Encyclopedias
Criminal justice 558
Women 407
Guides
Organizations 35
Handbooks 455
Offenders 455
Prevention 455
Victims 455
Offenders
Handbooks 455
Organizations
Guides 35
Prevention
Directories 452
Handbooks 455
Sex roles
Bibliographies 454, 470
Social attitudes
Bibliographies 453
Social services
Directories 418
Treatment
Directories 452
Victims
Bibliographies 453
Handbooks 455
Women
Almanacs 422
Bibliographies 408, 425, 432, 457
Encyclopedias 407

RECIDIVISM

SN Repeated relapse to criminal behavior
BT Law enforcement
Handbooks 197

REFUGEES

RT Immigrants
RT Migrants
Bibliographies
Acculturation 375
Mental health 375
Social services 375
Handbooks 358

REGIONAL STUDIES

Anthropology
Handbooks 99

REHABILITATION

BT Corrections
Bibliographies
Institutionalization 547
Directories
Organizations 560
Guides 555

REHABILITATION CENTERS

See Halfway houses

RELIGION

BT Belief systems
RT Sociology of religion
Bibliographies
Divorce 181
Elderly 340
Families 181
Marriage 181
Poverty 515
Social change 181
Social issues 181
Urban affairs 313

RELIGIOUS GROUPS

Elderly
Handbooks 336

REMARRIAGE

BT Marriage
RT Intermarriage
Bibliographies
One-parent families 216
Guides
Divorce 214

RESEARCH CENTERS

Directories
Anthropology 21
Ethnic groups 21, 350
Ethnology 21
Family studies 21
Folklore 21
Gerontology 21
Medical sociology 21
Mental health 21
Population 21
Race relations 21
Rural sociology 21
Social sciences 21
Social services 21
Sociology 21
Sociology of education 21
Sociology of religion 21
Sociology of sciences 21
Urban affairs 301, 311
Urban sociology 21

RESEARCH GUIDES

BT Guides
Alcoholism 198
American Indians 273
Youth 440
Criminal justice 552
Criminology 63
Social research 198
Statistics 198
Drug abuse 198
Elderly
Mexican-Americans 386
Ethnic groups
Mexican-Americans 386
Ethnicity
Youth 440
Families
Poverty 509
History
Youth 440
Immigration
Mexican-Americans 386
Mexican-Americans
Elderly 386
Ethnic groups 386
Immigration 386
Population 386
Statistics 386
Women 386
Population
Mexican-Americans 386
Statistics (International) 171
Poverty
Families 509
Social indicators 509
Social research 509
Social anthropology 63
Social indicators
Poverty 509
Social research
Criminology 198
Poverty 509
Social sciences 63
Statistics (International) 171
Social welfare
Statistics (International) 171
Sociology 63
Statistics

Criminology 198
Mexican-Americans 386
Statistics (International)
Population 171
Social sciences 171
Social welfare 171
Terrorism 489
Women
Mexican-Americans 386
Youth
American Indians 440
Ethnicity 440
History 440

RESEARCH METHODS

NT Quantitative methods
NT Survey methods
RT Social research
Anthropology
Handbooks 75
Archaeology
Bibliographies 102
Encyclopedias 103
Bibliographies 65
Archaeology 102
Ethnic relations 397
Families 221
Fertility 263
Marriage 221
Race relations 397
Social conflict 221
Social control 221
Social research 535
Social roles 221
Social stratification 147
Cultural anthropology
Handbooks 119
Demography
Handbooks 75
Dictionaries
Social sciences 66
Encyclopedias
Archaeology 103
Ethnic relations
Bibliographies 397
Families
Bibliographies 221
Fertility
Bibliographies 263
Guides 59
Sociology 71
Sociology of aging 182
Handbooks
Anthropology 75
Cultural anthropology 119
Demography 75
Social sciences 69, 72, 75
Sociology 69, 75, 154
Sociometry 69
Marriage
Bibliographies 221
Race relations
Bibliographies 397
Social conflict
Bibliographies 221
Social control
Bibliographies 221
Social research
Bibliographies 535
Social roles
Bibliographies 221
Social sciences
Handbooks 69, 72, 75
Social stratification
Bibliographies 147
Sociology
Guides 71
Handbooks 69, 75, 154
Sociology of aging
Guides 182
Sociometry
Handbooks 69

RESEARCH STUDIES

See Social research

RETIREMENT

BT Life events
RT Elderly
RT Gerontology
RT Leisure
RT Sociology of aging
Bibliographies
Elderly 321, 323, 326, 340
Gerontology 332
Social change 533
Directories
Organizations (Elderly) 339
Elderly
Bibliographies 321, 323, 326, 340
Handbooks 335

Gerontology
Bibliographies 332
Handbooks
Elderly 335
Organizations (Elderly)
Directories 339
Social change
Bibliographies 533

RIOTS

BT Social disorders
NT Prison riots
Bibliographies 531
Black-Americans 295
Poverty 505
Urban affairs 299, 308
Encyclopedias 488

RITUALS

SN Standardized actions performed on specific occasions
BT Social behavior
Social research
Bibliographies 95

ROLE MODELS

SN Individuals whose behavior in one of their roles is emulated by someone else
RT Social roles
Bibliographies
Ambition 411
Women 411

ROLES

See Social roles

ROMANIAN-AMERICANS

Bibliographies
Cultures 376
Ethnicity 376
Immigration 376

RURAL AREAS

RT Communal living
RT Suburbs
Bibliographies
Elderly 341
Poverty 505, 515

RURAL POVERTY

BT Poverty
RT Urban poverty
Bibliographies
Social work 512, 513

RURAL SOCIAL WELFARE

BT Social welfare
RT Child welfare
Guides
Community development 579
Elderly 579
Mental health 579
Social policy 579
Social research 579
Social services 579
Youth 579

RURAL SOCIOLOGY

BT Sociology
Encyclopedias 54
Guides 62
Indexes 148
Research centers
Directories 21

RUSSIAN-AMERICANS

BT Ethnic groups
Almanacs 348
Bibliographies
Immigration 375
Mental health 563

SCANDINAVIAN-AMERICANS

BT Ethnic groups
Bibliographies 345
Mental health 563

SECRET ORGANIZATIONS

BT Organizations
NT Ku Klux Klan
RT Criminal organizations
RT Fraternal organizations
Dictionaries 10

Handbooks 19

SEDATIVES

BT Drugs
NT Barbiturates
RT Depressants
RT Hallucinogens
RT Narcotics
RT Stimulants
Encyclopedias 502

SEGREGATION

SN Social separation based on race, religion or ethnic characteristics
UF Separatism
NT Racial segregation
RT Desegregation
RT Population distribution
Bibliographies
Black-Americans 287
Mexican-Americans 387
Minority groups 307

SEPARATION

See Marital separation

SEPARATISM

See Segregation

SEX CRIMES

BT Crime
Bibliographies 468

SEX DIFFERENCES

Bibliographies 471
American Indians 564
Sex research 469

SEX DISCRIMINATION

UF Discrimination, sexual
UF Sexual discrimination
BT Discrimination
Almanacs
Women 422
Bibliographies 471
Abortion 472
Family planning 472
Family relations 472
Minority groups 472
Sex roles 472
Women 412

SEX RESEARCH

BT Social research
Bibliographies
Sex differences 469
Social classes 469
Social conditions 469
Social sciences 469
Socialization 469
Sociology 469

SEX ROLES

BT Social roles
NT Fatherhood
NT Motherhood
Abstracts
Women 421
Almanacs
Women 422
Ambition
Bibliographies 411
American Indians
Bibliographies 275
Antisocial behavior
Bibliographies 466
Arab women
Bibliographies 437
Asian women
Bibliographies 429
Bibliographies 224, 225, 227, 471
Ambition 411
American Indians 275
Antisocial behavior 466
Arab women 437
Asian women 429
Black-Americans 284, 466
Chinese women 433
Communal living 304
Elderly 470, 473
Families 232
Fatherhood 466
Great Britain 144
Hispanics 466, 566
Homosexuality 461

Latin American women 435
Marriage 466
Men 466, 467
Mental health 466
Mexican-Americans 382
Pornography 470
Rape 454, 470
Sex discrimination 472
Socialization 466
Stereotypes 470
Television 518
Widowhood 199
Women 404, 408, 410-414, 417, 423, 425, 426, 432, 457, 470

Black-Americans
Bibliographies 284, 466

Chinese women
Bibliographies 433

Communal living
Bibliographies 304

Directories
Organizations 424

Elderly
Bibliographies 470, 473

Encyclopedias
Women 407

Families
Bibliographies 232

Fatherhood
Bibliographies 466

Great Britain
Bibliographies 144

Handbooks
Socialization 137

Hispanics
Bibliographies 466, 566

Homosexuality
Bibliographies 461

Indexes 126
Women 420

Latin American women
Bibliographies 435

Marriage
Bibliographies 466

Men
Bibliographies 466, 467

Mental health
Bibliographies 466

Mexican-Americans
Bibliographies 382

Organizations
Directories 424

Pornography
Bibliographies 470

Rape
Bibliographies 454, 470

Sex discrimination
Bibliographies 472

Socialization
Bibliographies 466
Handbooks 137

Stereotypes
Bibliographies 470

Television
Bibliographies 518

Widowhood
Bibliographies 199

Women
Abstracts 421
Almanacs 422
Bibliographies 404, 408, 410-414, 417, 423, 425, 426, 432, 457, 470
Encyclopedias 407
Indexes 420
World development 416

World development
Women 416

SEX-TYPED BEHAVIORS

UF Behaviors, sex-typed
BT Sexual stereotypes
RT Sex-typed occupations
Bibliographies 471
Television 520

SEX-TYPED OCCUPATIONS

UF Occupations, sex-typed
BT Sexual stereotypes
RT Sex-typed behaviors
Bibliographies 471

SEXUAL ABUSE

UF Sexual assault
BT Antisocial behavior
NT Child molesting
NT Incest
RT Child abuse

RT Physical abuse
RT Rape
RT Spouse abuse
Bibliographies 456
Youth 442
Guides 456
Organizations 35
Handbooks 455

SEXUAL ASSAULT

See Sexual abuse

SEXUAL DEVIANCE

BT Deviant behavior
RT Transsexualism
RT Transvestism
Social casework
Bibliographies 585

SEXUAL DISCRIMINATION

See Sex discrimination

SEXUAL RELATIONS

African women
Bibliographies 427

SEXUAL STEREOTYPES

BT Stereotypes
NT Sex-typed behaviors
NT Sex-typed occupations
Bibliographies 470
Women 423
Television 520

SEXUALITY

NT Homosexuality
NT Transsexualism
Abstracts
Women 421
Alcoholism
Bibliographies 475
Almanacs
Women 422
Asian women
Guides 439
Bibliographies
Alcoholism 475
Elderly 323, 326, 473
Homosexuality 465
Jews 228
Latin American women 435
Lesbians 474
Social research 465
Sociology 465
Women 404, 413, 414, 426, 474
Youth 474
Directories
Organizations 424
Organizations (Elderly) 339
Elderly
Bibliographies 323, 326, 473
Men 473
Women 473
Encyclopedias
Women 407
Guides
Asian women 439
Handicapped 39
Popular culture 522
Handicapped
Guides 39
Homosexuality
Bibliographies 465
Jews
Bibliographies 228
Latin American women
Bibliographies 435
Lesbians
Bibliographies 474
Men
Elderly 473
Organizations
Directories 424
Organizations (Elderly)
Directories 339
Popular culture
Guides 522
Social research
Bibliographies 465
Sociology
Bibliographies 465
Stereotypes
Television 520
Television
Stereotypes 520
Women
Abstracts 421
Almanacs 422
Bibliographies 404, 413, 414, 426, 474
Elderly 473

Encyclopedias 407
Youth
Bibliographies 474

SINGLE PARENTS

BT Parents
Families
Bibliographies 235

SLANG

UF Argot
UF Jargon
RT Sociolinguistics
Dictionaries
Alcoholism 480
Crime 487
Criminology 490
Drug abuse 498
Subcultures 490
Guides
Criminology 490
Subcultures 490

SLAVIC-AMERICANS

BT Ethnic groups
Bibliographies 345

SLUMS

BT Social conditions
RT Urban poverty
Bibliographies
Minority groups 307
Urbanization 317

SMALL GROUPS

RT Social group work
RT Sociometry
Handbooks
Deviant behavior 70
Social control 70
Social interaction 70
Social norms 70
Social research 70
Social roles 70

SOCIAL ADJUSTMENT

BT Social behavior
Mental retardation
Bibliographies 568

SOCIAL ADMINISTRATION

RT Assistance programs
RT Social welfare
Dictionaries 49

SOCIAL AGGRESSION

BT Antisocial behavior
RT Terrorism
RT Violence
Suicide
Bibliographies 209

SOCIAL ANTHROPOLOGY

UF Anthropology, social
BT Anthropology
American Indians
Handbooks 271
Bibliographies 122
Cross-cultural studies 84
History 89
New Guinea 81
South Asia 78, 79
Theses 92
Cross-cultural studies
Bibliographies 84
Death and dying
Handbooks 94
Encyclopedias 54, 121
Families
Handbooks 94
Guides 59
Publications 64
Handbooks 120
American Indians 271
Death and dying 94
Families 94
Kinship 94
Marriage 94
Social life 94
Social stratification 94
Social structures 94
History
Bibliographies 89
Indexes 28, 80
Kinship
Handbooks 94
Marriage
Handbooks 94
New Guinea
Bibliographies 81
Publications

Guides 64
Research guides 63
Social life
Handbooks 94
Social stratification
Handbooks 94
Social structures
Handbooks 94
South Asia
Bibliographies 78, 79
Theses
Bibliographies 92

SOCIAL ATTITUDES

NT Prejudice
NT Stereotypes
RT Public opinion
Bibliographies
Death and dying 201
Rape 453

SOCIAL BEHAVIOR

NT Collective behavior
NT Group behavior
NT Rituals
NT Social adjustment
NT Urban behavior
RT Antisocial behavior
Bibliographies
Death and dying 204
Juvenile delinquency 446
Marihuana 503
Urban affairs 315
Guides
Youth 445
Handbooks
Elderly 335

SOCIAL BIOLOGY

SN Application of biology to social sciences
RT Human ecology
Handbooks 175

SOCIAL CASEWORK

BT Social work
RT Social group work
Bibliographies
Alcoholism 585
Corrections 585
Drug abuse 585
Elderly 585
Family planning 585
Mental health 585
Minority groups 585
Sexual deviance 585
Women 585
Youth 585

SOCIAL CHANGE

UF Change, social
UF Societal change
NT Industrialization
NT Modernization
NT Prison reform
NT Urbanization
RT Cultural change
RT Societal development
Abstracts 510
Anthropology
Bibliographies 87
Asian women
Guides 439
Bereavement
Bibliographies 533
Bibliographies 57, 153, 529, 531
Anthropology 87
Bereavement 533
Black-Americans 127
Communal living 304
Crime 127
Drug abuse 127
Elderly 127, 341
Families 127, 574
Jewish-Americans 372
Juvenile delinquency 127
Latin America 55, 56
Population 127
Poverty 127
Publications 149
Religion 181
Retirement 533
Social classes 533
Social life 127
Social research 535
Social support 533
Social work 512, 513
Unemployment 533
Urban communities 314
Women 127, 412
Youth 533
Black-Americans
Bibliographies 127

Communal living
  Bibliographies 304
Crime
  Bibliographies 127
Dictionaries 532
Directories
  Publications 149
Drug abuse
  Bibliographies 127
Elderly
  Bibliographies 127, 341
Families
  Bibliographies 127, 574
Guides
  Asian women 439
  Linguistics 91
  Social research 262
  Urban affairs 306
Handbooks 138
Indexes 126, 139, 148
Jewish-Americans
  Bibliographies 372
Juvenile delinquency
  Bibliographies 127
Latin America
  Bibliographies 55, 56
Linguistics
  Guides 91
Population
  Bibliographies 127
Poverty
  Bibliographies 127
Publications
  Bibliographies 149
  Directories 149
Religion
  Bibliographies 181
Retirement
  Bibliographies 533
Social classes
  Bibliographies 533
Social life
  Bibliographies 127
Social research
  Bibliographies 535
  Guides 262
Social support
  Bibliographies 533
Social work
  Bibliographies 512, 513
Unemployment
  Bibliographies 533
Urban affairs
  Guides 306
Urban communities
  Bibliographies 314
Women
  Bibliographies 127, 412
Youth
  Bibliographies 533

SOCIAL CHARACTERISTICS

RT Social conditions
RT Social correlates
RT Social factors
Abortion
  Women 400
Alcoholism
  Bibliographies 483
Bibliographies
  Alcoholism 483
  Women 406
Congressional districts
  Statistics (U.S.) 157
Drug abuse
  Guides 500
Families
  Poverty 507
Guides
  Drug abuse 500
Population
  Social trends 507
  Statistics (U.S.) 507
Poverty
  Families 507
Social trends
  Population 507
Statistics (U.S.)
  Congressional districts 157
  Population 507
Women
  Abortion 400
  Bibliographies 406

SOCIAL CLASSES

BT Social groups
NT Middle classes
RT Social stratification
Adoption
  Bibliographies 234
Bibliographies 57, 151, 153
  Adoption 234
  Black-Americans 294
  Great Britain 144

Latin America 55, 56
Mental health 563
Poverty 514
Sex research 469
Social change 533
Social mobility 147
Urban affairs 315
Urban communities 314
Women 404, 413, 414
Black-Americans
Bibliographies 294
Great Britain
Bibliographies 144
Guides
Mental health 570
Radical sociology 60
Handbooks
Statistics (Eastern Europe) 162
Statistics (Soviet Union) 162
Indexes 551
Latin America
Bibliographies 55, 56
Mental health
Bibliographies 563
Guides 570
Poverty
Bibliographies 514
Radical sociology
Guides 60
Sex research
Bibliographies 469
Social change
Bibliographies 533
Social mobility
Bibliographies 147
Statistics (Eastern Europe)
Handbooks 162
Statistics (Soviet Union)
Handbooks 162
Urban affairs
Bibliographies 315
Urban communities
Bibliographies 314
Women
Bibliographies 404, 413, 414

SOCIAL CONDITIONS

NT Slums
RT Social characteristics
RT Social factors
Abstracts 510
Urban affairs 309
Asian women
Bibliographies 434
Bibliographies
Asian women 434
Black-Americans 294-296, 298
Dutch-Americans 362
Ethnic groups 352
Filipino-Americans 363, 373
German-Americans 364
Jewish-Americans 372
Mexican-Americans 382, 388
Publications 149
Puerto Ricans 391
Sex research 469
Black-Americans
Bibliographies 294-296, 298
Encyclopedias 292
Directories
Publications 149
Dutch-Americans
Bibliographies 362
Encyclopedias
Black-Americans 292
Ethnic groups
Bibliographies 352
Filipino-Americans
Bibliographies 363, 373
German-Americans
Bibliographies 364
Guides
Urban affairs 306
Indexes 26
Jewish-Americans
Bibliographies 372
Yearbooks 359
Mexican-Americans
Bibliographies 382, 388
Publications
Bibliographies 149
Directories 149
Puerto Ricans
Bibliographies 391
Sex research
Bibliographies 469
Statistics (Europe) 539
Urban affairs
Abstracts 309

Guides 306
Yearbooks
Jewish-Americans 359

SOCIAL CONFLICT

Bibliographies 530, 531
Latin America 55
Research methods 221
Social stratification 147
Women 412
Blacks (African)
Guides 98
Guides
Blacks (African) 98
Puerto Ricans 390
Latin America
Bibliographies 55
Puerto Ricans
Guides 390
Research methods
Bibliographies 221
Social stratification
Bibliographies 147
Women
Bibliographies 412

SOCIAL CONTROL

SN Formal and informal pressure to conform to social norms and traditions
RT Social norms
RT Socialization
Bibliographies
Research methods 221
Television 518
Blacks (African)
Guides 98
Guides
Blacks (African) 98
Social research 67
Handbooks 138, 197
Small groups 70
Indexes 148, 193, 551
Research methods
Bibliographies 221
Small groups
Handbooks 70
Social research
Guides 67
Television
Bibliographies 518

SOCIAL CORRELATES

RT Social characteristics
RT Social indicators
Alcoholism
Bibliographies 477

SOCIAL CUSTOMS

See Customs

SOCIAL DEMOGRAPHY

See Population studies

SOCIAL DEVELOPMENT

See Socialization

SOCIAL DEVIANCE

See Deviant behavior

SOCIAL DIFFERENTIATION

SN Development of social, cultural and status differences in society
RT Social organization
Indexes 148

SOCIAL DISCRIMINATION

UF Discrimination, social
BT Discrimination
RT Prejudice
Bibliographies 508

SOCIAL DISORDERS

NT Riots
Urban affairs
Bibliographies 299

SOCIAL DISORGANIZATION

SN Increase in social problems from a breakdown of social control and social structures
RT Social control
RT Social structures

Handbooks 138
Social research 68
Indexes 126

SOCIAL ECOLOGY

See Human ecology

SOCIAL FACTORS

RT Demographic factors
RT Social characteristics
RT Social conditions
Bibliographies
Baby boom 239
Child abuse 237, 441, 442
Suburbs 310
Television 518
Guides
Poverty 506

SOCIAL GERONTOLOGY

See Gerontology

SOCIAL GROUP WORK

BT Social work
RT Small groups
RT Social casework
RT Sociometry
Bibliographies
Corrections 575
Ethics 575
Group dynamics 575
Treatment 575
Handbooks 576

SOCIAL GROUPS

UF Groups, social
BT Cultures
NT Adults
NT College students
NT Elderly
NT Men
NT Parents
NT Social classes
NT Veterans
NT Women
NT Youth
Alcoholism
Treatment 482
Bibliographies
Race relations 393
Women 417
Guides
Mental health 570
Organizations
Encyclopedias 18

SOCIAL IDENTITY

RT Role models
RT Social roles
Bibliographies
Black-Americans 287
Ethnicity 110

SOCIAL IMPACT ASSESSMENT

Bibliographies 537

SOCIAL INDICATORS

NT Quality of life
RT Social characteristics
RT Social correlates
Abstracts
Social research 577
Urban affairs 312
Bibliographies 537
Crime 538
Families 538
Leisure 538
Population 538
Poverty 509, 538
Quality of life 538
Social mobility 538
Social policy 543
Socialization 538
Urban affairs 541
Urban communities 314
Youth 538
Crime
Bibliographies 538
Families
Bibliographies 538
Handbooks
Social patterns 542
Statistics (Eastern Europe) 162
Statistics (International) 542
Statistics (Soviet Union) 162, 536
Leisure
Bibliographies 538
Population

    Bibliographies 538
  Poverty
    Bibliographies 509, 538
    Research guides 509
  Quality of life 511
    Bibliographies 538
  Research guides
    Poverty 509
  Social mobility
    Bibliographies 538
  Social patterns
    Handbooks 542
  Social policy
    Bibliographies 543
  Social research
    Abstracts 577
  Socialization
    Bibliographies 538
  Statistics (Eastern Europe)
    Handbooks 162
  Statistics (Europe) 539
  Statistics (International) 511
    Handbooks 542
  Statistics (Soviet Union)
    Handbooks 162, 536
  Urban affairs
    Abstracts 312
    Bibliographies 541
  Urban communities
    Bibliographies 314
  Youth
    Bibliographies 538

SOCIAL INEQUALITY

  RT Social status
  RT Social stratification
  RT Socially disadvantaged
  Sociology of aging
    Guides 182

SOCIAL INSTITUTIONS

  SN Organizations satisfying economic, political or social needs or functions
  NT Mental health facilities
  RT Organizations
  RT Social programs
  RT Social structures
  Bibliographies
    Black-Americans 294
    Juvenile delinquency 446
  Guides
    Sociology of aging 182

SOCIAL INTERACTION

  NT Group dynamics
  RT Sociometry
  Bibliographies
    Marihuana 503
    Urban affairs 315
  Handbooks
    Small groups 70

SOCIAL ISOLATION

  SN Separation that inhibits communication, cooperation and other forms of interaction
  UF Isolation, social
  RT Alienation
  RT Anomie
  RT Social role loss
  Elderly
    Bibliographies 326, 327

SOCIAL ISSUES

  NT Abortion
  NT Antisocial behavior
  NT Crime
  NT Discrimination
  NT Divorce
  NT Drug abuse
  NT Homelessness
  NT Poverty
  NT Prostitution
  NT Unemployment
  Bibliographies 57, 188, 485
    Death and dying 204
    Families 235
    Juvenile delinquency 446
    Religion 181
    Urban affairs 534
    Urban communities 314
    Youth 231

UF-Used For, BT-Broader Term, NT-Narrower Term, RT-Related Term

Death and dying
Bibliographies 204
Families
Bibliographies 235
Guides 229
Guides 62
Families 229
Migration 246
Poverty 506
Publications 64
Sociology of aging 182
Urban affairs 306
Indexes 148
Public opinion 528
Juvenile delinquency
Bibliographies 446
Migration
Guides 246
Poverty
Guides 506
Public opinion
Indexes 528
Religion
Bibliographies 181
Sociology of aging
Guides 182
Urban affairs
Bibliographies 534
Guides 306
Urban communities
Bibliographies 314
Youth
Bibliographies 231

SOCIAL LIFE

UF Community life
NT Social participation
RT Dating
RT Leisure
American Indians
Bibliographies 274
Dictionaries 269
Encyclopedias 277
Guides 270
Appalachia
Women 428
Arab-Americans
Bibliographies 378
Bibliographies
American Indians 274
Arab-Americans 378
Black-Americans 282, 296
Chinese-Americans 378
Dutch-Americans 362
Elderly 326
Families 235
Filipino-Americans 378
German-Americans 364
Homosexuality 460, 461
Immigration 355
Indian-Americans 378
Italian-Americans 369
Japanese-Americans 378
Jews 228
Mental retardation 568
Mexican-Americans 388
Prisons 561
Puerto Ricans 391
Social change 127
Urban affairs 308
Urbanization 317
Women 413, 414, 432, 484
Black-Americans
Bibliographies 282, 296
Blacks (African)
Guides 98
Chinese-Americans
Bibliographies 378
Dictionaries
American Indians 269
Dutch-Americans
Bibliographies 362
Elderly
Bibliographies 326
Encyclopedias
American Indians 277
Ethnic groups 353
Ethnic groups
Encyclopedias 353
Families
Bibliographies 235
Filipino-Americans
Bibliographies 378
German-Americans
Bibliographies 364
Guides
American Indians 270
Blacks (African) 98
Migration 246
Handbooks
Social anthropology 94
Homosexuality
Bibliographies 460,

461
Immigration
Bibliographies 355
Indexes
Public opinion 523
Indian-Americans
Bibliographies 378
Italian-Americans
Bibliographies 369
Japanese-Americans
Bibliographies 378
Jewish-Americans
Yearbooks 359
Jews
Bibliographies 228
Mental retardation
Bibliographies 568
Mexican-Americans
Bibliographies 388
Migration
Guides 246
Prisons
Bibliographies 561
Public opinion
Indexes 523
Puerto Ricans
Bibliographies 391
Social anthropology
Handbooks 94
Social change
Bibliographies 127
Urban affairs
Bibliographies 308
Urbanization
Bibliographies 317
Women
Appalachia 428
Bibliographies 413, 414, 432, 484
Yearbooks
Jewish-Americans 359

SOCIAL MOBILITY

SN Movement from one social class to another
RT Social classes
RT Social status
Bibliographies 57, 153
Deviant behavior 147
Families 147
Fertility 147
Irish-Americans 368
Jewish-Americans 372
Leisure 147
Mental health 147
Social classes 147
Social indicators 538
Social values 147
Suicide 147
Ukrainian-Americans 379
Guides
Migration 246

SOCIAL MOVEMENTS

SN Organization of people to bring about or to resist social change
RT Collective behavior
RT Social change
Bibliographies 529

SOCIAL NETWORK ANALYSIS

Handbooks 120

SOCIAL NETWORKS

SN Communication linkages between people or groups
NT Invisible colleges
RT Social structures
RT Sociometry
Mental health
Bibliographies 569

SOCIAL NORMS

SN Common ideas which guide socially acceptable behavior
UF Norms
RT Customs
RT Social control
Bibliographies
Caribbean women 436
Fertility 263
Caribbean women
Bibliographies 436
Fertility
Bibliographies 263
Indexes 139
Small groups
Handbooks 70

SOCIAL ORGANIZATION

NT Community organization
NT Families
NT Social stratification
RT Social differentiation
RT Social structures
Aborigines
Guides 107
American Indians
Bibliographies 268
Guides 270
Asian-Americans
Guides 360
Atlases
Ethnography 5
Bibliographies
American Indians 268
Ethnic groups 351, 352
Jewish-Americans 372
Latin America 55, 56
Micronesia 93
Poverty 515
Theses 92
Blacks (African)
Guides 98
Encyclopedias 121
Ethnic groups 353
Ethnic groups
Bibliographies 351, 352
Encyclopedias 353
Ethnography
Atlases 5
Guides 59
Aborigines 107
American Indians 270
Asian-Americans 360
Blacks (African) 98
Handbooks 138
Social research 68
Jewish-Americans
Bibliographies 372
Latin America
Bibliographies 55, 56
Micronesia
Bibliographies 93
Poverty
Bibliographies 515
Social research
Handbooks 68
Theses
Bibliographies 92

SOCIAL PARTICIPATION

BT Social life
RT Community organization
Elderly
Bibliographies 341

SOCIAL PATTERNS

RT Social trends
Social indicators
Handbooks 542

SOCIAL PLANNING

RT Development planning
Bibliographies
Social work 512, 513
Handbooks 576

SOCIAL POLICY

NT Crime control policies
RT Population policy
Abstracts
Immigration 247
Australia
Guides 545
Bibliographies 57, 265
Drug abuse 543
Elderly 543
Ethnic groups 351
Families 238
Great Britain 144, 544
Migration 543
Population 543
Race relations 543
Social indicators 543
Social programs 543
Social welfare 543
Urban affairs 546
Women 412
Drug abuse
Bibliographies 543
Elderly
Bibliographies 543
Ethnic groups
Bibliographies 351
Families
Bibliographies 238
Great Britain
Bibliographies 144, 544
Guides
Australia 545

Rural social welfare 579
Immigration
Abstracts 247
Indexes 26
Migration
Bibliographies 543
Population
Bibliographies 543
Race relations
Bibliographies 543
Rural social welfare
Guides 579
Social indicators
Bibliographies 543
Social programs
Bibliographies 543
Social welfare
Bibliographies 543
Urban affairs
Bibliographies 546
Women
Bibliographies 412

SOCIAL PROBLEMS

See Social issues

SOCIAL PROGRAMS

RT Special programs
Bibliographies
Family planning 226
Social policy 543
Directories
Blindness 33
Elderly 33
Mental health 33
Mental retardation 33
Veterans 33
Youth 33
Family planning
Bibliographies 226
Guides
Poverty 506
Indexes
Public opinion 523
Poverty
Guides 506
Public opinion
Indexes 523
Social policy
Bibliographies 543

SOCIAL PSYCHOLOGY

SN Study of the influence of social factors on individual behavior
BT Sociology
RT Group dynamics
Bibliographies
Theses 150
Dictionaries 142
Guides 59
Indexes 148, 551
Theses
Bibliographies 150

SOCIAL RELATIONS

BT Interpersonal relations
NT Ethnic relations
NT Family relations
NT Race relations
Abstracts 190
American Indians
Bibliographies 275
Bibliographies
American Indians 275
Black-Americans 294
Ethnic groups 343
Suicide 209
Youth 231
Black-Americans
Bibliographies 294
Encyclopedias
Ethnic groups 353
Ethnic groups
Bibliographies 343
Encyclopedias 353
Jewish-Americans
Yearbooks 359
Public opinion 526
Suicide
Bibliographies 209
Yearbooks
Jewish-Americans 359
Youth
Bibliographies 231

SOCIAL RESEARCH

UF Research studies
NT Case studies
NT Field research
NT Sex research
NT Sociological research
RT Library research
RT Research methods

RT Theses
Abstracts
Alcoholism 577
Child abuse 577
Elderly 584
Family 577, 584
Foster families 577
Immigration 247
Juvenile delinquency 577
Mental health 577
Social indicators 577
Social services 577
Social systems 577
Social work 584
Youth 584
Acculturation
Handbooks 68
Alcoholism
Abstracts 577
Bibliographies 479
Anthropology 74
Arab women
Bibliographies 437
Arabs
Bibliographies 377
Bibliographies 65
Alcoholism 479
Arab women 437
Arabs 377
Child abuse 441
Countries of the world 535
Demography 535
Drug abuse 499
Families 535
Gerontology 535
Interpersonal relations 535
Mental health 563
Poverty 509, 535
Prisons 561
Quantitative methods 178
Research methods 535
Rituals 95
Sexuality 465
Social change 535
Social work 578
Suicide 207
Survey methods 535
Television 518
Child abuse
Abstracts 577
Bibliographies 441
Confidentiality
Guides 67
Countries of the world
Bibliographies 535
Criminology
Guides 192
Research guides 198
Demography
Bibliographies 535
Directories
Organizations 13, 572
Social welfare 572
Urban affairs 311
Drug abuse
Bibliographies 499
Guides 500
Elderly
Abstracts 584
Handbooks 335, 338
Ethics
Guides 67
Families
Abstracts 577, 584
Bibliographies 535
Guides 222
Foster families
Abstracts 577
Gerontology
Bibliographies 535
Guides
Anthropology 74
Confidentiality 67
Criminology 192
Drug abuse 500
Ethics 67
Families 222
Informed consent 67
Internal migration 262
Migrants 262
Migration 262
Population 74
Privacy 67
Rural social welfare 579
Social change 262
Social control 67
Social sciences 74
Sociology 74
Spouse abuse 449
Volunteerism 67
Handbooks
Acculturation 68
Elderly 335, 338
Migration 68
Small groups 70
Social disorganization

68
Social organization 68
Socialization 137
Urban affairs 68
Immigration
Abstracts 247
Indexes 139
Informed consent
Guides 67
Internal migration
Guides 262
Interpersonal relations
Bibliographies 535
Juvenile delinquency
Abstracts 577
Mental health
Abstracts 577
Bibliographies 563
Migrants
Guides 262
Migration
Guides 262
Handbooks 68
Organizations
Directories 13, 572
Population
Guides 74
Poverty
Bibliographies 509, 535
Research guides 509
Prisons
Bibliographies 561
Privacy
Guides 67
Quantitative methods
Bibliographies 178
Research guides
Criminology 198
Poverty 509
Research methods
Bibliographies 535
Rituals
Bibliographies 95
Rural social welfare
Guides 579
Sexuality
Bibliographies 465
Small groups
Handbooks 70
Social change
Bibliographies 535
Guides 262
Social control
Guides 67
Social disorganization
Handbooks 68
Social indicators
Abstracts 577
Social organization
Handbooks 68
Social sciences
Guides 74
Social services
Abstracts 577
Social systems
Abstracts 577
Social welfare
Directories 572
Social work
Abstracts 584
Bibliographies 578
Socialization
Handbooks 137
Sociology
Guides 74
Spouse abuse
Guides 449
Suicide
Bibliographies 207
Survey methods
Bibliographies 535
Television
Bibliographies 518
Urban affairs
Directories 311
Handbooks 68
Volunteerism
Guides 67
Youth
Abstracts 584

SOCIAL ROLE LOSS

RT Alienation
RT Anomie
RT Social isolation
RT Social roles

Elderly
Bibliographies 326

SOCIAL ROLES

SN Expected actions performed in social situations
UF Roles
NT Family roles
NT Sex roles
NT Work roles
RT Role models

RT Social role loss
Arab women
Bibliographies 431
Asian women
Bibliographies 429, 434
Bibliographies
Arab women 431
Asian women 429, 434
Ethnic groups 351
Families 232, 238
Men 467
Research methods 221
Elderly
Handbooks 335
Ethnic groups
Bibliographies 351
Families 219
Bibliographies 232, 238
Women 238
Guides
Linguistics 91
Mental health 570
Police 491
Handbooks
Elderly 335
Small groups 70
Indexes
Women 420
Linguistics
Guides 91
Men
Bibliographies 467
Mental health
Guides 570
Police
Guides 491
Research methods
Bibliographies 221
Small groups
Handbooks 70
Women
Families 238
Indexes 420

SOCIAL SCIENCES

NT Anthropology
NT Demography
NT Gerontology
NT History
NT Sociology
Bibliographies 57
Death and dying 201
Elderly 321
Publications 149
Sex research 469
Soviet Union 46
Biographies
Directories 45
Book reviews
Indexes 25
Citations
Indexes 27
Death and dying
Bibliographies 201
Dictionaries 47-49, 58
Research methods 66
Directories
Biographies 45
Grants 15
Organizations 12, 13, 23
Proceedings 50
Publications 37, 41, 149
Research centers 21
Elderly
Bibliographies 321
Handbooks 335
Encyclopedias 51, 54
Grant recipients
Indexes 16
Grants
Directories 15
Guides 17
Guides 52, 59, 61
Grants 17
Publications 64
Publishing 53
Social research 74
Writing 53
Handbooks
Elderly 335
Research methods 69, 72, 75
Statistics (Soviet Union) 536
Indexes 28
Book reviews 25
Citations 27
Grant recipients 16
Statistics (International) 159
Statistics (U.S.) 159
Women 420
Organizations
Directories 12, 13, 23
Proceedings
Directories 50

Publications
 Bibliographies 149
 Directories 37, 41,
 149
 Guides 64
Publishing
 Guides 53
Research centers
 Directories 21
Research guides 63
 Statistics (Interna-
 tional) 171
Research methods
 Handbooks 69, 72, 75
Sex research
 Bibliographies 469
Social research
 Guides 74
Soviet Union
 Bibliographies 46
Statistics (Internation-
 al)
 Indexes 159
 Research guides 171
Statistics (Soviet
 Union)
 Handbooks 536
Statistics (U.S.)
 Indexes 159
Women
 Indexes 420
Writing
 Guides 53

SOCIAL SCIENTISTS

 NT Anthropologists
 NT Sociologists
 Biographies 54

SOCIAL SERVICES

 UF Human services
 NT Child care
 RT Assistance programs
 RT Social welfare
 Abstracts
 Social research 577
 Urban affairs 309,
 312
 Alcoholism
 Handbooks 576
 Almanacs
 Statistics (Great
 Britain) 155
 Asian-Americans

 Guides 360
Australia
 Guides 545
Bibliographies
 Gerontology 332
 Information sources
 316
 Poverty 514
 Refugees 375
 Youth 448
Child abuse
 Guides 443
Directories 316
 Family planning 418
 Organizations 42,
 424, 581
 Organizations (Volun-
 tary) 571
 Rape 418
 Research centers 21
 Spouse abuse 418
 Women 418
Drug abuse
 Handbooks 576
Elderly
 Handbooks 576
Encyclopedias
 Organizations 580
Families
 Guides 229
 Handbooks 576
Family planning
 Directories 418
Gerontology
 Bibliographies 332
Guides
 Asian-Americans 360
 Australia 545
 Child abuse 443
 Families 229
 Rural social welfare
 579
 Statistics (Great
 Britain) 167
Handbooks
 Alcoholism 576
 Drug abuse 576
 Elderly 576
 Families 576
 Mental health 576
 Youth 576
Indexes
 Statistics (Interna-
 tional) 159
 Statistics (U.S.) 159
Information sources

Bibliographies 316
Mental health
Handbooks 576
Municipalities
Statistics (U.S.) 38
Organizations
Directories 42, 424, 581
Encyclopedias 580
Organizations (Voluntary)
Directories 571
Poverty
Bibliographies 514
Rape
Directories 418
Research centers
Directories 21
Rural social welfare
Guides 579
Social research
Abstracts 577
Spouse abuse
Directories 418
Statistics (Great Britain)
Almanacs 155
Guides 167
Statistics (International)
Indexes 159
Statistics (U.S.)
Indexes 159
Municipalities 38
Urban affairs
Abstracts 309, 312
Women
Directories 418
Youth
Bibliographies 448
Handbooks 576

SOCIAL STATUS

NT Marital status
RT Social mobility
American Indians
Bibliographies 275, 564
Arab women
Bibliographies 431, 437
Asian women
Bibliographies 429, 434
Bibliographies
American Indians 275, 564
Arab women 431, 437
Asian women 429, 434
Caribbean women 436
Chinese women 433
Ethnic groups 352
Irish-Americans 368
Mexican-Americans 387
Poverty 505
Urban affairs 546
Women 404, 413, 414, 417, 432
Caribbean women
Bibliographies 436
Chinese women
Bibliographies 433
Directories
Organizations 424
Elderly
Handbooks 335
Ethnic groups
Bibliographies 352
Guides
Mental health 570
Handbooks
Elderly 335
Indexes
Public opinion 528
Irish-Americans
Bibliographies 368
Mental health
Guides 570
Mexican-Americans
Bibliographies 387
Organizations
Directories 424
Poverty
Bibliographies 505
Public opinion
Indexes 528
Urban affairs
Bibliographies 546
Women
Bibliographies 404, 413, 414, 417, 432
World development 416
World development
Women 416

SOCIAL STRATIFICATION

SN Process of ranking of social status levels
BT Social organization
RT Social classes

RT Social inequality
Asian women
Bibliographies 429
Bibliographies 151, 529
Asian women 429
Ethnicity 110
Fertility 263
Minority groups 147
Research methods 147
Social conflict 147
Elderly
Handbooks 335
Ethnicity
Bibliographies 110
Fertility
Bibliographies 263
Handbooks 138
Elderly 335
Indexes 126
Minority groups
Bibliographies 147
Research methods
Bibliographies 147
Social anthropology
Handbooks 94
Social conflict
Bibliographies 147

SOCIAL STRUCTURES

SN Interrelated roles and statuses in society
BT Social systems
NT Family structures
RT Social institutions
RT Social networks
RT Structural functionalism
Abstracts 190
Asian-Americans
Guides 360
Asian women
Bibliographies 429
Bibliographies 140, 153
Asian women 429
Ethnic groups (Canadian) 344
Fertility 263
Italian-Americans 369
Latin America 56
Countries of the world
Guides 319
Encyclopedias
Ethnic groups 353
Ethnography 115
Ethnic groups
Encyclopedias 353
Ethnic groups (Canadian)
Bibliographies 344
Ethnography
Encyclopedias 115
Fertility
Bibliographies 263
Guides
Asian-Americans 360
Countries of the world 319
Migration 246
Handbooks
Social anthropology 94
Indexes 148, 193
Italian-Americans
Bibliographies 369
Latin America
Bibliographies 56
Migration
Guides 246
Social anthropology
Handbooks 94

SOCIAL SUPPORT

RT Assistance programs
RT Support groups
Elderly
Handbooks 335
Social change
Bibliographies 533

SOCIAL SUPPORT GROUPS

See Support groups

SOCIAL SYSTEMS

SN Two or more persons whose interaction has a common focus
NT Cultural areas
NT Prison systems
NT Social structures
Social research
Abstracts 577

SOCIAL THEORY

NT Sociological theory
Bibliographies
Ethnic groups 351
Ethnic relations 397

Race relations 397
Suicide 209
Ethnic groups
Bibliographies 351
Ethnic relations
Bibliographies 397
Guides 59
Sociology of aging 182
Handbooks
Socialization 137
Indexes 139
Race relations
Bibliographies 397
Socialization
Handbooks 137
Sociology of aging
Guides 182
Suicide
Bibliographies 209

SOCIAL TRENDS

UF Sociocultural patterns
UF Trends
NT Baby boom
NT Brain drain
RT Social patterns
Bibliographies
Families 232
Families
Bibliographies 232
Guides
Poverty 506
Population
Social characteristics 507
Statistics (Latin America) 251
Poverty
Guides 506
Statistics (U.S.) 507
Social characteristics
Population 507
Statistics (Latin America)
Population 251
Statistics (U.S.)
Poverty 507

SOCIAL VALUES

SN Standards of social interaction regarded as important by group members
RT Belief systems
Bibliographies
Social mobility 147
Caribbean women 436
Indexes
Public opinion 523, 528

SOCIAL WELFARE

UF Public welfare
NT Child welfare
NT Criminal justice
NT Mental health
NT Rural social welfare
NT Social work
RT Assistance programs
RT Social services
Abstracts 510
Almanacs
Women 422
Asian-Americans
Guides 360
Asian women
Bibliographies 434
Australia
Guides 545
Bibliographies 186
Asian women 434
Black-Americans 582
Death and dying 204
Elderly 340, 582
Ethnic groups 351
Families 582
History 582
Jews 228
Juvenile delinquency 582
Poverty 582
Social policy 543
South Asia 79
Theses 150
Youth 582
Black-Americans
Bibliographies 582
Death and dying
Bibliographies 204
Dictionaries 305
Directories
International grants 20
Organizations 572
Publications 37, 41
Social research 572
Urban affairs 301

Elderly
  Bibliographies 340, 582
Encyclopedias
  Organizations 580
Ethnic groups
  Bibliographies 351
Families
  Bibliographies 582
Guides 52
  Asian-Americans 360
  Australia 545
  Statistics (Great Britain) 167
  Urban affairs 306
Handbooks 576
History
  Bibliographies 582
Indexes 26
  Women 420
International grants
  Directories 20
Jews
  Bibliographies 228
Juvenile delinquency
  Bibliographies 582
Organizations
  Directories 572
  Encyclopedias 580
Poverty
  Bibliographies 582
Publications
  Directories 37, 41
Research guides
  Statistics (International) 171
Social policy
  Bibliographies 543
Social research
  Directories 572
South Asia
  Bibliographies 79
Statistics (Great Britain)
  Guides 167
Statistics (International)
  Research guides 171
  Yearbooks 32, 40
Theses
  Bibliographies 150
Urban affairs
  Directories 301
  Guides 306
Women
  Almanacs 422
  Indexes 420
Yearbooks
  Statistics (International) 32, 40
Youth
  Bibliographies 582

SOCIAL WORK

BT Social welfare
NT Social casework
NT Social group work
Abstracts 190
  Social research 584
Alcoholism
  Bibliographies 483
Bibliographies 57
  Alcoholism 483
  Child abuse 578
  Drug abuse 578
  Elderly 512, 513
  Ethnic groups 578
  Ethnicity 512, 513
  Families 512, 513, 578
  Great Britain 544
  Handicapped 578
  Mental health 578
  Minority groups 512, 513
  Poverty 512, 513
  Rural poverty 512, 513
  Social change 512, 513
  Social planning 512, 513
  Social research 578
  Urban poverty 512, 513
Canadian organizations
  Directories 11
Child abuse
  Bibliographies 578
Crime
  Encyclopedias 573
Dictionaries 49
Directories
  Canadian organizations 11
  Organizations 424
  Organizations (Voluntary) 571
  Proceedings 50
Drug abuse
  Bibliographies 578

Encyclopedias 573
Elderly
Bibliographies 512, 513
Encyclopedias 573
Encyclopedias
Crime 573
Drug abuse 573
Elderly 573
Families 573
Juvenile delinquency 573
Mental health 573
Minority groups 573
Poverty 573
Statistics (U.S.) 573
Youth 573
Ethnic groups
Bibliographies 578
Ethnicity
Bibliographies 512, 513
Families
Bibliographies 512, 513, 578
Encyclopedias 573
Great Britain
Bibliographies 544
Handbooks 576
Handicapped
Bibliographies 578
Indexes 551
Women 420
Juvenile delinquency
Encyclopedias 573
Mental health
Bibliographies 578
Encyclopedias 573
Minority groups
Bibliographies 512, 513
Encyclopedias 573
Organizations
Directories 424
Organizations (Voluntary)
Directories 571
Poverty
Bibliographies 512, 513
Encyclopedias 573
Proceedings
Directories 50
Rural poverty
Bibliographies 512, 513
Social change
Bibliographies 512, 513
Social planning
Bibliographies 512, 513
Social research
Abstracts 584
Bibliographies 578
Statistics (U.S.)
Encyclopedias 573
Urban poverty
Bibliographies 512, 513
Women
Indexes 420
Youth
Encyclopedias 573

SOCIAL WORK EDUCATION

BT Education
Bibliographies
Countries of the world 583
Field instruction 583
Minority groups 583

SOCIAL WORK PROGRAMS

Directories 586

SOCIAL WORK (RURAL)

See Rural social welfare

SOCIALIZATION

SN Process of learning the values and norms of a social group
UF Social development
RT Acculturation
RT Assimilation
Abstracts 190
Women 421
Adoption
Bibliographies 234
Adults
Handbooks 137
Anthropology
Bibliographies 87
Bibliographies 224, 225, 227
Adoption 234
Anthropology 87

Black-Americans 281
Communal living 304
Families 235
Latin American women 435
Mental health 563
Mental retardation 568
Race relations 393
Sex research 469
Sex roles 466
Social indicators 538
Television 518
Urban affairs 313
Women 403, 404, 413, 414, 417, 419, 426, 457
Youth 218
Black-Americans
Bibliographies 281
Communal living
Bibliographies 304
Families
Bibliographies 235
Guides 222
Guides
Families 222
Linguistics 91
Handbooks 138
Adults 137
Sex roles 137
Social research 137
Social theory 137
Youth 137
Indexes 148, 193
Theses 152
Latin American women
Bibliographies 435
Linguistics
Guides 91
Mental health
Bibliographies 563
Mental retardation
Bibliographies 568
Race relations
Bibliographies 393
Sex research
Bibliographies 469
Sex roles
Bibliographies 466
Handbooks 137
Social research
Handbooks 137
Social theory
Handbooks 137
Social indicators
Bibliographies 538
Television
Bibliographies 518
Theses
Indexes 152
Urban affairs
Bibliographies 313
Women
Abstracts 421
Bibliographies 403, 404, 413, 414, 417, 419, 426, 457
Youth
Bibliographies 218
Handbooks 137

SOCIALLY DISADVANTAGED

SN Those with low societal status for reasons of race, sex, economics, education, disabilities, etc.
UF Disadvantaged
RT Social inequality
RT Social status
Bibliographies 508

SOCIETAL CHANGE

See Social change

SOCIETAL DEVELOPMENT

NT Community development
NT Development planning
NT World development
Elderly
Handbooks 335

SOCIOCULTURAL PATTERNS

See Social trends

SOCIOLINGUISTICS

SN Study of language in society
BT Linguistics
RT Slang
Handbooks 120
Hispanics
Guides 392
South Asia
Bibliographies 79

SOCIOLOGICAL RESEARCH

BT Social research
RT Field research
Handbooks
Africa 136
Asia 136
Eastern Europe 136
Northern Europe 136
Southern Europe 136
Western Europe 136

SOCIOLOGICAL THEORISTS

BT Sociologists
Bibliographies 530

SOCIOLOGICAL THEORY

BT Social theory
NT Durkheimian school
NT Structural functionalism
Bibliographies 143
Durkheimian school 131
Soviet Union 46
Suicide 200
Dictionaries 142
Marxism 133

SOCIOLOGISTS

BT Social scientists
NT Sociological theorists
Biographies 51, 54

SOCIOLOGISTS (AMERICAN)

Directories 130

SOCIOLOGY

BT Social sciences
NT Applied sociology
NT Economic sociology
NT Mathematical sociology
NT Medical sociology
NT Political sociology
NT Radical sociology
NT Rural sociology
NT Social psychology
NT Sociology of aging
NT Sociology of death
NT Sociology of education
NT Sociology of human fertility
NT Sociology of knowledge
NT Sociology of law
NT Sociology of organizations
NT Sociology of poverty
NT Sociology of religion
NT Sociology of sciences
NT Sociology of the family
NT Urban sociology
Abstracts 190
Urban affairs 312
Africa
Bibliographies 318
Alcoholism
Bibliographies 496
American Indians
Indexes 272
Bibliographies
Africa 318
Alcoholism 496
Black-Americans
Divorce 212
Drug abuse 496, 499
Elderly 321
Ethnicity 110
Filipino-Americans 117
Homosexuality 458, 460
Incest 451
Marihuana 503
Prostitution 459
Publications 149
Sex research 469
Sexuality 465
Soviet Union 46, 153
Suicide 210
Theses 150
Urban affairs 303
Women 404, 406, 408, 410, 413, 414, 425, 426
Biographies
Directories 45
Black-Americans
Bibliographies 283
Encyclopedias 292
Citations
Indexes 27
Cuban-Americans

Guides 392
Dictionaries 47, 48, 58, 128, 141, 142, 145, 146
Graduate departments 135
Quotations 129
Directories
Biographies 45
Grants 15
International organizations 24
Organizations 12, 424
Proceedings 50
Publications 37, 41, 149
Research centers 21
Divorce
Bibliographies 212
Drug abuse
Bibliographies 496, 499
Elderly
Bibliographies 321
Encyclopedias 51, 54, 132, 141
Black-Americans 292
Organizations 14
Ethnicity
Bibliographies 110
Faculty
Graduate departments 135
Filipino-Americans
Bibliographies 117
Graduate departments
Dictionaries 135
Faculty 135
Special programs 135
Grant recipients
Indexes 16
Grants
Directories 15
Guides 17
Guides 52, 59, 61, 62
Cuban-Americans 392
Grants 17
Mexican-Americans 392
Publications 64, 125
Puerto Ricans 392
Research methods 71
Social research 74
Handbooks 138, 197
Research methods 69, 75, 154
Homosexuality
Bibliographies 458, 460
Incest
Bibliographies 451
Indexes 28, 126, 139, 148
American Indians 272
Citations 27
Grant recipients 16
Theses 152
International organizations
Directories 24
Marihuana
Bibliographies 503
Mexican-Americans
Guides 392
Organizations
Directories 12, 424
Encyclopedias 14
Yearbooks 44
Proceedings
Directories 50
Prostitution
Bibliographies 459
Publications
Bibliographies 149
Directories 37, 41, 149
Guides 64, 125
Puerto Ricans
Guides 392
Quotations
Dictionaries 129
Research centers
Directories 21
Research guides 63
Research methods
Guides 71
Handbooks 69, 75, 154
Sex research
Bibliographies 469
Sexuality
Bibliographies 465
Social research
Guides 74
Soviet Union
Bibliographies 46, 153
Special programs
Graduate departments 135
Suicide
Bibliographies 210
Theses
Bibliographies 150

Indexes 152
Urban affairs
Abstracts 312
Bibliographies 303
Women
Bibliographies 404, 406, 408, 410, 413, 414, 425, 426
Yearbooks
Organizations 44

SOCIOLOGY, EDUCATIONAL

See Sociology of education

SOCIOLOGY, MATHEMATICAL

See Mathematical sociology

SOCIOLOGY OF AGING

BT Sociology
RT Elderly
RT Gerontology
Guides
Research methods 182
Social inequality 182
Social institutions 182
Social problems 182
Social theory 182

SOCIOLOGY OF DEATH

BT Sociology
RT Death and dying
Bibliographies 205

SOCIOLOGY OF EDUCATION

UF Educational sociology
UF Sociology, educational
BT Sociology
Bibliographies 180
Black-Americans 183
Desegregation 183
Minority groups 183
Black-Americans
Bibliographies 183
Desegregation
Bibliographies 183
Guides 62, 180
Handbooks 176
Indexes 148
Minority groups
Bibliographies 183
Research centers
Directories 21

SOCIOLOGY OF HUMAN FERTILITY

BT Sociology
Bibliographies 263

SOCIOLOGY OF KNOWLEDGE

BT Sociology
Encyclopedias 54

SOCIOLOGY OF LAW

BT Sociology
Bibliographies 186
Encyclopedias 54

SOCIOLOGY OF MEDICINE

See Medical sociology

SOCIOLOGY OF ORGANIZATIONS

UF Organizational sociology
BT Sociology
Encyclopedias 54

SOCIOLOGY OF POVERTY

BT Sociology
RT Poverty
Bibliographies 184

SOCIOLOGY OF RELIGION

BT Sociology
RT Religion
Bibliographies 177, 181
Encyclopedias 54
Guides 62
Indexes 148
Research centers
Directories 21

SOCIOLOGY OF SCIENCES

BT Sociology
Bibliographies 185
Guides 62

Indexes 148
Research centers
Directories 21

SOCIOLOGY OF THE FAMILY

BT Sociology
Guides 62
Indexes 148

SOCIOMETRY

SN Study of group relations and structures in terms of personal preferences and degrees of attraction
RT Group dynamics
RT Social groups
RT Social interaction
RT Social networks
Encyclopedias 54
Research methods
Handbooks 69

SOCIOPATHY

SN Socially deviant behavior that is psychologically normal
RT Antisocial behavior
RT Deviant behavior
Indexes 193

SOUTH AFRICA

BT Africa
Indexes
Anthropology 83
Ethnicity 83

SOUTH AMERICA

RT Latin America
Bibliographies
Criminal justice 553
Ethnography 112

SOUTH ASIA

BT Asia
Bibliographies
Archaeology 78
Cultural anthropology 78, 79
Physical anthropology 78
Social anthropology 78, 79
Social welfare 79
Sociolinguistics 79
Urbanization 79

SOUTHERN EUROPE

BT Europe
RT Eastern Europe
RT Northern Europe
RT Western Europe
Sociological research
Handbooks 136

SOUTHERN WHITES

BT Racial groups
Bibliographies
Cultures 516
Folklore 516
Migration 516
Poverty 516
Race relations 516
Urbanization 516
Women 516

SOVIET UNION

BT Countries of the world
Bibliographies
Social sciences 46
Sociological theory 46
Sociology 46, 153
Demography
Handbooks 114
Dictionaries
Ethnic groups 116
Ethnography 116
Nationalities 116
Population 116
Ethnic groups
Dictionaries 116
Handbooks 116
Ethnography
Dictionaries 116
Handbooks 116
Handbooks
Demography 114
Ethnic groups 116
Ethnography 116

Immigration 114
Migration 114
Nationalities 114, 116
Population 114, 116
Statistics 114
Urbanization 114
Immigration
Handbooks 114
Migration
Handbooks 114
Nationalities
Dictionaries 116
Handbooks 114, 116
Population
Dictionaries 116
Handbooks 114, 116
Social sciences
Bibliographies 46
Sociological theory
Bibliographies 46
Sociology
Bibliographies 46, 153
Statistics
Handbooks 114
Urbanization
Handbooks 114

SPANISH-AMERICANS

BT Ethnic groups
Bibliographies 345

SPECIAL PROGRAMS

RT Social programs
Sociology
Graduate departments 135

SPOUSE ABUSE

UF Battered women
UF Wife abuse
BT Family violence
RT Physical abuse
Almanacs
Women 422
Appalachia
Women 428
Bibliographies 237
Women 412, 457
Directories
Organizations 581
Social services 418
Guides
Organizations 35, 449
Social research 449
Organizations
Directories 581
Guides 35, 449
Social research
Guides 449
Social services
Directories 418
Women
Almanacs 422
Appalachia 428
Bibliographies 412, 457

STATISTICS

RT Censuses
RT Social indicators
Almanacs
Black-Americans 293
Bibliographies
Latin American women 435
Mexican-Americans 381, 383
Black-Americans
Almanacs 293
Handbooks 291
Criminology
Research guides 198
Death and dying
Guides 208
Divorce
Guides 214
Guides
Death and dying 208
Divorce 214
Handbooks
Black-Americans 291
Social indicators 536
Soviet Union 114
Indexes
Public opinion 523, 528
Jewish-Americans
Yearbooks 359
Latin American women
Bibliographies 435
Leisure 521
Marriage
Yearbooks 32
Mexican-Americans
Bibliographies 381, 383

Research guides 386
Migration 164
Population
Social trends 251
Public opinion 524-527
Indexes 523, 528
Research guides
Criminology 198
Mexican-Americans 386
Soviet Union
Handbooks 114
Women
Black-Americans 409
Yearbooks
Jewish-Americans 359

STATISTICS (CANADA)

Crime 165
Elderly 165
Families 165
Leisure 165
Population 165
Almanacs 29
Urban affairs 165

STATISTICS (EASTERN EUROPE)

Handbooks
Occupations 162
Population 162
Social classes 162
Social indicators 162

STATISTICS (EUROPE)

Population 539
Social conditions 539
Social indicators 539

STATISTICS (GREAT BRITAIN)

Almanacs
Births 155
Crime 155
Deaths 155
Divorce 155
Families 155
Marriage 155
Migration 155
Population 155
Social services 155
Guides
Crime 167
Population 167
Social services 167
Social welfare 167

STATISTICS (INTERNATIONAL)

Abortion
Indexes 159
Yearbooks 160
Almanacs
Population 43
Bibliographies
Euthanasia 206
Suicide 210
Births
Indexes 159
Women 405
Yearbooks 32, 160, 170
Crime
Indexes 159
Yearbooks 40
Deaths
Indexes 159
Women 405
Yearbooks 32, 170
Demography
Yearbooks 160
Divorce
Yearbooks 160
Elderly
Handbooks 338
Ethnic groups
Yearbooks 32
Euthanasia
Bibliographies 206
Families
Guides 229
Fertility
Women 405
Yearbooks 160
Guides
Families 229
Handbooks
Elderly 338
Social indicators 542
Indexes
Abortion 159
Births 159
Crime 159
Deaths 159
Population 159
Social sciences 159
Social services 159
Suicide 159
Marriage
Women 405
Yearbooks 160

Migration
  Women 405
Mortality
  Yearbooks 160
Population
  Almanacs 43
  Indexes 159
  Research guides 171
  Yearbooks 32, 40, 160, 170
Research guides
  Population 171
  Social sciences 171
  Social welfare 171
Social indicators 511
  Handbooks 542
Social sciences
  Indexes 159
  Research guides 171
Social services
  Indexes 159
Social welfare
  Research guides 171
  Yearbooks 32, 40
Suicide
  Bibliographies 210
  Indexes 159
Women
  Births 405
  Deaths 405
  Fertility 405
  Marriage 405
  Migration 405
Yearbooks
  Abortion 160
  Births 32, 160, 170
  Crime 40
  Deaths 32, 170
  Demography 160
  Divorce 160
  Ethnic groups 32
  Fertility 160
  Marriage 160
  Mortality 160
  Organizations 44
  Population 32, 40, 160, 170
  Social welfare 32, 40

STATISTICS (LATIN AMERICA)

Social trends
  Population 251
Urbanization 251

STATISTICS (SOVIET UNION)

Handbooks
  Demography 536
  Occupations 162
  Populations 162
  Social classes 162
  Social indicators 162
  Social sciences 536

STATISTICS (U.S.)

Abortion
  Almanacs 43, 169
  Indexes 159
Abstracts
  Black-Americans 297
  Population 166
Almanacs
  Abortion 43, 169
  Births 43, 168, 169
  Crime 43, 168
  Deaths 43, 168, 169
  Divorce 43, 168, 169
  Drug abuse 43
  Families 43, 220
  Immigration 43
  Marriage 43, 168, 169
  Migration 169
  Population 43, 168, 169
American Indians
  Directories 161
  Women 409
Asian-Americans
  Women 409
Bibliographies
  Divorce 212, 213
  Suicide 209
Births 173
  Almanacs 43, 168, 169
  Cities 158
  Counties 158
  History 163
  Indexes 159
Black-Americans
  Abstracts 297
  Directories 161
  Urban affairs 9
  Women 409
Censuses
  Population 260, 261
Child abuse
  Guides 443
Chinese-Americans
  Directories 161
Cities
  Births 158

Crime 158
Deaths 158
Divorce 158
Families 158
Marriage 158
Population 158
Congressional districts
Demography 156
Population 156, 157
Racial composition 156
Social characteristics 157
Counties
Age composition 3
Births 158
Crime 158
Deaths 158
Divorce 158
Families 158
Marriage 158
Population 158
Population density 3
Racial composition 3
Crime
Almanacs 43, 168
Cities 158
Counties 158
Directories 161
Indexes 159
Women 409
Criminal justice
Encyclopedias 558
Guides 562
Deaths 173
Almanacs 43, 168, 169
Cities 158
Counties 158
History 163
Indexes 159
Demography
Congressional districts 156
Poverty 506
Directories
American Indians 161
Black-Americans 161
Chinese-Americans 161
Crime 161
Ethnic groups 161
Families 161
Filipino-Americans 161
Japanese-Americans 161
Local areas 161
Population 161
Puerto Ricans 161
Divorce 173, 540
Almanacs 43, 168, 169
Bibliographies 212, 213
Cities 158
Counties 158
History 163
Drug abuse
Almanacs 43
Elderly
Guides 330, 342
Municipalities 38
Urban affairs 9
Encyclopedias
Criminal justice 558
Social work 573
Ethnic groups
Directories 161
Families 164, 540
Almanacs 43, 220
Cities 158
Counties 158
Directories 161
Fertility 164, 173, 540
Women 409
Filipino-Americans
Directories 161
Guides
Child abuse 443
Criminal justice 562
Elderly 330, 342
Prisoners 555
Puerto Ricans 390
Handicapped
Municipalities 38
Hispanics
Women 409
History
Births 163
Crime 163
Deaths 163
Divorce 163
Marriage 163
Migration 163
Population 163
Immigration
Almanacs 43
Indexes
Abortion 159
Births 159
Crime 159
Deaths 159
Population 159

Social sciences 159
Social services 159
Suicide 159
Japanese-Americans
Directories 161
Leisure 540
Local areas
Directories 161
Marital status
Women 409
Marriage 173, 540
Almanacs 43, 168, 169
Cities 158
Counties 158
History 163
Migration 540
Almanacs 169
History 163
Minority groups
Municipalities 38
Mortality 173
Women 409
Municipalities
Elderly 38
Handicapped 38
Minority groups 38
Social services 38
Yearbooks 38
Natality 173
Population 164, 540
Abstracts 166
Almanacs 168, 169
Censuses 260, 261
Cities 158
Congressional districts 156, 157
Counties 158
Directories 161
History 163
Indexes 159
Social characteristics 507
Urban affairs 9
Population density
Counties 3
Poverty 164
Demography 506
Social trends 507
Women 409
Prisoners
Guides 555
Puerto Ricans
Guides 390
Puerto Rico
Directories 161
Racial composition
Congressional districts 156
Counties 3
Social characteristics
Congressional districts 157
Population 507
Social sciences
Indexes 159
Social services
Indexes 159
Municipalities 38
Social trends
Poverty 507
Social work
Encyclopedias 573
Suicide
Bibliographies 209
Indexes 159
Urban affairs
Black-Americans 9
Elderly 9
Population 9
Youth 9
Women
American Indians 409
Asian-Americans 409
Crime 409
Fertility 409
Hispanics 409
Marital status 409
Mortality 409
Poverty 409
Yearbooks
Municipalities 38
Youth
Urban affairs 9

STEPFAMILIES

SN Related individuals resulting from parental remarriage
BT Families
RT Foster families
RT One-parent families
RT Two-career families
Youth
Bibliographies 211

STEREOTYPES

BT Social attitudes
NT Sexual stereotypes
Sex roles
Bibliographies 470

Television
Elderly 520
Handicapped 520
Minority groups 520
Sexuality 520
Women 520

STIMULANTS

BT Drugs
NT Amphetamines
NT Cocaine
NT Tobacco
RT Depressants
RT Hallucinogens
RT Narcotics
RT Sedatives
Bibliographies 494, 495

STRUCTURAL ANTHROPOLOGY

UF Anthropology, structural
BT Anthropology
Handbooks 120

STRUCTURAL FUNCTIONALISM

BT Sociological theory
RT Durkheimian school
RT Social structures
RT Social systems
Indexes 139

SUBCULTURES

BT Cultures
RT Ethnicity
Dictionaries
Slang 490
Guides
Police 491
Slang 490

SUBURBS

RT Cities
RT Rural areas
Bibliographies
Migration 310
Population studies 310
Social factors 310
Urban affairs 300, 546

SUICIDE

RT Death and dying
RT Mortality
Alcohol
Bibliographies 200
Alcoholism
Bibliographies 209
American Indians
Bibliographies 278
Bibliographies 201, 205, 206
Alcohol 200
Alcoholism 209
American Indians 278
Drug abuse 200, 210
Elderly 210
Families 200
Interpersonal relations 210
Mental health 209, 563
Parent-child separation 230
Prevention 210
Social aggression 209
Social mobility 147
Social relations 209
Social research 207
Social theory 209
Sociological theory 200
Sociology 210
Statistics (International) 210
Statistics (U.S.) 209
Treatment 210
Women 412, 484
Youth 210
Crisis intervention
Directories 36
Death education
Guides 203
Directories
Crisis intervention 36
Drug abuse
Bibliographies 200, 210
Elderly
Bibliographies 210
Families
Bibliographies 200
Guides
Death education 203
Handbooks 202

Indexes
Statistics (International) 159
Statistics (U.S.) 159
Interpersonal relations
Bibliographies 210
Mental health
Bibliographies 209, 563
Parent-child separation
Bibliographies 230
Prevention
Bibliographies 210
Social aggression
Bibliographies 209
Social mobility
Bibliographies 147
Social relations
Bibliographies 209
Social research
Bibliographies 207
Social theory
Bibliographies 209
Sociological theory
Bibliographies 200
Sociology
Bibliographies 210
Statistics (International)
Bibliographies 210
Indexes 159
Statistics (U.S.)
Bibliographies 209
Indexes 159
Treatment
Bibliographies 210
Women
Bibliographies 412, 484
Youth
Bibliographies 210

SUICIDE PREVENTION

RT Assistance programs
RT Crisis intervention
Organizations
Guides 35

SUMMARIES

See Abstracts

SUPPORT GROUPS

UF Social support groups
RT Social networks
RT Social support
Mental health
Bibliographies 569

SURVEY METHODS

BT Research methods
RT Quantitative methods
Encyclopedias 54
Social research
Bibliographies 535

SWEDISH-AMERICANS

BT Ethnic groups
Almanacs 348
Bibliographies 361
Mental health 563

SWISS-AMERICANS

BT Ethnic groups
Bibliographies
Mental health 563

SYNOPSES

See Abstracts

TELEVISION

Bibliographies
Black-Americans 517
Families 518
Leisure 518
Sex roles 518
Social control 518
Social factors 518
Social research 518
Socialization 518
Violence 518
Youth 518
Black-Americans 517
Elderly
Stereotypes 520
Families
Bibliographies 518
Handicapped
Stereotypes 520
Leisure 521
Bibliographies 518
Minority groups
Stereotypes 520
Sex roles
Bibliographies 518

Sex stereotypes 520
Sex-typed behaviors 520
Sexuality
Stereotypes 520
Social control
Bibliographies 518
Social factors
Bibliographies 518
Social research
Bibliographies 518
Socialization
Bibliographies 518
Stereotypes
Elderly 520
Handicapped 520
Minority groups 520
Sexuality 520
Women 520
Violence
Bibliographies 518
Women
Stereotypes 520
Youth
Bibliographies 518

TERRORISM

BT Antisocial behavior
RT Social aggression
RT Violence
Bibliographies 489
Research guides 489

THERAPY

See Treatment

THESAURI

RT Dictionaries
RT Glossaries
RT Polyglots
Archaeology 106

THESES

UF Dissertations
RT Graduate departments
RT Social research
Bibliographies
Acculturation 92
Anthropology 92
Anthropometry 92
Archaeology 92
Criminology 150
Cultural anthropology 92
Demography 150
Ethnography 92
Ethnology 92
Gerontology 150
Juvenile delinquency 150
Physical anthropology 92
Social anthropology 92
Social organization 92
Social psychology 150
Social welfare 150
Sociology 150
Indexes
Poverty 152
Socialization 152
Sociology 152
Italian-Americans
Acculturation 370
Assimilation 370
Ethnicity 370
Immigration 370

THIRD WORLD

UF Developing nations
RT Countries of the world
Population
Guides 257

TOBACCO

BT Stimulants
Bibliographies 494, 495

TOWNS

See Cities

TOWNSHIPS

RT Local areas
RT Minor Civil Divisions
RT Municipalities
Atlases 172

TRANSPORTATION

Urban affairs
Bibliographies 313

TRANSRACIAL ADOPTIONS

  BT Adoptions
   Bibliographies 217, 234

TRANSSEXUALISM

  SN Sexual change through surgery
  BT Sexuality
  RT Homosexuality
  RT Sexual deviance
   Bibliographies 458

TRANSVESTISM

  SN Practice of dressing in the manner of the opposite sex
  RT Sexual deviance
   Bibliographies 458

TREATMENT

  UF Counseling
  UF Therapy
  RT Rehabilitation
   Alcoholism
     Bibliographies 477, 496
     Encyclopedias 482, 502
     Guides 478
     Social groups 482
   Bibliographies
     Alcoholism 477, 496
     Child abuse 237, 442
     Drug abuse 494-496, 501
     Families 574
     Incest 450
     Social group work 575
     Suicide 210
   Child abuse
     Bibliographies 237, 442
   Directories
     Mental health 567
     Rape 452
   Drug abuse
     Bibliographies 494-496, 501
     Encyclopedias 502
   Encyclopedias
     Alcoholism 482, 502
     Drug abuse 502
   Families
     Bibliographies 574
   Guides
     Alcoholism 478
   Incest
     Bibliographies 450
   Mental health
     Directories 567
   Organizations
     Guides 35
   Rape
     Directories 452
   Social group work
     Bibliographies 575
   Social groups
     Alcoholism 482
   Suicide
     Bibliographies 210

TRENDS

  See Social trends

TRIBAL GROUPS

  RT African cultures
  RT American Indians
  RT Blacks (African)
   Aborigines
     Guides 107
   Almanacs
     American Indians 267
   American Indians
     Almanacs 267
     Bibliographies 274
     Dictionaries 269
   Bibliographies
     American Indians 274
     Ethnography 111, 112
   Blacks (African)
     Bibliographies 77
   Dictionaries
     American Indians 269
   Ethnography
     Bibliographies 111, 112
   Guides
     Aborigines 107

TWO-CAREER FAMILIES

  UF Dual-career families
  BT Families
  RT Foster families
  RT One-parent families
  RT Step families
   Bibliographies 236

UKRAINIAN-AMERICANS

BT Ethnic groups
Bibliographies
Cultures 379
Ethnicity 379
Immigration 379
Social mobility 379

UNEMPLOYMENT

BT Social issues
Social change
Bibliographies 533

UNION LISTS

Family planning 264
Population periodicals 264

URBAN AFFAIRS

RT Cities
RT Urban communities
Abstracts
Crime 309, 312
Demography 312
Elderly 312
Handicapped 312
Social conditions 309
Social indicators 312
Social services 309, 312
Sociology 312
Women 312
Youth 312
American Indians
Bibliographies 564
Indexes 272
Anthropology
Bibliographies 303
Atlases
Black-Americans 9
Elderly 9
Population 9
Youth 9
Australia
Guides 545
Bibliographies
American Indians 564
Anthropology 303
Black-Americans 299, 300, 308, 541, 546
Crime 299, 300, 308, 541, 546
Desegregation 308
Discrimination 308
Education 313
Ethnic groups 300, 308, 546
Ethnicity 313
Families 315, 534
Industrialization 534
Interpersonal relations 299
Migration 541
Minority groups 308, 546
Modernization 534
Population 256, 541, 546
Poverty 299, 300, 514, 515
Privacy 315
Race relations 308
Racism 299
Religion 313
Riots 299, 308
Social behavior 315
Social classes 315
Social disorders 299
Social indicators 541
Social interaction 315
Social issues 534
Social life 308
Social policy 546
Social status 546
Socialization 313
Sociology 303
Suburbs 300, 546
Transportation 313
Urban sociology 300
Urbanization 300
Women 541
Youth 315
Black-Americans
Atlases 9
Bibliographies 299, 300, 308, 541, 546
Statistics (U.S.) 9
Community development
Guides 306
Crime
Abstracts 309, 312
Bibliographies 299, 300, 308, 541, 546
Directories 301
Guides 306
Demography
Abstracts 312

    Guides 306
  Desegregation
    Bibliographies 308
  Dictionaries 305
  Directories
    Crime 301
    Drug abuse 301
    Juvenile delinquency 301
    Minority groups 301
    Population 301
    Poverty 301
    Race relations 301
    Research centers 301, 311
    Social research 311
    Social welfare 301
  Discrimination
    Bibliographies 308
  Drug abuse
    Directories 301
  Education
    Bibliographies 313
  Elderly
    Abstracts 312
    Atlases 9
    Statistics (U.S.) 9
  Encyclopedias
    Population 302
  Ethnic groups
    Bibliographies 300, 308, 546
  Ethnicity
    Bibliographies 313
  Families
    Bibliographies 315, 534
  Guides 62
    Australia 545
    Community development 306
    Crime 306
    Demography 306
    Juvenile delinquency 306
    Latin America 306
    Migration 306
    Radical sociology 60
    Social change 306
    Social conditions 306
    Social issues 306
    Social welfare 306
  Handbooks
    Social research 68
  Handicapped
    Abstracts 312
  Indexes 26
    American Indians 272
  Industrialization
    Bibliographies 534
  Interpersonal relations
    Bibliographies 299
  Juvenile delinquency
    Directories 301
    Guides 306
  Latin America
    Guides 306
  Migration
    Guides 306
  Minority groups
    Bibliographies 308, 541, 546
    Directories 301
  Modernization
    Bibliographies 534
  Population
    Atlases 9
    Bibliographies 256, 541, 546
    Directories 301
    Encyclopedias 302
    Statistics (U.S.) 9
  Poverty
    Bibliographies 299, 300, 514, 515
    Directories 301
  Privacy
    Bibliographies 315
  Race relations
    Bibliographies 308
    Directories 301
  Racism
    Bibliographies 299
  Radical sociology
    Guides 60
  Religion
    Bibliographies 313
  Research centers
    Directories 301, 311
  Riots
    Bibliographies 299, 308
  Social behavior
    Bibliographies 315
  Social change
    Guides 306
  Social classes
    Bibliographies 315
  Social conditions
    Abstracts 309
    Guides 306
  Social disorders

Bibliographies 299
Social indicators
Abstracts 312
Bibliographies 541
Social interaction
Bibliographies 315
Social issues
Bibliographies 534
Guides 306
Social life
Bibliographies 308
Social policy
Bibliographies 546
Social research
Directories 311
Handbooks 68
Social services
Abstracts 309, 312
Social status
Bibliographies 546
Social welfare
Directories 301
Guides 306
Socialization
Bibliographies 313
Sociology
Abstracts 312
Bibliographies 303
Statistics (Canada) 165
Statistics (U.S.)
Black-Americans 9
Elderly 9
Population 9
Youth 9
Suburbs
Bibliographies 300, 546
Transportation
Bibliographies 313
Urban sociology
Bibliographies 300
Urbanization
Bibliographies 300
Women
Abstracts 312
Bibliographies 541
Youth
Abstracts 312
Atlases 9
Bibliographies 315
Statistics (U.S.) 9

URBAN ANTHROPOLOGY

UF Anthropology, urban
BT Anthropology
RT Village studies
Cross-cultural studies
Bibliographies 84
Handbooks 120

URBAN BEHAVIOR

BT Social behavior
RT Collective behavior
RT Group behavior
Encyclopedias 121

URBAN COMMUNITIES

RT Cities
RT Suburbs
RT Urban affairs
Bibliographies
Black-Americans 314
Crime 314
Cultures 314
Elderly 314
Ethnicity 314
Population 314
Poverty 314
Publications 149
Race relations 393
Racial segregation 314
Social change 314
Social classes 314
Social indicators 314
Social issues 314
Directories
Publications 149

URBAN ENVIRONMENT

Bibliographies 313

URBAN POVERTY

BT Poverty
RT Rural poverty
RT Slums
Bibliographies
Social work 512, 513

URBAN SOCIOLOGY

BT Sociology
NT Human ecology
Bibliographies
Urban affairs 300
Encyclopedias 54
Indexes 139

UF-Used For, BT-Broader Term, NT-Narrower Term, RT-Related Term

Research centers
Directories 21

URBAN STUDIES

RT Family studies
African women
Bibliographies 427

URBANIZATION

BT Social change
RT Industrialization
RT Modernization
RT Population density
Africa
Bibliographies 318
American Indians
Bibliographies 278, 279, 564
Arabs
Bibliographies 377
Bibliographies 534
Africa 318
American Indians 278, 279, 564
Arabs 377
Black-Americans 290
Cultural life 317
Demography 303
Fertility 317
Great Britain 144
Mexican-Americans 387
Migration 303, 317
Minority groups 346
Mortality 317
Population 303, 317
Slums 317
Social life 317
Southern whites 516
Women 415
Black-Americans
Bibliographies 290
Cultural life
Bibliographies 317
Demography
Bibliographies 303
Encyclopedias 302
Fertility
Bibliographies 317
Great Britain
Bibliographies 144
Guides 306
Migration 246
Handbooks
Soviet Union 114
Mexican-Americans
Bibliographies 387
Migration
Bibliographies 303, 317
Guides 246
Minority groups
Bibliographies 346
Mortality
Bibliographies 317
Population
Bibliographies 303, 317
Slums
Bibliographies 317
Social life
Bibliographies 317
South Asia
Bibliographies 79
Southern whites
Bibliographies 516
Soviet Union
Handbooks 114
Statistics (Latin America) 251
Urban affairs
Bibliographies 300
Women
Bibliographies 415

VETERANS

BT Social groups
RT Military (U.S.)
Social programs
Directories 33

VICTIMIZATION

RT Physical abuse
Elderly
Guides 320

VICTIMS

RT Child abuse
RT Spouse abuse
Rape
Bibliographies 453
Handbooks 455

VIETNAMESE-AMERICANS

BT Ethnic groups
Bibliographies
Acculturation 378

Adoption 217

VILLAGE STUDIES

RT Cultural anthropology
RT Ethnography
RT Urban anthropology
Countries of the world
Guides 319

VIOLENCE

BT Antisocial behavior
NT Family violence
RT Social aggression
RT Terrorism
RT Warfare
Television
Bibliographies 518

VOCATIONS

See Occupations

VOLUNTEERISM

RT Assistance programs
Guides
Organizations 35
Social research 67

WARFARE

RT Military (U.S.)
RT Social conflict
RT Violence
Bibliographies
Demographic factors 100
Social factors 100

WESTERN EUROPE

BT Europe
RT Eastern Europe
RT Northern Europe
RT Southern Europe
Sociological research
Handbooks 136

WHITE COLLAR CRIME

BT Crime
NT Computer crime
Bibliographies 191

WIDOWHOOD

RT Bereavement
RT Death and dying
Bibliographies 432
Bereavement 199
Elderly 326, 341
One-parent families 216
Sex roles 199
Guides
Death education 203

WIFE ABUSE

See Spouse abuse

WINE

BT Alcohol
RT Beer
Encyclopedias 482

WOMEN

UF Females
BT Social groups
NT African women
NT Arab women
NT Asian women
NT Caribbean women
NT Chinese women
NT Indian women
NT Latin American women
NT Working women
RT Lesbians
RT Motherhood
Aborigines
Guides 107
Abortion
Abstracts 421
Almanacs 422
Bibliographies 419, 423, 432
Encyclopedias 407
Social characteristics 400
Abstracts
Abortion 421
Families 421
Family planning 421
Mental health 421
Sex roles 421
Sexuality 421
Socialization 421
Urban affairs 312

Africa
  Bibliographies 404
Alcoholism
  Bibliographies 412, 477, 484
Almanacs 220
  Abortion 422
  Criminal justice 422
  Divorce 422
  Families 422
  Family planning 422
  Homosexuals 422
  Incest 422
  Marriage 422
  Pornography 422
  Poverty 422
  Prostitution 422
  Rape 422
  Sex discrimination 422
  Sex roles 422
  Sexuality 422
  Social welfare 422
  Spouse abuse 422
Ambition
  Bibliographies 411
American Indians
  Bibliographies 275, 406, 410
  Indexes 272
  Statistics (U.S.) 409
Anthropology
  Bibliographies 404, 406, 408, 410, 413, 414, 425, 426
  Encyclopedias 407
  Indexes 420
Appalachia
  Child abuse 428
  Folklore 428
  Social life 428
  Spouse abuse 428
Arabs
  Bibliographies 377
Archaeology
  Bibliographies 406
  Indexes 420
Asian-Americans
  Bibliographies 406
  Statistics (U.S.) 409
Bibliographies 151
  Abortion 419, 423, 432
  Africa 404
  Alcoholism 412, 477, 484
  Ambition 411
  American Indians 275, 406, 410
  Anthropology 404, 406, 408, 410, 413, 414, 425, 426
  Arabs 377
  Archaeology 406
  Asian-Americans 406
  Black-Americans 283, 289, 296, 404, 406, 410, 423, 426, 432
  Child abuse 457
  Child care 408, 417, 432
  Communal living 304
  Crime 408, 432
  Criminology 425
  Cross-cultural studies 419
  Deaths 484
  Demography 406
  Deviant behavior 484
  Discrimination 417
  Divorce 212, 413, 414, 419, 432
  Drug abuse 408, 412, 499
  Elderly 341, 426
  Ethnic groups 408, 410, 417
  Ethnicity 406
  Ethnology 406
  Families 238, 404, 408, 410, 413-415, 417, 419, 423, 426
  Family planning 403, 413, 414, 432
  Family violence 457
  Fertility 403, 415, 423
  Hispanics 406, 410
  Homosexuality 404, 408, 419, 425, 426
  Immigrants 432
  Incest 457
  Lesbianism 412
  Marital status 417
  Marriage 404, 408, 410, 413, 414, 419, 423, 432
  Mental health 412
  Mexican-Americans 382, 383
  Migration 403
  Minority groups 406

Occupations 417
Population 256
Pornography 457
Poverty 412, 417, 432
Prostitution 419, 425, 432
Racial groups 410
Rape 408, 425, 432, 457
Role models 411
Sex discrimination 412
Sex roles 404, 408, 410-414, 417, 423, 425, 426, 432, 457, 470
Sexual stereotypes 423
Sexuality 404, 413, 414, 426, 474
Social casework 585
Social change 127, 412
Social characteristics 406
Social classes 404, 413, 414
Social conflict 412
Social groups 417
Social life 413, 414, 432, 484
Social policy 412
Social status 404, 413, 414, 417, 432
Socialization 403, 404, 413, 414, 417, 419, 426, 457
Sociology 404, 406, 408, 410, 413, 414, 425, 426
Southern whites 516
Spouse abuse 412, 457
Suicide 412, 484
Urban affairs 541
Urbanization 415

Births
Statistics (International) 405

Black-Americans
Bibliographies 283, 289, 296, 404, 406, 410, 423, 426, 432
Encyclopedias 280
Handbooks 291
Statistics (U.S.) 409

Child abuse
Appalachia 428
Bibliographies 457

Child care
Bibliographies 408, 417, 432

Communal living
Bibliographies 304

Crime
Bibliographies 408, 432
Statistics (U.S.) 409

Criminal justice
Almanacs 422

Criminology
Bibliographies 425

Cross-cultural studies
Bibliographies 419

Deaths
Bibliographies 484
Statistics (International) 405

Demography
Bibliographies 406

Deviant behavior
Bibliographies 484

Directories
Organizations 255, 424
Organizations (Elderly) 339
Social services 418

Discrimination
Bibliographies 417

Divorce
Almanacs 422
Bibliographies 212, 413, 414, 419, 432

Drug abuse
Bibliographies 408, 412, 499
Guides 500

Elderly
Bibliographies 341, 426
Sexuality 473

Encyclopedias
Abortion 407
Anthropology 407
Black-Americans 280
Ethnography 115
Ethnology 407
Families 407
Family planning 407
Marriage 407
Rape 407
Sex roles 407

Sexuality 407
Ethnic groups
Bibliographies 408, 410, 417
Ethnicity
Bibliographies 406
Ethnography
Encyclopedias 115
Ethnology
Bibliographies 406
Encyclopedias 407
Families
Abstracts 421
Almanacs 422
Bibliographies 238, 404, 408, 410, 413-415, 417, 419, 423, 426
Encyclopedias 407
Social roles 238
Family planning
Abstracts 421
Almanacs 422
Bibliographies 403, 413, 414, 432,
Encyclopedias 407
World development 416
Family violence
Bibliographies 457
Fertility
Bibliographies 403, 415, 423,
Statistics (International) 405
Statistics (U.S.) 409
World development 416
Folklore
Appalachia 428
Grants
Guides 22
Guides
Aborigines 107
Drug abuse 500
Grants 22
Popular culture 522
Radical sociology 60
Handbooks
Black-Americans 291
Hispanics
Bibliographies 406, 410
Statistics (U.S.) 409
Homosexuality
Bibliographies 404, 408, 419, 425, 426
Homosexuals
Almanacs 422
Immigrants
Bibliographies 432
Incest
Almanacs 422
Bibliographies 457
Indexes
American Indians 272
Anthropology 420
Archaeology 420
Sex roles 420
Social roles 420
Social sciences 420
Social welfare 420
Social work 420
Lesbianism
Bibliographies 412
Marital status
Bibliographies 417
Statistics (U.S.) 409
Marriage
Almanacs 422
Bibliographies 404, 408, 410, 413, 414, 419, 423, 432
Encyclopedias 407
Statistics (International) 405
Mental health
Abstracts 421
Bibliographies 412
Mexican-Americans
Bibliographies 382, 383
Research guides 386
Migration
Bibliographies 403
Statistics (International) 405
Minority groups
Bibliographies 406
Mortality
Statistics (U.S.) 409
Occupations
Bibliographies 417
Organizations
Directories 255, 424
Organizations (Elderly)
Directories 339
Popular culture
Guides 522
Population
Bibliographies 256
Pornography
Almanacs 422
Bibliographies 457

Poverty
  Almanacs 422
  Bibliographies 412, 417, 432
  Statistics (U.S.) 409
Prostitution
  Almanacs 422
  Bibliographies 419, 425, 432
Public opinion 524
Racial groups
  Bibliographies 410
Radical sociology
  Guides 60
Rape
  Almanacs 422
  Bibliographies 408, 425, 432, 457
  Encyclopedias 407
Research guides
  Mexican-Americans 386
Role models
  Bibliographies 411
Sex discrimination
  Almanacs 422
  Bibliographies 412
Sex roles
  Abstracts 421
  Almanacs 422
  Bibliographies 404, 408, 410-414, 417, 423, 425, 426, 432, 457, 470
  Encyclopedias 407
  Indexes 420
  World development 416
Sexual stereotypes
  Bibliographies 423
Sexuality
  Abstracts 421
  Almanacs 422
  Bibliographies 404, 413, 414, 426, 474
  Elderly 473
  Encyclopedias 407
Social casework
  Bibliographies 585
Social change
  Bibliographies 127, 412
Social characteristics
  Abortion 400
  Bibliographies 406
Social classes
  Bibliographies 404, 413, 414
Social conflict
  Bibliographies 412
Social groups
  Bibliographies 417
Social life
  Appalachia 428
  Bibliographies 413, 414, 432, 484
Social policy
  Bibliographies 412
Social roles
  Families 238
  Indexes 420
Social sciences
  Indexes 420
Social services
  Directories 418
Social status
  Bibliographies 404, 413, 414, 417, 432
  World development 416
Social welfare
  Almanacs 422
  Indexes 420
Social work
  Indexes 420
Socialization
  Abstracts 421
  Bibliographies 403, 404, 413, 414, 417, 419, 426, 457
Sociology
  Bibliographies 404, 406, 408, 410, 413, 414, 425, 426
Southern whites
  Bibliographies 516
Spouse abuse
  Almanacs 422
  Appalachia 428
  Bibliographies 412, 457
Statistics (International)
  Births 405
  Deaths 405
  Fertility 405
  Marriage 405
  Migration 405
Statistics (U.S.)
  American Indians 409
  Asian-Americans 409
  Black-Americans 409
  Crime 409
  Fertility 409
  Hispanics 409

Marital status 409
Mortality 409
Poverty 409
Stereotypes
Television 520
Suicide
Bibliographies 412,
484
Television
Stereotypes 520
Urban affairs
Abstracts 312
Urbanization
Bibliographies 415,
541
World development
Family planning 416
Fertility 416
Sex roles 416
Social status 416

WORK RELEASE

BT Corrections
RT Community-based
corrections
RT Halfway houses
Institutionalization
Bibliographies 547

WORK ROLES

BT Social roles
RT Family roles
RT Occupations
RT Sex roles
Families
Bibliographies 238

WORKING WOMEN

BT Women
RT Maternal employment
Families
Bibliographies 402

WORLD DEVELOPMENT

BT Societal development
RT Community development
RT Development planning
Population
Guides 257
Women
Family planning 416
Fertility 416

Sex roles 416
Social status 416

WRITING

RT Linguistics
Social sciences
Guides 53

YEARBOOKS

Abortion
Statistics (Interna-
tional) 160
Anthropology
Organizations 44
Archaeology
Organizations 44
Births
Statistics (Interna-
tional) 32, 160, 170
Crime
Statistics (Interna-
tional) 40
Deaths
Statistics (Interna-
tional) 32, 170
Demography
Statistics (Interna-
tional) 160
Divorce
Statistics (Interna-
tional) 160
Ethnic groups
Statistics (Interna-
tional) 32
Fertility
Statistics (Interna-
tional) 160
Jewish-Americans
Population 359
Social conditions 359
Social life 359
Social relations 359
Statistics 359
Marriage
Statistics (Interna-
tional) 32, 160
Mortality
Statistics (Interna-
tional) 160
Municipalities
Statistics (U.S.) 38
Organizations
Anthropology 44
Archaeology 44

Sociology 44
Statistics (International) 44
Population
Jewish-Americans 359
Statistics (International) 32, 40, 160, 170
Social conditions
Jewish-Americans 359
Social life
Jewish-Americans 359
Social relations
Jewish-Americans 359
Social welfare
Statistics (International) 32, 40
Sociology
Organizations 44
Statistics
Jewish-Americans 359
Statistics (International)
Abortion 160
Births 32, 160, 170
Crime 40
Deaths 32, 170
Demography 160
Divorce 160
Ethnic groups 32
Fertility 160
Marriage 32, 160
Mortality 160
Organizations 44
Population 32, 40, 160, 170
Social welfare 32, 40
Statistics (U.S.)
Municipalities 38

YOUTH

UF Adolescents
UF Children
BT Social groups
RT College students
Abstracts
Social research 584
Urban affairs 312
Alcoholism
Bibliographies 477, 483
Guides 478
Almanacs 220
American Indians
Handbooks 440
Research guides 440
Atlases
Urban affairs 9
Bibliographies 494, 495
Alcoholism 477, 483
Black-Americans 281, 282, 284
Child abuse 218
Community development 448
Day care 218
Death and dying 201, 205
Deaths 231
Divorce 212, 213, 215, 231
Drug abuse 448, 494, 495, 499, 501
Families 211, 218
Handicapped 448
Homosexuality 460, 461
Incest 451
Juvenile delinquency 448
Leisure 448
Marihuana 503
Mental health 218
One-parent families 231
Polish-Americans 374
Poverty 514
Race relations 393
Sexual abuse 442
Sexuality 474
Social casework 585
Social change 533
Social indicators 538
Social issues 231
Social relations 231
Social services 448
Social welfare 582
Socialization 218
Stepfamilies 211
Suicide 210
Television 518
Urban affairs 315
Black-Americans
Bibliographies 281, 282, 284
Encyclopedias 280
Canadian organizations
Directories 11
Child abuse
Bibliographies 218
Community development

Bibliographies 448
Day care
Bibliographies 218
Death and dying
Bibliographies 201, 205
Handbooks 202
Death education
Guides 203
Deaths
Bibliographies 231
Directories
Canadian organizations 11
Organizations 13, 30, 42
Social programs 33
Divorce
Bibliographies 211-213, 215, 231
Guides 214
Drug abuse
Bibliographies 448, 494, 495, 499, 501
Guides 500
Encyclopedias
Black-Americans 280
Social work 573
Ethnicity
Handbooks 440
Research guides 440
Families
Bibliographies 211, 218
Grants
Guides 22
Guides
Alcoholism 478
Death education 203
Divorce 214
Drug abuse 500
Grants 22
Marihuana 497
Mental health 570
Migration 246
Organizations 35
Rural social welfare 579
Social behavior 445
Handbooks
American Indians 440
Death and dying 202
Ethnicity 440
History 440
Social services 576
Socialization 137
Handicapped
Bibliographies 448
History
Handbooks 440
Research guides 440
Homosexuality
Bibliographies 460, 461
Incest
Bibliographies 451
Juvenile delinquency
Bibliographies 448
Leisure
Bibliographies 448
Marihuana
Bibliographies 503
Guides 497
Mental health
Bibliographies 218
Guides 570
Migration
Guides 246
One-parent families
Bibliographies 231
Organizations
Directories 13, 30, 42
Guides 35
Polish-Americans
Bibliographies 374
Poverty
Bibliographies 514
Race relations
Bibliographies 393
Research guides
American Indians 440
Ethnicity 440
History 440
Rural social welfare
Guides 579
Sexual abuse
Bibliographies 442
Sexuality
Bibliographies 474
Social behavior
Guides 445
Social casework
Bibliographies 585
Social change
Bibliographies 533
Social indicators
Bibliographies 538
Social issues
Bibliographies 231
Social programs
Directories 33

Social relations
  Bibliographies 231
Social research
  Abstracts 584
Social services
  Bibliographies 448
  Handbooks 576
Social welfare
  Bibliographies 582
Social work
  Encyclopedias 573
Socialization
  Bibliographies 218
  Handbooks 137
Statistics (U.S.)
  Urban affairs 9
Stepfamilies
  Bibliographies 211
Suicide
  Bibliographies 210
Television
  Bibliographies 518
Urban affairs
  Abstracts 312
  Atlases 9
  Bibliographies 315

About the Compiler

SAMUEL R. BROWN is a Ph.D. candidate in Sociology at the University of Pennsylvania. Formerly he was a reference librarian at Spring Hill College, Mobile, Alabama.